MEANS and ENDS

IN

AMERICAN
ABOLITIONISM

*Garrison and His Critics on
Strategy and Tactics, 1834–1850*

BY

Aileen S. Kraditor

*VINTAGE BOOKS
A Division of Random House, New York*

Library of Congress Catalog Card Number: 68-26046

The first part of Chapter 2 of this book is based on the article "A
Note on Elkins and the Abolitionists," which was published in the
December 1967 issue of *Civil War History*.

Manufactured in the United States of America

FIRST VINTAGE BOOKS EDITION, AUGUST 1970

For Doris

Preface

*U*NTIL *ABOUT* fifteen years ago many scholars thought American abolitionism as a field for research and interpretation had been plowed, planted, cultivated, and harvested so thoroughly that there was not much left to learn about it. By now we know better, and new studies continue to pour off the presses and out of the graduate schools in such abundance that one feels it almost presumptuous to offer another monograph on the subject. But as every historian has discovered to his great joy, the more closely he explores a historical field, the more avenues for further exploration open out across it, avenues no less inviting because he knows they will cross and recross others that his predecessors have traveled.

There are no newly discovered sources in this book. The selected incidents have all been discussed before. I assume that the reader is familiar with them and include them only as it is necessary to my purpose of indicating how they reflected and affected the abolitionists' attitudes toward the strategy and tactics of their movement. Not included are several topics, relevant to a study of abolitionist tactical thinking, which have been dealt with extensively by other students of the movement —topics such as the petition campaign, the struggle against the annexation of Texas, and the agitation against recapture of fugitive slaves.

This study is limited to the period between 1834 and 1850 because most of the major tactical problems that arose in the entire history of the abolitionist movement were thrashed out within those seventeen years. It is true that the question of violence came up again very sharply when John Brown raided Harpers Ferry, but the premises of that later debate had all been worked out long before. After I had decided to make 1850 the cutoff year I was pleased to discover that Louis Ruchames had, on the same ground, included few post-1850 selections in his splendid anthology, *The Abolitionists* (1964). In the Preface he explains that it was during the 1830s and early 1840s

> that the Abolitionist movement made its greatest contribution to American life and faced its most difficult tasks: to awaken public opinion to the horror of slavery and to stimulate it to take action against the evil. It was during those formative years that the leadership and philosophy of the movement crystallized. On the one hand, issues which were to split the movement into two were born then; on the other, the philosophy and strategy of each of the contending factions took form within that period and were not to undergo any significant change until the Civil War.

As an explanation of why a study of abolitionist tactics can stop at about 1850, this quotation cannot be improved upon.

I chose 1834 as the starting point because it was then that the American Anti-Slavery Society, founded at the end of 1833, began its activities. Until then the movement existed in the form of a few local and regional societies, and tactical problems arose principally as issues that a few individual leaders, mainly William Lloyd Garrison, had to cope with. Garrison's chief tactical decisions before 1834 were three: to rally a movement around the slogan of immediate and unconditional emancipation; to use absolutely frank and unsparing language in his *Liberator;* and to discredit colonizationism, the program of the American Colonization Society (to which many slaveholders belonged) to send manumitted slaves to Liberia. The first two policies were fully discussed within the nationwide movement after 1833, and after 1834 the third was largely subsumed in the movement's struggle against race prejudice. Consequently I felt justified in omitting the bulk of the pre-1834 sources that would otherwise have been relevant, thus reducing the material to more manageable proportions.

I started this project with a rather negative opinion of Garrison. This is understandable, since all I had read about him was the secondary literature. Merrill's biography of Garrison is excellent; Thomas's is brilliant. Yet one cannot read them through and retain any affection or much respect for their subject. Admiration will be more than balanced by the conviction that he was bullheaded, arrogant, vindictive, and incredibly blind to some obvious truths. Then I turned to Garrison's own writings, published and epistolary, and the more I read the more I became convinced that I was meeting the man for the first time. I read editorials in *The Liberator* in which he frankly expressed uncertainty about his opinions on given issues and asked for discussion in his columns which, he suggested, might change his mind. I encountered private letters in which he tried to calm the hot tempers of correspondents with understanding words of conciliation. I had to chuckle at occasional displays of wit, sometimes at his own expense. Most of all I was increasingly struck by the logical consistency of his thought on all subjects. This is not to say his opinions did not change between the cutoff dates of my research. But the changes themselves represented a logical development, and I discovered no mutually invalidating convictions or torturings of logic to fit the needs of his position in the internecine warfare in the abolitionist movement. The primary sources that changed my opinion of Garrison and my interpretation of the abolitionist movement were so different from what the standard works in the field had led me to expect that I decided to break a rule of good monograph-writing and quote them at length, so the reader may read for himself significant documents otherwise unavailable. I set down these observations at the start to make it clear that although the picture of Garrison that emerges in the following pages is far more favorable than is common even now when the abolitionists are being rehabilitated, I did not set out to paint it that way. It is a truism that a historian reads the evidence in the light of his preconceptions. I do not claim to have brought to the task a tabula rasa, but my original bias in the abolitionists' (though not in Garrison's) favor did not require me to gloss over their faults. However, it predisposed me to give more than customary weight to such evidences of consistency, tactical acumen, foresight, percipience, occasional humility, and humor as exist in the sources.

The phrase "abolitionist humor" will, I know, strike readers as a contradiction in terms, but I use it advisedly. By now, Samuel Eliot Morison and Edmund S. Morgan have liberated students of American history from the distorting notion of the Puritan as a steeple-hatted, long-faced fanatic who sought his diversion in "planning a witch-hunt or a battue of Quakers."[1] The current new look at the antislavery movement has not yet succeeded in dispelling the equally false idea that the abolitionists were a fiercely humorless band of fanatics who met weekly to preach jeremiads at their countrymen and sought their recreation in planning verbal battues of slaveholders. A reading of the private letters of abolitionists Abby Kimber and Sarah Pugh is a sheer delight; Wendell Phillips was a master of gentle wit; and not all of Garrison's innumerable puns were labored and obvious. True, I have found no trace of humor in the writings of James G. Birney and Lewis Tappan, but Henry B. Stanton's and James A. Thome's letters teem with uproarious metaphors. Morison and Morgan have taught us that the old portrait of the Puritans revealed more about the painters than it did about their subjects. I suggest that the same is true of the traditional picture of the abolitionists, and that in time a new picture will emerge of a group of people intensely earnest in their struggle against slavery but also capable of poking fun at their own seriousness and laughing at their own vagaries.

A certain amount of repetition in the following chapters could not be avoided, since my purpose was best served by a topical rather than a chronological analysis of events that overlapped in time. If I had dealt in chronological sequence with the disputes over the woman question, religion, and political

[1] Morison, "The Faith of a Historian," *American Historical Review*, LVI (January 1951), 272, as quoted in Edward N. Saveth, *Understanding the American Past* (Boston, 1954), p. 67.

action, I could not have given them the separate analyses they warranted, whereas if I had excluded all repetitions in the topical discussions, I would have distorted the events by making too great a separation, even for analysis, among themes that were not separated in fact or in the actors' minds.

Chapters 3 through 8 divide naturally into two groups. Chapters 3, 4, and 5 discuss differences that arose within the movement over questions of ends and means and as abolitionists worked out divergent theories about who should belong to their societies, how those societies should operate, and what image they should present to the American public. Chapters 6, 7, and 8 deal with problems of agitation and conversion that the movement encountered within American society, and how theories of ends and means were worked out to cope with those problems.

I incurred many debts in the years I worked on this book. Miss Mary Heneghan and Miss Marion Ricketson, both formerly of the Providence Public Library, and Mr. William Ewing of the William L. Clements Library of the University of Michigan were extraordinarily helpful. Mr. Selby U. Gration, former director of the Rhode Island College library, repeatedly offered his aid in securing interlibrary loans of unpublished material. Mr. André Schiffrin of Pantheon suggested major revisions that resulted in a vast improvement of the manuscript. Professors Sydney Rosen and James M. Mc-Pherson and my former students, Mr. Jean L. Girard and Miss Florence Leduc (Mrs. Denis L. Girard), read all or parts of the manuscript, and their comments and criticisms were very important in helping me work out my conclusions. Those conclusions are of course my own, and my debt to these friends is not diminished by my not having taken all the suggestions they offered. Most of all I want to thank Professors Eugene D. Genovese and Doris W. Dashew, the former for having suggested the project, the latter for working with me chapter by chapter and problem by problem, and both for having read and criticized the entire manuscript with infinite care.

A.S.K.

Abbreviations Used in Citations

AAS   American Antiquarian Society, Worcester, Mass.

BPL   Boston Public Library

LC   Library of Congress, Manuscript Division

NYHS   New-York Historical Society, New York, N.Y.

NYPL   New York Public Library, New York, N.Y.

SU   Syracuse University Library, Syracuse, N.Y.

UM   William L. Clements Library, University of Michigan, Ann Arbor, Mich.

AASS   American Anti-Slavery Society

A & F American and Foreign Anti-Slavery Society

CONTENTS

Means and Ends in
American Abolitionism

1

INTRODUCTION

AMERICAN HISTORIOGRAPHY, as well as modern movements for change, badly need, first, analyses of the philosophic assumptions behind the tactical differences that have plagued American reform and radical movements, and second, studies of the efficacy in different historical situations of the various tactics adopted by these movements. Until we have both kinds of study, any analogies between present and past movements must be tentative at best. Once we have a sufficient number of both kinds, however, current movements for change will be able to benefit by the lessons of their predecessors' successes and failures.

The present work is of the first sort: an examination of certain strategies and tactics adopted by the abolitionists; it makes no attempt to gauge how effective the strategies and tactics were. And although this study is not intended as a history of the abolitionist movement between 1834 and 1850, it is appropriate at the outset to summarize certain major events in that history, in order to indicate the context within which the tactical thinking took place.

It is customary to date the beginning of abolitionism from January 1, 1831, when the first issue of Garrison's *Liberator* appeared in Boston. Antislavery organizations had existed in this country prior to that time, and Garrison himself had worked for two years in Baltimore with Benjamin Lundy on the latter's gradual-emancipationist paper, *The Genius of Universal Emancipation*. What was new in 1831 was the abandonment of the gradualism and moderation that had characterized the earlier efforts.

The twenty-five-year-old Garrison began *The Liberator* without capital, and almost all his early subscribers and supporters were Northern free Negroes. However, his paper, which continued publication without interruption through 1865, and his other writings circulated beyond New England and helped to bring new recruits into the movement—including men who later became anti-Garrisonians. This was particularly true of his pamphlet *Thoughts on African Colonization;* published in 1832, this pamphlet helped to discredit the American Colonization Society among people sincerely committed to abolition. The object of the ACS, organized fifteen years earlier and including prominent slaveholders such as Henry Clay, was to encourage manumission of slaves with compensation to their owners and to finance the deportation of the former slaves and of free Negroes to Africa, where they could develop their own society unmolested. Garrison argued that this program was racist in spirit; it assumed that whites and blacks could not live together in a biracial society. As evidence, he quoted statements by leading colonizationists assuring slaveholders that the ACS had no desire to tamper with their human property and expressing horror at the prospect of a large free black population in the United States. Furthermore, Garrison showed that the project was impractical in any case, for many more blacks were born in this country each year than could possibly be transported to Liberia. He argued that they were Americans with as much right as the whites to remain in their native land. And he ended by demonstrating the strong opposition of blacks to the ACS.

The first abolitionist association to reflect the new uncompromising approach, demanding immediate, unconditional abolition of slavery without expatriation, was the New-England Anti-Slavery Society, founded in Boston in January 1832. After a few years, when there were enough abolitionists in

New England to require the organization of state societies with local affiliates, the New-England Society changed its name to the Massachusetts Anti-Slavery Society. In December 1833, abolitionists from nine states met in Philadelphia, founded the American Anti-Slavery Society (AASS), and adopted a constitution and Declaration of Sentiments written by Garrison.[1]

Among the ten articles in the constitution, the second, third, fourth, and tenth are of particular relevance here:

The object of this Society is the entire abolition of slavery in the United States. While it admits that each State, in which slavery exists, has, by the Constitution of the United States, exclusive right to *legislate* in regard to its abolition in this State, it shall aim to convince all our fellow-citizens, by arguments addressed to their under-standings and consciences, that slave-holding is a heinous crime in the sight of God, and that the duty, safety, and best interests of all concerned, require its *immediate abandonment*, without expatriation. The Society will also endeavor, in a constitutional way, to influence Congress to put an end to the domestic slave-trade, and to abolish slavery in all those portions of our common country, which come under its control, especially in the District of Columbia, and likewise to prevent the extension of it to any State that may be hereafter admitted to the Union. . . . This Society shall aim to elevate the charac-ter and condition of the people of color, by encouraging their intellectual, moral, and religious improvement, and by removing public prejudice, that thus they may, ac-cording to their intellectual and moral worth, share an equality with the whites, of civil and religious privileges; but this Society will never, in any way, countenance the oppressed in vindicating their rights by resorting to physical force. . . . Any person who consents to the principles of this Constitution, who contributes to the funds of this Society, and is not a slave-holder, may be a member of this Society, and shall be entitled to vote at the meetings. . . . This Constitution may be amended at any annual meeting of the Society, by a vote of two-thirds of the members present, provided the amendments proposed have been previously submitted, in writing, to the Executive Committee.[2]

The first annual convention of the AASS took place in New York in May 1834, and thereafter the association met annually in the same city and month. It grew quickly, and "by 1838, there were 1,350 societies in the national organization, with a membership of about 250,000. In Massachusetts, in 1837, there were 145 local societies, in New York 274 societies, and in Ohio, the most ardent anti-slavery state in the West, 213."[3]

Its success in recruiting members did not mean that the AASS had yet won popular acceptance. Its traveling lecturers were regularly mobbed throughout the 1830s; the climax of the violence came in November 1837 when Elijah Lovejoy, editor of an antislavery paper in Alton, Illinois, was killed while defending his press from a mob. In addition to physical violence, the abolitionist movement was subjected to other forms of repression, the most important of which was the reaction of Congress to the AASS's petition campaign. By 1836 the petitions for abolition of slavery, collected in enormous numbers by abolitionists, mainly women, with the object of forcing the issue onto the nation's chief political forum, had reached such volume that the House of Representatives voted to table them automatically upon presentation. This was the notorious "gag rule," and it was repassed at each session thereafter; in 1840 it was made a permanent rule. The effort to silence the abolitionists received presidential endorsement when Andrew Jackson, in his message to Congress in December 1835, asked for a law to prohibit the mailing of "incendiary publications intended to instigate the slaves to insurrection." Actually, abolitionist literature sent South was directed to whites and never recommended violence. Jackson was in effect endorsing the action of his Postmaster General, Amos Kendall, who had written to the postmaster in Charleston, South Carolina, approving of the recent burning of abolitionist mail in that city. The most significant result of the repression was the growing willingness of many Northerners to identify abolitionism with the rights of freedom of speech and petition, a willingness antislavery propagandists diligently encouraged. Many Americans who did not feel strongly about slavery began to believe that if abolitionists could be mobbed with impunity and prevented from having their petitions considered by Congress, the rights of all Americans were in danger.

The AASS won increasing public toleration as a result of the repression, but the beginning of real acceptance came after the passage of the Fugitive Slave Law of 1850. Several provisions of that act alarmed large numbers of people who had always considered slavery a distant problem. For one thing, it placed the burden of proof of freedom on the individual claimed as a slave; as the abolitionists pointed out, this meant that any Northerner, including the swarthy Daniel Webster (who defended the law), could be claimed by a slave hunter in Massachusetts, dragged before a federal commissioner, and taken South into slavery, unless he could prove his free status. No Northerner, regardless of his color, was secure, since many slaves were lighter than their masters. Among the other objectionable provisions was a clause stating that the commissioner should receive ten dollars if he decided the claimed person was a slave and only five dollars if he found him to be free.

[The public reaction against the Fugitive Slave Law, however, took place after the period covered in this study. It was in an atmosphere of repression that the AASS worked out its strategies and tactics, and the disputes within the organization over policies to be adopted must be understood in part as responses to both the movement's unpopularity and its need to convert large numbers of hostile people to its cause.] In the course of these disputes deep differences emerged, not only over policy but also in basic philosophic assumptions, beginning in 1837 and culminating in 1840, when the two major factions split and one group withdrew from the AASS to organize a rival association, the American and Foreign Anti-Slavery Society (A & F).

IN THE LITERATURE on abolitionism, certain terms frequently appear—such as Garrisonian and anti-Garrisonian, conservative and radical, and so on—whose implicit definitions vary with the authors' attitudes toward Garrison and their interpretations of the issues that divided the movement. Since these are value-loaded terms and not merely neutral designations for universally agreed-upon referents, I should make clear the meanings attached to them in the following pages. I apply the term *abolitionist* to a man or woman who belonged to an antislavery society in the years covered by this study and who believed that slavery was a sin, that slaves should be freed immediately, unconditionally, and without expatriation or compensation to the owners, and who subscribed at least in theory to the doctrine of race equality. By *Garrisonian* I mean an abolitionist who, while not necessarily agreeing with Garrison's teachings on religion, politics, or the woman question, supported Garrison's belief that an antislavery society should be "broad" in the sense that it should include members with all religious, social, and political views, united only by their devotion to abolitionist principles as above defined. An *anti-Garrisonian* abolitionist was one who, from about 1837 on, desired to "narrow" the antislavery societies to include only those abolitionists whose views on religious and social questions not directly connected with antislavery were not such as to alienate the general Northern public, and who, from 1839 on, believed that the societies should officially endorse political action. I call *radical* those abolitionists who, like Garrison, believed that American society, North as well as South, was fundamentally immoral, with slavery only the worst of its many sins, and who looked forward to a thoroughgoing change in its institutional structure and ideology. I call *conservative* those abolitionists who were reformers rather than radicals in that they considered Northern society fundamentally good and believed that abolition of slavery would eliminate a deviation from its essential goodness and thereby strengthen and preserve its basically moral arrangements. The radical-conservative and Garrisonian–anti-Garrisonian divisions were not identical, although they overlapped to a considerable degree. That is, there were conservative abolitionists who were Garrisonians on the question of the breadth of the antislavery societies' membership. [Nevertheless, it should be noted that, as with other movements for change in American history, the radical and reformist wings of the abolitionist movement did not simply occupy different locations on a single continuum. It would be misleading to portray them as two groups, one more and the other less extreme, but fundamentally heading in the same direction. On certain issues they did appear in that way. But in a deeper sense their differences were not quantitative but qualitative; to one faction abolition would preserve and strengthen the American social order, and to the other it would be a step toward the subversion of that social order and its replacement by a new one.] I believe that the failure by some students of abolitionism to analyze these theoretical distinctions has encouraged them to attribute the factional disputes too much to personality conflicts. While such conflicts certainly played a role, I have generally ignored them in the following pages in order to redirect attention to what I believe are the more significant causes of the split in the movement.

Thesis

[It is the explanation of these causes that constitutes the principal thesis of this book. I shall argue, first, that the split was due fundamentally to the fact that some of the leaders were radical in social philosophy and others were reformist. Second, the conflict in theory was reflected in a conflict in practice: each faction had a different conception of the proper mode of agitating for emancipation. The two factions approached in different and finally mutually exclusive ways the tactical problem of alliances with political groups and other sectors of the nonabolitionist public. Third, since the two chief factions had mutually exclusive attitudes toward American society, the problem of alliances existed *within* the abolitionist organization as well: On what terms should a radical abolitionist work with a reformist abolitionist, and on what terms should a reformist work with a radical? Other ways of asking that question would be: What should be the nature of the antislavery organization be? What should be the conditions for membership? Each faction must answer these questions with a formula that would permit it to combine forces with the other if that would strengthen the antislavery movement; and the formula must not permit the social philosophy of the other faction to be identified with the movement.]

When the AASS was formed in December 1833, these questions had not yet arisen. For one thing, the abolitionists were a tiny and despised movement, and questions of alliance with others were far in the future. Furthermore, Garrison and his group had not yet become radicals in social philosophy, and so the question of alliances within the movement did not yet exist. Both problems began to appear about the middle of 1837 and by 1840 had become insoluble. By then the radical and conservative factions could no longer agree on a formula by which they could work together in a single organization, and had widely differing ideas about how to agitate their common cause of emancipation among their fellow Americans. The struggles that occurred within the AASS before the split at the annual convention in May 1840—struggles over the role of women in the movement and over religious and political questions—were, it will be argued, manifestations of the more basic radical-conservative conflict. After May 1840 the two groups of abolitionists worked separately, each group deriving its tactics of alliance and propaganda from its underlying attitude toward American society.

NOTES

[1] The "Roll of the Convention," in *Proceedings of the Anti-Slavery Convention Assembled in Philadelphia, December 4, 5, and 6, 1833* (New York, 1833), contains the names of 63 men, including several Negroes. No women are listed, but a few attended the meeting.

[2] *First Annual Report of the American Anti-Slavery Society* (New York, 1834), p. 66. The wording differs slightly from the version in the *Proceedings* of the Philadelphia convention.

[3] Louis Ruchames, ed., "Introduction," *The Abolitionists: A Collection of Their Writing* (New York, 1964), p. 20.

2

THE ABOLITIONIST
AS AGITATOR

MOST MONOGRAPHS about the abolitionists emphasize the difference between abolitionism and other movements for change. Their scholarly critics have singled them out as a major cause of the worst catastrophe this nation has ever experienced; their scholarly admirers have credited them with awakening the American conscience to the worst crime the nation has ever committed. While I willingly accord the abolitionists a unique and honored place in American history, I believe there is much to be learned by studying certain problems that they faced in common with other radical and reform groups: the relation of ends to means, of goals to tactics.

Historians who have stressed the uniqueness of the abolitionist movement have often done more than ignore these common problems; frequently they have distorted abolitionism as well as the other mid-nineteenth-century movements for change by emphasizing their esoteric aspects. For example, one of the qualities that makes Alice Felt Tyler's *Freedom's Ferment* such entertaining reading is its abundance of detail concerning the oddities of the antebellum religious cults; it pays less attention to the more sober denominations than

their importance warrants.[1] The same fate has befallen the
abolitionists: the personal and ideological idiosyncrasies of William Lloyd Garrison have been used to set the tone for discussions of the whole movement. Gilbert H. Barnes's *The Anti-
slavery Impulse, 1830–1844* (1933) and Dwight L. Dumond's
Antislavery: The Crusade for Freedom in America (1961) are
in a way thoroughly within the same scholarly tradition as
those historians who tarred the entire abolitionist movement
with the Garrisonian brush. Accepting the conventional interpretation of Garrison, they "rehabilitate" the movement by
denying that the fanatic Garrison played a leading role in it.
One of the principal theses of this study is that the older and
the Barnes-Dumond interpretations are both half right: the
older in accepting Garrison's key importance in the movement, and Barnes and Dumond in refusing to identify the
entire movement with its radical wing. At the same time, I will
argue that both schools have misunderstood Garrison's role in
the movement.

A sophisticated interpretation that perpetuates the old error
of equating the entire movement with its radical wing is
offered by Stanley Elkins in his book *Slavery*, published in
1959. If Elkins's identification of the abolitionist movement
with its radical sector were justified and if his interpretation of
its ideology were correct, there would be no point in discussing the tactics of abolitionism beyond the scope of an article,
for a movement such as he describes could hardly be said to
have notions of tactics.

Elkins contrasts the structure of American society with that
of English society in the middle of the nineteenth century, and
finds that by then the power of many American institutions
had melted away. The church had broken into denominational
fragments. The legal profession was not the strong institution
it was in England. Political parties were dissolving and changing their forms. Old classes were declining and new ones
rising. As a result, according to Elkins, institutions were so
weak, fragmented, and shifting that it was easy for Americans
of the time to imagine that institutions as such were not necessary to a society's stability. "In the America of the 1830's and

1840's there was no other symbol of vitality to be found than the individual, and it was to the individual, with all his promise, that the thinker, like everyone else, would inexorably orient himself." Individualism, self-reliance, abstractionism, disregard of the responsibilities and uses of power—"Such was the state of mind in which Americans faced the gravest social problem that had yet confronted them as an established nation": slavery.²

Elkins seems unable to decide whether to blame the abolitionists for approaching slavery in this state of mind. On one hand he argues that there were insufficient institutional arrangements within which they could have worked to rid the country of this problem in a gradual and peaceful manner. On the other, he obviously disapproves of their alleged anti-institutional bias, of their seeing the question as "*all* moral," and declares that there was,

> in principle if not in fact, an alternative philosophical mode. Slavery might have been approached not as a problem in pure morality but as a question of institutional arrangements—a question of those institutions which make the crucial difference in men's relationships with one another. . . .³

[The question is whether the abolitionists as a group did have an anti-institutional bias.] Elkins prejudges the issue in his query, "Why should the American of, say, 1830 have been so insensitive to institutions and their function?"⁴ "The American," according to the evidence Elkins provides, turns out to be a tiny group of transcendentalists and a handful of abolitionists whose ideas and attitudes were uncharacteristic not only of the overwhelming majority of Americans but even of the majority of abolitionists. What was called the "Transcendental Club" of the mid-1830s, comprising the best-known transcendentalists, was small enough—including perhaps a dozen men and women—to meet in Ralph Waldo Emerson's study in Concord, Massachusetts. The term "transcendentalist" can be applied to a somewhat larger number of former clergymen, journalists, and other intellectuals, mostly in New

England. Transcendentalism is a loose term designating a faith rather than a philosophy, a concern for man's spiritual nature that was being crushed by American commercialism, a revolt against the institutions that confined the human spirit, an assertion of the divinity of the human soul, the immanence of God in the universe, and the efficacy of intuition as a way of apprehending truth. But the "movement's" religious heresy, its fascination with German and Eastern philosophy, and its calm toleration of radical social ideas were as successful in alienating its contemporaries as they have been in attracting the interest of historians.

Elkins discusses such transcendentalists as Emerson and Theodore Parker and their refusal to use institutional means to effect reforms and to think in institutional terms,[5] and he admits that "their relationship with abolition societies was never anything but equivocal."[6] But although the transcendentalists did not generally join abolition societies, their intellectual affinities with the abolitionists, according to Elkins, were very significant. It would seem, then, that he discusses the transcendentalists in order to provide a foundation for his contention that the abolitionists themselves were anti-institutionalists. This inference is strengthened by his reference[7] to "Transcendentalism and other reform movements," despite the notorious fact that the transcendentalists lacked the commitment to action that characterizes movements for change. Stating that any other movement concerned with social policy "would have" found no better source of wisdom than the transcendentalists, that a formidable abolitionist movement "might thus have" gathered both strength and weakness from them, and that the abolitionists "could not have duplicated the intellectual pattern of the Transcendentalists more precisely if they tried," Elkins then transforms all those conditionals into declaratives.[8] Moreover, he believes it significant that "the very time at which they [the transcendentalists] flourished coincides with the launching of the great reform impulses." We are half persuaded already; the transcendentalists, it appears, were both logical models for and contemporaries of the abolitionists. Evidence from the abolitionists' own writings is almost superfluous.

[But "evidence" is furnished, from the speeches and writings of Garrison, Wendell Phillips,[9] and Stephen S. Foster,[10] and from the doctrines of Nathaniel P. Rogers,[11] the last two of whom were undoubtedly anti-institutionalists; and from the writings of Theodore D. Weld,[12] William Jay,[13] and James G. Birney,[14] who were not. A thorough study of the latter three and even a cursory glance at the scores of political abolitionists who worked through such institutions as the Democratic and Whig parties, or who formed new institutions such as the Liberty party and the Liberty League,[15] would have destroyed Elkins's thesis.]

To discover whether most abolitionists were anti-institutionalists we ought to begin with a definition of institutions. Elkins does not provide one, but he describes them as follows:

> . . . institutions define a society's culture, . . . they provide the stable channels, for better or worse, within which the intellectual must have his business—if, that is, his work is to have real consequences for society and if he himself is to have a positive function there. Institutions with power produce the "things" not only upon which one leans but also against which one pushes; they provide the standards whereby, for men of sensibility, one part of society may be judged and tested against another. The lack of them, moreover, removes the thinker not only from the places where power resides but also from the very *idea* of power and how it is used.[16]

Elkins's application of this analysis to the transcendentalists, and by later implication and logical leap to the abolitionists, is suggested in the title of the next section of the same chapter: "Intellectuals without Responsibility." The picture is completed in "The Abolitionist as Transcendentalist," a section containing many highly anti-institutionalistic quotations from some abolitionists as well as quotations that could be interpreted otherwise.

All this might justify Elkins's generalizations concerning abolitionist anti-institutionalism if the bulk of the movement had shared Garrison's repudiation of human government (as construed by Elkins), withdrawn from all organized churches as Foster did, and relied solely on moral suasion to induce slaveholders to repent their sin. Unfortunately for the theory, this was not the case. The Rogerses and Fosters were a tiny minority of the movement even in New England, their stronghold. The Garrisonian radicals (who, incidentally, insisted they were not anti-institutionalists) were but a small coterie even in Massachusetts. The overwhelming majority of members of antislavery societies evidently believed that slavery would not be abolished unless the political power of the slaveowners was destroyed by political means, for they continued to work within the major parties and later in the Free Soil and Republican parties. Most of them believed that the respectability and influence of the slaveowners would be destroyed not by withdrawing from the compromising churches but by working within them, to persuade them to exert pressure on their Southern wings and refuse fellowship with slaveowning clergymen and members. In other words, the vast majority of abolitionists did not repudiate institutions or institutional means to effect the desired change; they valued them as potential weapons, and where existing institutions seemed too corrupted, they tried to replace them with new ones by which collective efforts could be exerted. Most abolitionists harbored no illusions about the possibility of convincing the slaveowners, by mere exhortation, of the error of their ways. When they advocated moral pressure on the owners, they usually explained that this meant worldwide ostracism, disruption of economic and social contacts, and an unremitting propaganda offensive—something quite different from the naive sermons on brotherhood that some historians claim they were content to rely on.[17] And most abolitionists who advocated these tactics urged that they be accompanied by efforts to win elections, pass laws, dominate political parties, reform the churches, and use other institutional means to destroy slavery.

How much extreme individualism and "disregard of the

responsibilities and uses of power" can be read into the following sentiments expressed by James G. Birney, abolitionist
candidate for President?

> We have nothing in our political structure that is stable.
> Stability is an *essential* in governments. With us every
> thing is unstable because subject to popular excitements,
> and popular excitements can be generated and used by
> demagogues at their pleasure. No people, I am sure, can
> advance in moral refinement and true civilization under
> the univ'l Suffrage.

On another occasion he wrote that changes such as an increase
or decrease in tariff rates ought to be gradual because, he said,
reforms should not be sudden where lawful interests were at
stake.[18]

[Far from repudiating institutions, most abolitionists wished
to purify them.]Consider, for example, a passage from William
Goodell's *Slavery and Anti-Slavery* (1852), an extremely influential book by a prominent abolitionist:

> This great question is to be decided, mainly, by the
> concurrent action of the two great social institutions of
> the country, the Church, and the State, the ecclesiastical
> and the civil power.
>   It is for THE PEOPLE of the non-slaveholding States
> to say whether these two social institutions shall be re-
> deemed from the foul embraces of slavery, and wielded
> for their heaven-appointed ends, or whether they shall
> remain, as at present, in the hands of their enemies.[19]

Such statements abound in antislavery literature. Even the
Garrisonian James S. Gibbons could write, "Organization,
Concert, is at the base of the divine economy."[20]

Another sort of statement that abounds in the literature is
the accusation by some abolitionists that others were anti-institutionalists. At the height of the controversy over the woman
question and religious heresy, the Rev. James T. Woodbury,
an abolitionist, asserted that in the opinion of Garrison and his
friends, "Slavery is not merely to be abolished, but nearly
everything else. . . . *We* are not willing, for the sake of kill-

ing the rats, to burn the house down with all it contains."[21]
The "Appeal" of some abolitionists at Andover Theological
Seminary, published in *The Liberator* of August 25, 1837, included the statement that the appellants had read, in antislavery publications, "speculations which lead inevitably to dis-
organization and anarchy, unsettling the domestic economy,
removing the landmarks of society, and unhinging the machinery of government."[22] The targets of these accusations
pleaded innocent[23] (sometimes, in my opinion, convincingly),
but Elkins himself could not have penned a severer indictment
of anti-institutionalism than this group of abolitionists directed
against another. While many non-Garrisonians thought the
Andover Appeal in bad taste, they agreed with its substance.
What inferences, then, can be drawn concerning the thinking
of the movement as a whole?

Only a minority of abolitionists reacted to the hostility they
encountered by rejecting not the *compromising* churches and
the *proslavery* government but churches and governments—
institutions per se. The vast majority never did so. And when
the Northern wings of some churches and parties and later the
federal government moved closer to their position, that majority and even some of the minority ceased their attacks. When
abolitionists supported the Union in the Civil War, it was
because the institutions, not the abolitionists, by and large, had
changed positions.

Radicals have always been accused of wanting to undermine
institutions. What is true of most radicals, including most Garrisonians and many other abolitionists, is that they did not
share the conservatives' reverence for institutions as such.
Specific traditions, customs, and institutions they were willing
to judge by transcendent ethical criteria and condemn if found
wanting. The radical abolitionists repeatedly disclaimed hostility to, for example, the clergy and the church per se and
reiterated that they deplored only the perversions of these
institutions.[24] It may be objected that they were anti-institutionalists despite their disclaimers. In the case of Henry C.
Wright, I think that is true. In other cases it is a matter of
definition. This question is peripheral, because if the radicals

did not represent the entire movement, Elkins's discussion of
their attitude toward institutions proves nothing about American abolitionism as a whole. The bulk of the movement, those
who followed the more conservative leaders such as Birney
and the Tappan brothers, found no need even to make public
disclaimers. Unless a desire to abolish an inherently evil institution like slavery and an insistence that all other institutions be
purged of its influence are defined as anti-institutionalism, the
majority of abolitionists do not merit that label. If such desire
and insistence do add up to anti-institutionalism, the label must
be applied to every movement for change that does not visual-
ize the proposed change as piecemeal, gradual, reformist. But
to do that is to contradict the word's denotation and to attach
to it an invidious connotation in the guise of objective historiography.

Elkins regrets that slavery was not ended gradually, by
piecemeal adjustments of the institutional arrangements that
supported it. He offers "a catalogue of preliminaries—a series
of separate short-term reforms rather than root-and-branch
abolition" that might have solved the problem. For example,
the churches could have insisted that slaves be instructed in
Christian morality and be given a dignified spiritual life. They
could have required regular marriage and guaranteed the
sanctity of the family. Laws could have been passed to mitigate cruelty and recognize the slaves' humanity. Slaves might
have been given the right to earn enough money to buy their
freedom.[25] He points out that such schemes were in fact
proposed in the United States, and were put into practice in
the British West Indies and in Latin America with the result
that slavery died peacefully there. But, he adds, this process was
not possible here. There was no national church, no national
focus of social and financial power, no national bar, no other
national institutions such as existed in other slaveholding coun-
tries that could have mediated the conflicting interests or
wielded the necessary power. The absence of such institutions
forced the opponents of slavery to see it in abstract terms, in
terms of "sin" on the part of the slaveholders and of "guilt" on
the part of Northerners. Since this view of the abolitionists'

conception of sin, guilt, and morality is a principal corollary of Elkins's anti-institutionalism thesis, it is appropriate at this point to consider its validity.

The contrast between the United States and other nations in which slavery existed is valid up to a point; certainly institutions here were much more fluid and, in the period under discussion, were changing drastically. But no society, however structured, provides institutional means or moral justifications for its own subversion.[26] The significant point is not that American society was relatively "devoid of structure," as Elkins correctly states,[27] but that slavery was part of what structure it had, such an integral part that a movement to destroy it was not a reform movement but a radical one; it judged the institution of slavery not by the moral criteria of the society within which slavery had a legitimate place, but by a higher law that rejected those very criteria. Slavery was not only inextricably involved in the economic and political structure of the entire nation, but was also the social and economic base of a class that wielded total power in its own section and tremendous influence in the North and in the federal government. The abolitionists' situation was, therefore, different from that of all the other movements for change in that day— women's rights, temperance, trade-unionism, prison reform, and so on. They were reform movements; abolitionism was radical.[28] The reformers' goals were attainable without touching the basic structure of American society; abolitionism's goal would be attained only by overturning that structure in part of the country and shifting power drastically in the remainder.

Elkins thus misconstrues what he regards as the abolitionists' penchant for moral abstractionism, their moral absolutism, and their guilt feelings. He blames these attitudes on a society so unstructured that it exaggerated each individual's sense of his own responsibility.

> Reforming energy, or a sense of social responsibility, could be designated in terms other than "guilt." But the conditions of American society have made such energy peculiarly a personal, an individual, phenomenon. It is the

absence of clear channels for the harnessing of these drives that has made it so. . . . Guilt must be borne as an individual burden to a degree not to be observed elsewhere.[29]

I would suggest a less psychological explanation for the abolitionists' guilt feelings. If slavery was an integral part of the institutional structure of the nation as a whole, the average Northerner had as realistic a basis for guilt feelings as the average German in the 1930s. By the same token the minority of Northerners who were aware of their section's complicity in the crime of slavery and worked in a variety of ways to publicize that complicity and end it were no more pathological than German antifascists thirty years ago. The unrealism was not the abolitionists' for feeling guilty but their neighbors' for *not* feeling guilty.

Frank Tannenbaum, in his brilliant study *Slave and Citizen: The Negro in the Americas*, argues that the piecemeal and peaceful ending of slavery in the United States was impossible

because the gap between the Negro and the white man had been made so impassable and so absolute that it could not be bridged by any means of transition, by any natural growth and adaptation. Revolution was the result because change as a principle had been denied.[30]

Elkins cites the Tannenbaum volume, and his own emphasis on the fluidity of American society might have provided him with insights suggested by this passage, for it was in the United States, more than in any other slaveholding nation, that the contrast between the status of the slave and that of every other inhabitant was sharpest. The anomaly of the most rigid, institutionalized form of slavery existing within the most fluid, least institutionalized social structure had to make slavery seem morally wrong to those whites who took the Declaration of Independence seriously. This anomaly suggests that the abolitionists' reaction was realistic, not a pathological attitude forced on them by the absence of institutionalized ways to oppose a social anachronism, and whatever one may say of the tactics they employed, they were correct in insisting that individuals who shut their eyes to the crime of slavery were to that extent guilty of its perpetuation. It may be argued that slavery was objectively a moral problem precisely because it was anomalous and anachronistic and involved basic questions of men's relations with one another.[31] And if that is so, a movement to abolish it could not, without distorting the nature of the problem, have dealt with it otherwise than as largely a moral problem. That is, the charge of abstractionism could be leveled at a movement that did *not* make the moral aspect central.

The moral aspect of slavery was thus not something the abolitionists superimposed on a problem that was difficult enough to solve without it, nor was it imposed by the lack of institutional structure in the abolitionists' society; it was inherent in the nature of slavery itself. And it appealed with irresistible force to those who took literally the teachings of their religion that God created all men in his own image and that Christ died for all. The central place that the abolitionists gave to the religious and moral aspect of their crusade also shows why they always accompanied their demand for abolition with the demand for equal rights for the Negro and the ending of racial prejudice. Chattel slavery was simply the worst form of the sin they wanted to eradicate, the sin of denying the humanity of the Negro and the equality of all men as children of God. But Elkins's advice was followed a century before it was offered: the nation failed to respond to the moral appeal and preferred to approach the problem of slavery "as a question of institutional arrangements." This meant separating what the abolitionists insisted on combining —the legal status of the Negro, and the moral condition of American society as reflected in its treatment of him. When the nation altered the former and left the latter unchanged, it distorted the nature of the problem and ensured fulfillment of an ominous prophecy (somewhat exaggerated) uttered by Lydia Maria Child twenty-three years before the Thirteenth Amendment was ratified:

Great political changes may be forced by the pressure of external circumstances, without a corresponding change in the moral sentiment of a nation; but in all such cases, the change is worse than useless; the evil reappears, and usually in a more exaggerated form.[32]

LET US RETURN for a moment to the transcendentalists. If exaggeration of their affinities with abolitionists causes the latter to be misunderstood, a glance at the profound differences between the two movements can yield important insights. It was no mere difference in temperament (although it was that too) that kept most of the transcendentalists from joining with abolitionists in the struggle against an institution both groups abhorred. They were separated by a religious-philosophical chasm as wide as that between the immanent God whose "Revelation is the disclosure of the soul"[33] and the transcendent God whose will is revealed in the Bible (supplemented, for the Quakers, by direct illumination). The transcendentalist epistemology did not necessarily beget social passivity, yet it seems to have exerted a strong influence in that direction.[34] The reason is expressed eloquently by Arthur M. Schlesinger, Jr.:

> . . . transcendentalism . . . was infinitely individualistic, providing no means for reconciling the diverse intuitions of different men and deciding which was better and which worse. This did not worry most transcendentalists, who would allow Nicholas Biddle the authority of his inner voice and asked only to be allowed equally the authority of their own.[35]

Schlesinger is contrasting the transcendentalists with the Jacksonian Democrats; hence the reference to Biddle. For Jackson's adversary substitute "the slaveholder," and one needs no further explanation of the absurdity of classing the transcendentalist with the abolitionist. Whatever a historian a century later may concede about the validity of the slaveholder's intuitions, a crusader against slavery, accepting persecution and perhaps death for the sake of his cause, could not afford such luxury.

Schlesinger suggests that the typical transcendentalist was rationalizing a refusal to accept the responsibilities of politics.[36] Whether or not that is so, his rule-proving exception, Henry David Thoreau, is all the more significant. Thoreau was the one transcendentalist who, according to Schlesinger, accepted responsibility for his personal share in the state of American society, in his writings, his Walden experiment, and his refusal to pay taxes. For present purposes, the point to note is that Thoreau did so in true transcendentalist fashion, temporarily seceding from an iniquitous society and bearing solitary witness against its sins. The abolitionists, like secular radicals and reformers of other times, could agree on a common task because they accepted a source of value and obligation that was objective—external to themselves and valid for all men, even though not all men recognized it. For the abolitionists that source was the God who commanded men to love their neighbors as themselves and to do unto others as they would have others do unto them. They had a bond that no transcendentalist could have with any other person, even another transcendentalist, despite the purely abstract share of each man in the Oversoul. Thus, while it is true, as Frothingham insists, that transcendentalism should not be equated with dreaminess and withdrawal,[37] it is also true that the spirit of transcendentalism was hostile to a *movement* for change.

A related difference between the two groups is that the transcendentalist, disapproving of slavery, yet having no objective standard by which he could deny the slaveholders' own version of truth, could, if so inclined, accept a social philosophy that assumed that all things worked for ultimate good with or without much help from him; the abolitionist knew in his very soul that God worked through human instrumentalities[38] and that if these failed to fulfill their obligations, evil would remain and disobedient men would suffer the consequences of their own free choice of the wicked path. Most abolitionists rejected the doctrine of man's helplessness to overcome innate depravity. None of them, however, believed in automatic progress. While many of them saw man as free to earn salvation by his own efforts (although some, like Wendell

Phillips, were Calvinists), they saw him as equally free to earn God's wrath if he willfully rejected the clear injunctions of the gospel. What social progress would occur would be the fruit of unremitting struggle against sin, and the greatest sin of their time, they knew, was slavery.

In addition to the abolitionist and transcendentalist episte-mologies, there was a third one relevant here: that implicit in Jacksonian Democracy. The abolitionist and the transcenden-talist agreed at least on the possible validity of an individual's or small minority's perception of truth and duty as opposed to that of the majority. This the Jacksonian theorist denied on principle. George Bancroft, for example, argued:

> If it be true, that the gifts of mind and heart are univer-sally diffused, if the sentiment of truth, justice, love, and beauty exists in every one, then it follows, as a necessary consequence, that the common judgment in taste, poli-tics, and religion, is the highest authority on earth, and the nearest possible approach to an infallible decision. . . . The decrees of the universal conscience are the nearest approach to the presence of God in the soul of man.[39]

Ironically, the transcendentalist's extreme individualism and the Jacksonian's worship of public opinion as the voice of God could both rationalize absence of the urge to reform in the face of majority opposition. The abolitionist, sharing the tran-scendentalist's refusal to accept the dictum *vox populi vox dei*, had to carry that refusal one step further: public opinion at any given time before the establishment of God's kingdom on earth could never be the voice of God, and if it were, the reformer would lose his vocation.[40] The voice of the reform-ing minority was the voice of God.[41] But the majority was also teachable; the reformer was God's instrument to teach the nation the truth and the vanguard in its march to a better social order. Where the Jacksonian desiring to know the will of God might conduct a referendum (among white male adults, at any rate), the abolitionist would insist that truth is not ascertained by public-opinion polls, and he would point out that the majority in the 1830s and 1840s would vote against abolition of slavery, against prohibition (a few abolitionists would too), for capital punishment, and for Jim Crow laws in the free states. The laws, customs, even the Constitution, reflecting the general will in its unregenerate state, could not be the authority on which the reformer based his claim to the role of teacher. His authority was the higher law as embodied in the Bible and conveniently set forth, in part, in the first sentence of the second paragraph of the Declaration of Independence. The corrupt majority prevailed not because it was right but because it could enforce its will. "Might makes right" was in the abolitionist's view logically deducible from the principle of majority rule.[42]

It follows that the reforming minority, while necessary, must always be unpopular. As Wendell Phillips put it, when explaining why even abolitionists who employed conciliatory and moderate language "found every man's hand against them": ". . . our unpopularity is no fault of ours, but flows necessarily and unavoidably from our position."[43] Accordingly, hostility did not shake the abolitionists' conviction of the righteousness of their course; public acceptance could not be their criterion. (Those abolitionists who carried this logic to its conclusion would suggest, rather, that public acceptance would be a sign that their duty was to move on to a new unpopular position.) In fact, the more they were execrated, especially by defenders of slavery, the more certain they were that they were attacking slavery at its weakest points.[44]

It also follows, from the abolitionist's conception of his role in society, that the goal for which he agitated was not likely to be immediately realizable. Its realization must follow conversion of an enormous number of people, and the struggle must take place in the face of the hostility that inevitably met the agitator for an unpopular cause. Hence he would be denounced not only as a contemner of the general will but also as a visionary. The abolitionists knew as well as their later scholarly critics that immediate and unconditional emancipation could not occur for a long time. But unlike those critics they were sure it would never come unless it were agitated for during the long period in which it was impracticable. The

Rev. Samuel J. May, a prominent Unitarian abolitionist, expressed this thought clearly when he wrote, concerning the demand for *immediate* abolition:

> We must hold fast to that adjective. It expresses the only sound doctrine. The more I think of it the more I am satisfied we shall put every thing at hazard if we relinquish the great truth for which we have hitherto plead [*sic*] with so much effect. Nothing can be done for the improvement of the Slaves until their *rights as men* are recognized and secured—and when their rights as men are acknowledged, Slavery will be ipso facto abolished. Whatever restraints the commonweal may render it necessary to impose upon the liberated slaves—they cannot bear any resemblance to that abject bondage of body & soul from which we are pledged by the grace of God to redeem them.[45]

[To have dropped the demand for *immediate* emancipation because it was unrealizable at the time would have been to alter the nature of the change for which the abolitionists were agitating. That is, even those who would have gladly accepted gradual and conditional emancipation had to agitate for immediate and unconditional abolition of slavery because that demand was required by their goal of demonstrating to white Americans that Negroes were their brothers. Once the nation had been converted on that point, conditions and plans might have been made.] Many documents indicate that most abolitionists would have accepted such conditions; most of them did in fact accept a moderate policy after the Civil War. Before the war, they refused to be drawn into discussions on the problems that sudden emancipation might create or on "plans" for easing the transition to freedom, for implicit in such discussions, they felt, was an assumption that Negro inferiority rather than white racism would produce the problems. This would not be so if the discussions were carried on by a society free of racism but merely anxious that the change in the Negro's status be as smooth as possible. But among whites unready to accept the Negro as inherently their equal, any such debate would feed the prevalent prejudice and provide an anaesthetic for consciences that were beginning to hurt. This is why Garrison's first great campaign was to discredit colonizationism; that movement diverted attention from the principle of equality and had proved an effective salve on potentially antislavery consciences. That is also why some abolitionists later could not accept free-soilism as a tactic to strangle slavery to death in the Southeast; while they might recognize the practical utility of the tactic, they could not admit the legitimacy of slavery in any part of the country without denying their movement's fundamental principle.[46]

Their refusal to water down their "visionary" slogan was, in their eyes, eminently practical, much more so than the course of the antislavery senators and congressmen who often wrote letters to abolitionist leaders justifying their adaptation of antislavery demands to what was attainable.[47] The abolitionist, while criticizing such compromises, would insist that his own intransigence made favorable compromises possible. He might have stated his position thus: If politics is the art of the possible, agitation is the art of the desirable. The practice of each must be judged by criteria appropriate to its goal. Agitation by the reformer or radical helps define one possible policy as more desirable than another, and if skillful and uncompromising, the agitation may help make the desirable possible. To criticize the agitator for not trimming his demands to the immediately realizable—that is, for not acting as a politician—is to miss the point. The demand for a change that is not politically possible does not stamp the agitator as unrealistic. For one thing, it can be useful to the political bargainer; the more extreme demand of the agitator makes the politician's demand seem acceptable and perhaps desirable in the sense that the adversary may prefer to give up half a loaf rather than the whole. Also, the agitator helps define the value, the principle, for which the politician bargains. The ethical values placed on various possible political courses are put there partly by agitators working on the public opinion that creates political possibilities.

Here again is seen the significance of the slogan of immediate and unconditional emancipation. In addition to being the

"end" of the movement, it was also a means; in fact, throughout the life of the movement, it was used primarily as a means,
a tool for reaching the conscience of the hearer. The AASS
stated in its first annual report that the well-meaning gradual-
ists in Kentucky and Tennessee misunderstood human nature.

> . . . we think that they are themselves a practical illus-
> tration of the power of abstract truths, when urged upon
> the conscience, to influence the conduct. We have no
> doubt that they themselves are impelled to effort by the
> powerful array of true principles which has already been
> made before the whole American people. Let them,
> therefore, if they would be successful, urge the naked
> truth. Let them insist upon reformation *now*. After the
> sternest immediatism of doctrine, the practical reforma-
> tion will be sufficiently gradual.[48]

And Garrison explained: "We have never said that slavery
would be overthrown by a single blow; that it ought to be, we
shall always contend."[49]

Garrison pursued the same tactic in his later agitation for
perfectionism, which in his version meant the denial of innate
depravity and the conviction that men were free literally to
obey the injunction "Be ye perfect even as your heavenly
Father is perfect." Like the immediatism slogan of the abolitionist movement, his slogan of the duty to struggle to free
oneself of all sin did not imply confusion between what is in
principle obligatory and what is immediately realizable. On the
contrary, he insisted that to refrain from propagating the full
truth or from struggling to do what he believed was the
Christian's duty, because perfection was not realizable, would
be to refrain from taking the first step toward its realization.
Historians have commented on the curious paradox between
Garrison's uncompromising and unsparing language in public
and his evident sweetness of disposition in personal relations.
The paradox evaporates when one understands that the public
image resulted from a consciously adopted tactic, one which
all abolitionists accepted in theory, but which he carried out
further in practice than most[50]—the tactic of always stating
the principle toward which public opinion must be educated,

no matter how far ahead of present public opinion it might be.

When the radical and conservative abolitionists diverged in the manner in which they carried out the tactic approved by both groups, they revealed more than a difference of temperament. As time went on, it became more and more apparent that conflicting interpretations of the role of the abolitionist in American society were developing within a movement that had begun by agreeing on ends and on rudimentary means. In the first years of the AASS, when the movement's main task was to get a hearing and when the most moderate and soft-spoken abolitionists were as execrated as Garrison was, differences in tactical approaches could not arise. But when it became possible for antislavery congressmen to be elected, and when some sections of the public were at least willing to listen, a wing of the abolitionist movement felt the time had come to adapt the movement's tactics to the new situation. The radical wing, on the contrary, believed that as public opinion was educated, they must take even more advanced positions; the same agitational methods that had produced a limited amount of public acceptance would produce even more. In any case, they felt, the limited public acceptance which the movement had won by the late 1830s reflected a growth in understanding of how white Americans were endangered by the aggressions of the slave power, but it did not reflect a reformation of white Americans' attitudes toward the Negro. And since race prejudice had corrupted all Northern institutions, they insisted that the abolitionist movement must struggle primarily to effect a profound change in Northern ideology. The conservative abolitionists, on the other hand, while accepting both goals of the movement—emancipation *and* eradication of race prejudice—wished to demonstrate to the potentially friendly sections of the white population that abolitionism was compatible with most customs and institutions, and they were willing to accept partial gains as steps toward the ultimate goals.

The two theories collided most spectacularly on the question of political action. The radicals pointed out that a politician cannot, in the nature of the case, demand what is far in advance of public opinion. Clearly, Northern whites in the late 1830s were more ready to listen to denunciations of slavery than to pleas to accept the Negro into their schools and to abolish the "Negro pew" in their churches. And when the "gag rules," the attempts in Congress to silence the antislavery congressmen Joshua Giddings and John Quincy Adams,[51] the insulting treatment of Massachusetts's emissary Samuel Hoar in South Carolina, the Prigg and Latimer cases,[52] the annexation of Texas, and the Mexican War made many Northerners begin to ponder sympathetically the abolitionist analysis of the nature of slave power, the danger, as the Garrisonians saw it, became ever more real. If abolitionists transferred their main operations to the political arena in this situation, they felt, the very successes they would achieve, in coalition with antislavery but not abolitionist politicians,[53] would have the effect of further splitting the movement's two goals. The political abolitionists, of course, denied this was likely. Historians usually consider them the more "realistic" of the factions, and if abolition of slavery had been the movement's only goal, I might agree. Historians have, however, played down the other goal, and that other goal obviously could not be attained through political action. Whether the Garrisonians' methods of educating public opinion to root out race prejudice were themselves "realistic" is a matter of opinion and ought to be investigated.[54] But I think they were correct in warning the political abolitionists that to work primarily in the political arena would encourage them to emphasize the more easily attainable results at the cost of the wider goal. Perhaps historians have been misled by tempting, though inaccurate, analogies of abolitionism with reform movements that succeeded in politics. Certainly laws themselves have proved to be educational devices, but only when they pointed in the direction in which public opinion was moving. When that was not the case, as with prohibition, the legislation failed. Certain limited legislated reforms could succeed in the antebellum North, such as the repeal of the law against interracial marriages in Massachusetts, the one state throughout which abolitionism had had a strong impact on public opinion.[55] But in the free states as a whole such reforms were out of the question and the education of public opinion to accept race equality had not even begun. In such a situation, the antipolitical abolitionists predicted that if antislavery sentiment became popular without being accompanied by real progress on the race question, the reflection of that sentiment in congressional action would create a frightful danger to the nation. Abolition of slavery could conceivably be forced eventually by a white North aroused to protect its own interests, but that very abolition would make the achievement of the abolitionists' other goal more difficult. It could be argued that that is precisely what happened.[56]

NOTES

[1] One historian who has noted this imbalance is Timothy Smith, *Revivalism and Social Reform in Mid-Nineteenth Century America* (New York, 1957), p. 79, quoted approvingly in David E. Smith, "Millenarian Scholarship in America," *American Quarterly*, XVII (Fall 1965), 537.

[2] Stanley Elkins, *Slavery* (Chicago, 1959), pp. 27-34.

[3] *Ibid.*, p. 28. Italics in original.

[4] *Ibid.*

[5] *Ibid.*, pp. 164-75. I might add that they refused to use *any* means to effect reforms; few of them were activists. This point will be amplified on pages 23-26 below.

[6] *Ibid.*, p. 168.

[7] *Ibid.*, p. 166.

[8] *Ibid.*, pp. 164-65.

[9] Phillips (1811-1884) made an interesting contrast with his friend Garrison, who was the son of a ne'er-do-well sailor and grew up in poverty in Newburyport, Massachusetts. Phillips was a Boston Brahmin, son of the first mayor of Boston, a Harvard graduate, and at the time of his joining the abolitionist movement in 1837, a member of the Boston bar. A consistent Garrisonian throughout the period covered in this book, he never espoused Garrison's nonresistance or religious heresies. Phillips's chief contribution to the abolition cause was as an orator.

[10] Foster (1809-1881), a New Hampshire-born graduate of Dartmouth, was a Congregationalist minister until 1839, when he became a nonresistant (or what would now be called an extreme pacifist). He became an antislavery lecturer in 1840 as a disciple of Garrison, but his views were more radical than his mentor's. He is known chiefly for his practice of interrupting religious services, denouncing the churches for collaborating with the slave power, and calling upon the members to

withdraw. He was usually thrown out. In 1845 he married Abby Kelley, whose views coincided with his.

11 Rogers (1794–1846), a Dartmouth graduate, was a New Hampshire abolitionist and editor of the weekly *Herald of Freedom*. An "ultraist" like Foster, Rogers carried pacifism to an extreme, finally deciding that even the organization of a meeting, with officers and rules of order, constituted "coercion," and he advocated freedom for anyone to rise and speak at any time on any subject he pleased.

12 Weld (1803–1895), born in Connecticut, was converted to Presbyterianism by the evangelist Charles G. Finney in 1825. By 1830 he was a committed abolitionist, associated with the New York group led by the Tappan brothers. He was the leader of the "Lane Rebels," the students at Lane Seminary in Cincinnati who in 1834 organized an antislavery society and then withdrew from the school when the trustees ordered it disbanded. Later that year he became an itinerant lecturer for the AASS and in 1836 the trainer and leader of "The Seventy," the society's band of traveling agents. In 1838 he married Angelina Grimké and in the same year wrote *Slavery as It Is*, one of the most important abolitionist tracts. In 1841–1843, after a couple of years of full-time work in the New York office of the AASS, he went to Washington to help the antislavery members of Congress, and then, convinced that his particular mission had been accomplished, he withdrew from abolitionist work and remained in private life thereafter.

13 Jay (1789–1858), son of John Jay, first Chief Justice of the United States Supreme Court, was a New York-born graduate of Yale, a justice of the Westchester County Court until 1843, and a supporter of many religious and philanthropic causes. He was conservative on the race question and on most other issues, but the Mexican War crisis converted him to the doctrine of disunionism. His chief contribution to the abolitionist movement was as a writer of very influential tracts, especially *A View of the Action of the Federal Government, in Behalf of Slavery* (1839), commonly referred to as *Jay's View.*

14 Birney (1792–1857), the son of a wealthy slaveholder in Kentucky, attended Princeton, started his own plantation in Alabama, and entered Alabama politics. He was converted to Presbyterianism and by the late 1820s had come to oppose slavery. Birney became an agent for the American Colonization Society in 1832, and in 1833, having moved back to Kentucky, he helped to found the Kentucky Society for the Gradual Relief of the State from Slavery; but in 1834 he was converted to immediate abolitionism. In the fall of that year Birney became a full-time agent for the AASS and in 1835 a vice-president. Local harassment convinced him he could no longer work effectively in a slave state, and in 1835 he moved to Cincinnati. There he published *The Philanthropist* from 1836 until the fall of 1837, when he moved to New York to become a corresponding secretary of the AASS. During the factional struggles that began about the same time, Birney was one of the bitterest of Garrison's adversaries and led the movement to force the radicals out of the organization. He was the Liberty party's candidate for President of the United States in 1840 and 1844. In 1841 he had moved to Michigan, eventually settling in the frontier town of Lower Saginaw. In 1845 he

was thrown from a horse and never recovered completely from his injuries. He withdrew from public activity but continued to correspond with other abolitionists, until with declining health and increasing pessimism and irritability in his last years, he shifted his interest more and more to religious questions.

15 These organizations will be discussed in Chapter 6 below.

16 Elkins, *Slavery*, p. 143.

17 One call for this sort of moral pressure is "To the Abolitionists of Massachusetts," an open letter from the board of managers of the Massachusetts Anti-Slavery Society, in *The Liberator*, August 10, 1838: "We would make the public sentiment of the North a tonic, instead of an opiate to southern conscience, we would unite and concentrate it, until it shall tell, in a manner perfectly irresistible, upon the sense of right, the pride of social standing, and character, even upon the interest of the slaveholder, until it shall help to make real to his mind, and he shall feel, in the air around him, the guilt, the danger, the deep disgrace, the ruinous impolicy of the relation he sustains. . . ." Frederick Douglass's writings are full of such statements. Another theme frequently found in abolitionist writings is that abolitionists should endeavor to ostracize slaveholders at Northern resorts like Newport.

18 Birney to Gamaliel Bailey, April 16, 1843, and to Russell Errett, August 5, 1844, in Dwight L. Dumond, ed., *Letters of James Gillespie Birney* (New York, 1938), II, 733, 832.

19 Goodell, p. 584.

20 Gibbons to Garrison, March 30, 1841, Anti-Slavery Letters, BPL. Several such statements appear in abolitionist writings, evoked especially by the distaste for concerted action expressed by transcendentalists who opposed slavery. See, for example, *Thirteenth Annual Report, Presented to the Massachusetts Anti-Slavery Society, by Its Board of Managers* (Boston, 1845), pp. 56–58: "Knowing from the universal experience of mankind that men effect more by concert and union of action, than by their disconnected efforts," the report notes, abolitionists had organized societies, and experience had vindicated their action, since defenders of slavery had tried to destroy the antislavery societies. But proslavery had found an unexpected ally in the late Dr. William Ellery Channing. "This distinguished gentleman was the first to broach the doctrine that organized action is hostile to individual freedom, and he exhorted the Abolitionists to disband their Societies. . . ." Channing is one of the transcendentalists discussed by Elkins. Since attitudes toward the use of institutional means to effect reforms constituted such a crucial difference between transcendentalists and abolitionists, this passage clearly shows the error of deducing the ideology of the latter from that of the former.

21 *The Liberator*, September 1, 1837. Emphasis added.

22 See also letter from "Alethea," *ibid.*, May 26, 1837, and Elizur Wright, Jr., "Judge Lawless and the Law," *Quarterly Anti-Slavery Magazine* (New York), I (July 1836), 400–409, especially pp. 400–402. Many other examples could be cited.

23 See, for example, Garrison's "Reply to Dr. Osgood," *The Libera-*

tor, August 2, 1839, and "To the Abolitionists of Massachusetts," cited in footnote 17 above.

24 See, for example, Garrison's editorial "Clerical Protest, No. 2," *ibid.*, September 8, 1837; and "To the Abolitionists of Massachusetts," cited in note 17 above: ". . . the abolitionists form the only great party, in our age, who, aiming at a wide social reform, and operating on and through social institutions, yet rest their efforts and their hopes professedly on religious grounds. . . ." The abolitionist Unitarian Rev. Samuel May, Jr., wrote, "Mr. Garrison has never denied that there has been, is, and should be *a church*; yet has he been represented as aiming to overthrow the Church, Ministry, Gospel, and all. He *has* plainly & vehemently . . . denied that there was a Church of *Christ* which excused Slaveholding & Slave-trading, . . . which apologised for these, nay which claimed for them the sanction of the Old Testament, and the permission at least of the New!" (May to J. B. Estlin, December 29, 1845, May Papers, BPL)

25 Elkins, *Slavery*, pp. 194-96. Cf. Barrington Moore, Jr., *Social Origins of Dictatorship and Democracy* (Boston, 1966), p. 132n; listing Elkins's "catalogue of preliminaries," Moore comments, "These measures still seem to me highly reactionary, a form of tokenism within the framework of slavery." See also *ibid.*, pp. 131–32. (I am indebted to Eugene D. Genovese for calling this passage to my attention.)

26 The contrast between the fluidity of American society and the institutional stability of British society should not be exaggerated. In Britain too the period was one of unaccustomed change and shifting of institutions. As to the reasons why slavery ended peacefully in the West Indies and Brazil, Eugene D. Genovese comments on this in his critique of Elkins's book in *Science & Society*, XXV (Winter 1961), 47: "The peaceful solution in the British Caribbean . . . followed from the political weakness of the ruling planters. In Brazil, the slaveowners lacked a contiguous territory and were isolated and subjected to a crushing defeatism by the failure of the Confederate cause."

27 Elkins, *Slavery*, p. 173.

28 This is not to say that all abolitionists realized the radical nature of their cause. That the majority were in fact temperamentally and ideologically reformers rather than radicals is a major thesis in the analysis, in the following chapters, of the factionalism in the abolitionist movement.

29 Elkins, *Slavery*, p. 161.

30 New York, 1946, pp. 109–10.

31 Acceptance of the objective validity of the moral aspect of slavery is gaining increasing currency among historians. The most recent statements of it are in David Brion Davis, *The Problem of Slavery in Western Culture* (Ithaca, N.Y., 1966); for example: "Despite great historical diversity in such matters as employment, manumission, and the differentiation of bondsmen from other classes, the very ways of defining and regulating the institution show that slavery has always raised certain fundamental problems that originate in the simple fact that the slave is a man" (p. 31).

32 "Dissolution of the Union," reprinted from *The National Anti-Slavery Standard* in *The Liberator*, May 20, 1842.

33 Emerson, "The Over-Soul." Another passage from the same essay: "We see the world piece by piece, as the sun, the moon, the animal, the tree; but the whole, of which these are the shining parts, is the soul."

34 Cause and effect may be reversed here: perhaps thinkers who were averse to activism were predisposed to find persuasive an epistemology that could justify their aversion. The Quakers, after all, looked inward for divine revelation; yet many Quakers were active abolitionists. Although the two groups believed in an inner source of truth, they emphasized different implications of the doctrine. The abolitionist Quakers emphasized the equalitarian implications of the "inner light" doctrine and deduced the need to oppose chattel slavery because it denied the equality of all men as potential recipients of that light; the transcendentalists stressed the individualist and anti-institutionalist implications, as noted in the text. The Quakers, in believing the Bible an inspired (but not the only) source of revelation, had a criterion, which the transcendentalists did not, for choosing between the abolitionist's and the slaveholder's intuitions.

35 *The Age of Jackson* (Boston, 1945), p. 381.

36 *Ibid.*, p. 382.

37 "Transcendentalism certainly did produce its share of idle, dreamy people. . . . But its legitimate fruit was earnestness, aspiration and enthusiastic energy." Octavius B. Frothingham, *Transcendentalism in New England* (New York, 1876, 1959), p. 143.

38 "We are told, we must not agitate this subject—let it alone, and it will remedy itself. This is not the course of Providence. Such reformations are never accomplished without human means. God will not indulge us in our indolence, and do the work without our instrumentality." Charles Follen, in an address before the Massachusetts Anti-Slavery Society, 1836, in Ruchames, ed., *The Abolitionists*, p. 135.

39 *Literary and Historical Miscellanies* (New York, 1840), as reprinted in Edwin C. Rozwenc, ed., *Ideology and Power in the Age of Jackson* (New York, 1964), pp. 294, 298.

40 This may be one source of the oft-noted Whig bias of the abolitionists, although of course there were others. The abolitionists, including those who favored low tariffs, an independent treasury, and other Democratic-type projects, were closer spiritually to the pre-1840 Whigs in their distrust of majorities. The most extreme were James G. Birney and Beriah Green, prominent abolitionists who opposed universal manhood suffrage. (See several letters in *Birney Letters*, Vol. II: Birney to Gamaliel Bailey, April 16, 1843, pp. 733–34; Birney to Samuel Lewis, July 13, 1843, pp. 744–45; Green to Birney, April 23, 1847, pp. 1066–67, among others.)

41 Ralph V. Harlow, in *Gerrit Smith, Philanthropist and Reformer* (New York, 1939), p. 88, cites a letter Smith wrote in 1852 in which he argued that government ought not merely to reflect public opinion; a legislator should obey the will of God regardless of his constituents' wishes. See also Lysander Spooner, *The Unconstitutionality of Slavery* (Boston, 1860; first published in 1845), p. 8n. Although Spooner was not

a prominent abolitionist, his book expressed the views of many who were.

42 "What is the goverment [*sic*] of a majority in reality, but a contrivance to find out which side is in a wordly sense the strongest . . . [?]" Maria Weston Chapman to John A. Collins, February 23, 1841, Anti-Slavery Letters, BPL. Garrison, in "James G. Birney—The Liberty Party," *The Liberator*, March 13, 1846, writes that Birney "complains of the profligacy of the Whig and Democratic parties. . . . That is true; but their profligacy is the necessary consequence of political action, based on the 'might makes right,' alias 'the majority shall rule' principle, which principle is also the foundation of the Liberty party, and will just as certainly corrupt that party in due time. . . ." See also first resolution introduced by Garrison at the 1842 convention of the Non-Resistance Society, as reported *ibid.*, October 28, 1842; editorial, "The Massachusetts Quarterly Review," *ibid.*, March 10, 1848. Cf. the opinion of Wendell Phillips in his letter to Sidney Howard Gay, reprinted from *The National Anti-Slavery Standard* in *The Liberator*, October 25, 1844.

43 "Philosophy of the Abolition Movement" (1853), in Ruchames, ed., *The Abolitionists*, p. 223.

44 See, for example, James G. Birney's speech reported in *Fourth Annual Report of the American Anti-Slavery Society* (New York, 1837), pp. 4–7; and Garrison, "The Anti-Slavery Standard," *The Liberator*, May 19, 1843. Historians have sometimes interpreted the abolitionists' reaction to persecution as evidence of a martyr complex (see especially Hazel C. Wolf, *On Freedom's Altar: The Martyr Complex in the Abolitionist Movement* [Madison, Wis., 1952]). To me the evidence shows *willingness* to suffer for the cause as a probably necessary price to be paid, rather than a *desire* to suffer.

45 May to Amos A. Phelps, March 18, 1834, Phelps Papers, BPL. Samuel J. May (1797–1871) should not be confused with his cousin Samuel May, Jr., who was thirteen years younger and like his kinsman a Unitarian minister. The elder May, a Harvard graduate, became an agent for the New-England Anti-Slavery Society in 1835. He was one of Garrison's first converts and later a consistent supporter, although he lacked Garrison's relish for controversy.

46 The religious implications of the refusal to discuss "plans" will be discussed in Chapter 4 below. The assertion that the principle of race equality was fundamental to the movement is not meant to deny the fact, well documented by several historians, that many abolitionists found it hard to put that principle into practice.

47 See, for example, several letters from Seth M. Gates to Gerrit Smith, especially that of August 28, 1839, Gerrit Smith Miller Collection, SU.

48 *First Annual Report of the American Anti-Slavery Society*, p. 50.

49 Quoted in Louis Filler, *The Crusade against Slavery, 1830–1860* (New York, 1960), p. 611.

50 His style was blandly benevolent compared to Stephen S. Foster's, but Foster did not edit a paper.

51 The Whigs Giddings of Ohio and Adams of Massachusetts led the

antislavery members of Congress in the presentation of petitions gathered by abolitionists. Their insurgency endangered the unity of the Whig party, which included Southerners as well as Northerners, and in January 1842 the Whigs initiated a resolution to censure the aged former President. Adams conducted his own defense, and the resolution was tabled. Shortly afterward, the House censured Giddings, who resigned his seat and was triumphantly re-elected by his constituents in the antislavery Western Reserve.

52 In *Prigg v. Pennsylvania* (1842), which dealt with the Fugitive Slave Law of 1793, the Supreme Court denied the right of states to legislate in regard to fugitive slaves. At first sight this decision seemed to help the South, but some Northerners reasoned that the decision gave the states an excuse for refusing to help federal authorities recapture fugitives; consequently a number of states passed "personal liberty laws" intended to hinder slave catchers within their borders. The Latimer case came soon after, when a fugitive, George Latimer, was captured in Boston and abolitionists mobilized their forces to prevent his extradition to Virginia. The abolitionists made sure that the legal proceedings would cost the owner more than the slave was worth, and they were able to purchase his freedom.

53 Such as, for instance, Senator Thomas Morris, who favored abolition but opposed Negro suffrage.

54 Howard Zinn, in his provocative article "Abolitionists, Freedom Riders, and the Tactics of Agitation" in Martin Duberman, ed., *The Antislavery Vanguard: New Essays on the Abolitionists* (Princeton, 1965), states on pp. 436–37: "We have the historical record as a check on whether the vituperative language of Garrison, the intemperate appeals of Wendell Phillips, hurt or advanced the popular sentiment against slavery. In the 1830's a handful of men cried out against slavery and were beaten, stoned, and shot to death by their Northern compatriots. By 1849, antislavery sentiment was clearly increasing, and some of the greatest minds and voices in America were speaking out for abolition." I would suggest this is *post hoc* reasoning. Perhaps the change in sentiment was due to the agitation, but this must be shown by analysis of public opinion in those two decades; the change itself proves nothing about the efficacy of the agitation.

55 Without a study of Massachusetts public opinion, one cannot say whether the agitation created the support for the legislation or whether the enlightened public opinion that helped produce the legislation also produced widespread support for the abolitionists who in turn were thereby able to agitate successfully for the law.

56 See Merton L. Dillon, "The Failure of the American Abolitionists," *Journal of Southern History*, XXV (May 1959), 159–77. See also Lydia Maria Child's editorial "Dissolution of the Union," quoted on page 23 above.

3

THE WOMAN QUESTION

ONE OF THE stranger ironies in American intellectual history appears when the relation between the antebellum movements for Negro rights and women's rights is compared with the relation between those movements in the Progressive Era. In both periods both movements based their claims in part on identical principles of natural rights, justice, and the Declaration of Independence. But the period in which woman suffrage became historically possible coincided with what Rayford Logan has called "the nadir" in the status of the Negro.[1] If the suffragists of 1900 had defended the Southern Negro's right to vote (an impossible supposition in view of their own attitudes on the race question) they would have split the suffrage movement, destroyed its Southern wing, alienated many Northern supporters, and delayed passage of the Nineteenth Amendment.[2] Aside from questions of justice and consistency, the suffragists had to consider the expediency of any position they might adopt on Negro rights. The abolitionists confronted the same problem in their day, but in reverse. Aside from questions of justice and consistency, they had to consider the expediency of any position they might adopt on women's rights in a period in which abolitionism was gaining

many converts who would be repelled by anything so absurd
as the equality of the sexes. In both periods the convenient
divorce of the two causes was facilitated by the fact that most
advocates of the more popular reform endorsed the prevailing
disapproval of the other. The suffragist leaders of 1900–1920
were too young to have been motivated by a desire for re-
venge on the Negro's earlier friends for having compromised
with public opinion on the woman question; the state of public
opinion in their own generation and the recurrent tactical
problems of all reform movements sufficiently explain the
ironic reversal.[3]

Another irony can be seen in the reactions of historians:
today few historians reading about the suffragists' accommoda-
tion to racism during the "nadir" period would justify it; the
suffragists' compromise of their own movement's principles is
obvious. Most historians, on the other hand, ridicule that
minority of abolitionists who advocated women's rights for
having tacked an "extraneous" issue onto the antislavery
movement. Since the tactical problems as well as the questions
of consistency and principle in the two cases were at least
similar, the respective reactions tell as much about the historians' attitudes toward sex equality and race equality, respectively, as about the subjects of their studies, just as the tactical
solutions proposed by abolitionists and suffragists reflected
their own feelings about the less popular issues at least as much
as they reflected their considered judgments on the ideals and
needs of their own causes.

It may be argued that the reason why and the manner in
which a reformer deviates from his professed principles tell
more about what he really means by those principles than his
activities in clear support of them. One can study at length the
suffragists' speeches between 1900 and 1920 urging wider
application of the principles of the hallowed Declaration, but
begin to learn what they really meant only when one comes to
those passages where the women explained, "But of course this
applies only to whites." Then, upon investigating this anomaly, one discovers that "the consent of the governed" must be

qualified by restriction of the vote to the "fit," for the sake of social stability and progress, and that fitness was much more common among white Protestant men and women, especially "Anglo-Saxons," than among other segments of the American population.

Before 1837 all abolitionists castigated unmercifully those who applied the Declaration of Independence to themselves but not to Negroes and who preferred the proslavery letter of parts of the Bible to its antislavery spirit. The woman question, precisely because it raised the same questions in regard to the status of women and thus forced some abolitionists to qualify their construction of the Declaration and the Bible, provides an excellent angle from which to study basic abolitionist principles and the ways in which those principles affected tactics.[4]

When Sarah and Angelina Grimké began, in 1837, to lecture on abolitionism to mixed audiences of men and women, they did not see themselves as nineteenth-century Pandoras opening a box of troubles that would in three years help to split the antislavery movement. To some abolitionists the parallel between these gentle Quakers from South Carolina and the woman sent by Zeus to bring calamities to mankind would have seemed uncannily close.[5] Throughout the ensuing controversy, however, the advocates of women's rights insisted that not they but their adversaries within the antislavery societies had created the problem, for those adversaries denounced efforts to tack feminism onto abolitionism when no one had tried to do so. In fact, the abstract question of women's rights, involving the pros and cons of such reforms as the right of women to vote for and become government officials, never did become an issue in the antislavery societies. Historians who state that it did are accepting as real a straw man erected by the conservative abolitionists who knew that the principles the Garrisonians did defend in the organization were more difficult to oppose.

THE GRIMKÉS' activity did not mark the entrance of women into the antislavery movement. At the founding con-

vention of the American Anti-Slavery Society in December
1833, women were present, and a few of them spoke, after
asking permission to do so.[6] Separate women's clubs were
organized within the national society, and their valuable work
in circulating petitions and raising money is well known. Even
that activity was not unprecedented; women had been encouraged by their churches to engage in organized fund-raising and educational work, also through separate clubs and
under the supervision of their pastors or the managers of the
all-male missionary and Bible societies. [What was unprecedented in the antislavery societies was the unplanned and unforeseen coalescing of the hitherto separate spheres of work of
men and women members.]

The wall between those spheres began to crumble when and
where it did because the most interesting lecturers on slavery,
in New England, just happened to be women. As former slaveholders and members of a famous family, the Grimké sisters
attracted larger audiences than any Northerner could. Their
descriptions of slavery had an authenticity that no others
could have except those of former slaves. If the Grimkés had
been men, lecturing in New England in 1837, they would have
drawn crowds; Angelina, at least, was a far more effective
speaker than James G. Birney, also a converted slaveholder.
That they happened to be women increased their appeal to a
curious public, especially since their talks were announced as
being for women only. Inevitably men began to show up at
the back of the lecture halls or in the doorways and then to
take seats, and it was not long before the sisters found
themselves speaking to what were then called "promiscuous
assemblies."[7] Despite their shyness and stage fright,[8] they did
not feel inhibited by the presence of male auditors.[9] The talks
were so successful that the sisters found themselves becoming
itinerant lecturers, traveling from town to town usually in
response to invitations from ladies' antislavery societies, something women simply did not do in those days.

The Congregational clergy of Massachusetts took alarm and
issued the notorious Pastoral Letter, declaring:

When the mild, dependant [*sic*] influence of woman upon the sternness of man's opinions is fully exercised, society feels the effects of it in a thousand forms. The power of woman is in her dependence, flowing from the consciousness of that weakness which God has given her for her protection. . . . But when she assumes the place and tone of man as a public reformer, our care and protection of her seem unnecessary. . . . If the vine, whose strength and beauty is to lean upon the trellis work and half conceal its clusters, thinks to assume the independence and overshadowing nature of the elm, it will not only cease to bear fruit, but fall in shame and dishonor in the dust.[10]

The sisters never considered stopping their open lectures. They were, after all, obeying what they believed to be a call from God to testify against slavery.[11] The only question was whether they should ignore the ever more frequent clerical denunciations[12] or reply to them and defend the propriety of their activity. Theodore D. Weld, who married Angelina the following year, urged the former course. Later the moderate Garrisonian Lydia Maria Child[13] revealed that she too had believed they should exercise but not defend their right to speak.[14] Garrison and his fellow radical Henry C. Wright[15] agreed with the Grimkés that if they did not defend their course their audiences would dwindle after the novelty of women lecturers had worn off.[16]

The arguments that the ministers used were almost impossible to ignore, aside from their probable effect on the size of the sisters' audiences.[17] First, Saint Paul had said that it was a shame for a woman to speak in church and that wives must be subject to their husbands.[18] Second, the Grimkés' activity defied custom and propriety and would, if large numbers of women followed their example, endanger the family. Inevitably, some abolitionists noticed that both these arguments echoed the principal defenses of Negro slavery.[19]

For many years abolitionists had been hearing tiresome repetitions of quotations from the Bible to justify slavery and Negro inferiority: the patriarchs of the Old Testament had

owned slaves, the curse on Ham was bequeathed to his de-
scendants, Saint Paul had returned Onesimus to his master, and
so on. The abolitionists, when they could not dispute the interpretations of the cited passages, invariably pointed out that
the spirit of the Bible if not always the letter proclaimed the
brotherhood and equality of all men.[20]

[Ironically, antifeminist abolitionists, who interpreted the
Bible allegorically when the issue was slavery, became fundamentalists when the issue was women's rights.]Henry Grew of
Philadelphia, in a public exchange of letters with Henry C.
Wright on the "nonresistance" issue, wrote: "You observe,
'We cannot obey God and man.' Then the Word of God
requires an impossibility, for it certainly requires obedience
to both. Wives are commanded to obey their husbands, and
children their parents. . . ."[21] The Rev. Amos A. Phelps[22]
argued that women were unfitted, by physiological nature and
divine command, for public life. He dismissed the feminists'
citations of exceptional women in the Bible on the ground that
those women *were* exceptional; that was the reason they were
mentioned. He would not silence those few modern women
who displayed unusual talents for public speaking; but when
they urged that public life be accepted as proper for any
woman, he felt he must protest.[23] Sarah Douglass, a Negro
abolitionist, admitted that although she felt humiliated by the
subjection of women, she believed it was divinely ordained as
punishment for Eve's sin.[24]

To the Grimkés and their friends it appeared that unless
they demonstrated that the biblical arguments used against
women's speaking were similar to those used against the Negro's equality, they would be undermining the abolitionist
rationale itself. They made some attempts to marshall New
Testament verses on their side of the question. Sarah Grimké
pointed out that the Scriptures had been translated and interpreted by men. If women were permitted to study Greek and
Hebrew and publish their translations, she predicted, they
would produce some different readings. Even the standard
version, she said, contained verses that could be cited against
those who would make woman inferior to man.[25] But the

most common reply to the biblical argument was not to match text for text; it was, after all, difficult to "reinterpret" the plain statements of Saint Paul. Far preferable was an appeal to the spirit of the New Testament as a whole, which the defenders of women's rights insisted favored equality of the sexes as well as of the races. As Angelina Grimké explained, all human beings have the same rights because they are all moral beings. To suppose that sex gave a man more rights and responsibilities than a woman "would be to deny the self-evident truth, that 'the physical constitution is the mere instrument of the moral nature.' " Sex, she insisted, had no more to do with rights than did color.

> This regulation of duty by the mere circumstance of sex, rather than by the fundamental principle of moral being, has led to all that multifarious train of evils flowing out of the anti-christian doctrine of masculine and feminine virtues. By this doctrine, man has been converted into the warrior, and clothed with sternness, and those other kindred qualities, which, in the eyes of many, belong to his character as a man; whilst woman has been taught to lean upon an arm of flesh, to sit as a doll arrayed in 'gold, and pearls, and costly array,' to be admired for her personal charms, and caressed and humored like a spoiled child, or converted into a mere drudge to suit the convenience of her lord and master.

There are no men's or women's rights; there are only human rights.[26] [The chief way, then, to dispose of the arguments against women's rights was to show that they derived from principles which, if made universal, would undermine abolitionism itself.]

The same tactic was used in the customary reply to another argument against the Grimkés' activity, that it was contrary to the usages of civilized society.[27] Wholesale emancipation of the slaves was also opposed on grounds of custom and the need to preserve the social fabric. If abolitionists resorted to similar arguments to condemn women's public lecturing or membership in mixed conventions, how could they consistently advocate such social innovations as Negro freedom and the equality of the races? James Mott of Philadelphia, commenting on the objections that had been made to Abby Kelley's participation in the recent New England Anti-Slavery Convention, wryly observed:

> . . . verily some of our northern gentlemen abolitionists are as jealous of any interference in rights they have long considered as belonging to them exclusively, as the southern slaveholder is, in the right of holding his slaves, —both are to be broken up, & *human* rights alone recognized.[28]

Another circumstance made explicit reply to the argument from custom necessary, in the eyes of the Garrisonian abolitionists. Antislavery propaganda always proclaimed that slaves could not legally marry, that slave families could be and were separated by sale, and that slave women were driven to work in the fields under the lash of brutal drivers, were sold on auction blocks like animals, and were helpless to defend their virtue against masters and overseers. These abolitionists could not forbear to cry hypocrite when clergymen who did not denounce these outrages denounced as immoral the public lectures of female abolitionists who were motivated in part by empathy with slave women.[29]

Abolitionists who favored an open defense of the Grimkés' speaking to "promiscuous assemblies" understood that the discussion of woman's sphere would frighten away many people who might otherwise be converted to abolition. They felt that a few people converted to the cause of human rights for all, regardless of sex or color, were more valuable in the long run than many people converted to antislavery alone, especially since antislavery alone could be compatible with racism. And as Garrison's disciple Maria Weston Chapman suggested, "the women whose efforts for the cause could not be hindered by men, were more valuable auxiliaries than the men whose dignity forbade them to be fellow-laborers with women."[30] Their approach to this tactical question was a consistent part of an over-all approach to the problem of weighing short-term losses against long-term gains. How their tactic would have worked

out in this instance will never be known; the "woman question," which had begun as an argument over a tactic, very
soon became itself a tactic, that is, a weapon that both sides in
a different factional dispute used against each other.[31] In any
event, Pandora's box was empty. One champion of "human
rights for all" preferred a different legend to illustrate her
view of what had happened: Mrs. Child wrote of the German
wizard who by certain incantations

> could cause a broom to become a man, and rapidly bring
> buckets of water from a neighboring river; and when the
> required work was completed, another spell transformed
> him to a broom again. The wizard's apprentice, being one
> day left with a charge to wash the shop and tools very
> thoroughly, thought he would avail himself of the ser-
> vice of the broom. He succeeded in repeating the first
> spell correctly; and to his great joy, saw arms and feet
> start forth to do his bidding. With supernatural activity,
> the bewitched household utensil brought water, water,
> water, till tubs were filled, the floor overflowed, the
> furniture was deluged. "Stop! stop!" cried the terrified
> apprentice: "We shall all be drowned, if you don't stop!"
> But, unfortunately, he had forgotten the backward spell,
> and the animated tool went on with frightful diligence.
>   Thus it is with those who urged women to become
> missionaries, and form tract societies. They have changed
> the household utensil to a living, energetic being; and
> they have no spell to turn it into a broom again.[32]

THE LEGENDS of Pandora and the sorcerer's apprentice
agree at several points: the events they describe were irreversi-
ble, unforeseen, and productive of cumulative results—and so
were the innovations in the status of women abolitionists. But
could the two factions not have subordinated their differences
on this issue to their common dedication to the cause of anti-
slavery? Each side asked this question and insisted that its
proposed answer would serve the common end.

The form in which the woman question became a divisive
issue within the AASS was both inevitable and guaranteed to
make it insoluble; it arose as a problem in constitutional inter-

pretation. The constitution of the national society stated that all "persons" except slaveholders who subscribed to the principles of the society and supported it financially were eligible for membership.[33] For the first few years no one thought of defining "persons," and custom determined the respective roles of men and women members. The women organized their own clubs, although nothing in the constitution technically precluded their joining the same clubs as the men. Quarterly and annual meetings of the regional and national associations were open to all members; the conventions were not delegated bodies, and all members present could vote. Under the constitution, could women speak and serve on committees at the conventions? Technically yes, if they were persons, and not even the most inveterate quoter of Saint Paul denied that.

Those who buttressed their view of female propriety by citing the letter of the New Testament contended that the actual words of the constitution were irrelevant, because in December 1833 when it was written no one anticipated that the Grimkés would become public lecturers or that Abby Kelley and other women would be willing to serve on committees.[34] The faction that relied on the spirit of the New Testament replied that the constitution meant precisely what it said. Both sides were, in different senses, "right," and as is clear from the debates, both knew perfectly well that they were carrying on in constitutional terms a debate that really involved much more than the "true" interpretation of the society's charter.[35]

At first the executive committee of the national society tried to localize the growing dispute in Massachusetts between the advocates of women's rights and the clerical remonstrants. It issued a statement from its New York headquarters asking the public not to identify the movement with a few individuals who had unorthodox notions of woman's sphere. It quoted the society's constitution on the qualifications for membership and pointed out that the organization had no authority to interfere with its members' views. And it bravely added that diversity of opinion was a sign of strength, because it showed that abolitionism was not restricted to one sect or party.[36] Garrison took the same position. He published a reply to the Rev. James T. Woodbury, who had announced that he had never "swallowed" Garrison; the editor of *The Liberator* retorted that no one had ever been expected to and that abolitionists were not obliged to accept one another's views on such questions as women's rights.[37]

The first showdown occurred at the annual New England Anti-Slavery Convention in the spring of 1838, when women were given permission to participate in its proceedings. Several members asked to have their names expunged from the roll of the convention. They spoke through the Rev. Charles T. Torrey[38] in a statement complaining that the convention's action deviated from previous usage and had hurt the cause of the slave by connecting it with a foreign subject and by furnishing a precedent for associating it with other irrelevant topics.[39]

An anonymous "Member of the Convention," in a letter to *The Liberator*, pointed out that the convention had not debated the rights, duties, or status of women in American society. To the slight extent that these subjects had been admitted into the discussion the convention had erred. But, he contended, the real issue in dispute *was* germane: whether women should be allowed to become equal members. Suppose a temperance convention voted to admit anyone who pledged abstinence from liquor, he wrote, and some Negroes claimed seats and some whites objected on the grounds that their admission would be unprecedented, that it was wrong for the races to mix on a basis of equality, and that the innovation would give the association bad publicity and cause other members to resign. Would it not be proper for those on the other side to offer their reasons why Negroes ought to be admitted? Would it not be relevant to the purposes for which the convention had met?[40]

This answered Torrey's objection on the ground of "irrelevance," but it did not meet his objection that the convention's vote admitting women reversed accepted policy in regard to convention membership. To deal with that question, the Garrisonians repeatedly pointed out that the women had come forward of their own accord and that the meetings had had to choose either to silence some members at the behest of others or to accord all members the equal status that the constitution seemed to give them.[41] At the time of the split in the national society, the Massachusetts Anti-Slavery Society's board of managers sent an address to its agents explaining that the organization had tried to deal with the woman-question issue

> *in a practical, inoffensive, and common sense way.* Those members appeared at our meetings, and claimed the right to vote and speak. *Their right was questioned. . . .* It thus became necessary to settle it. . . . We turned to the constitution of our society. We there found that all persons, who were members of the society, had equal rights in its meetings. Unless, therefore, we were prepared to vote that women are not *persons,* we could not deny them the common privileges of membership. Sparingly as our sisters in the cause have exercised their right to speak, our acknowledging that the right existed is put prominently forward as good cause for breaking up the anti-slavery organization in this State!

If a member disagrees with the constitution, the address went on, he should try to have it amended. If instead he resigns, "we can only say that *he is acting on a narrow principle, that would make all organized effort impossible, or very short-lived,*" because perfect agreement at all times is impossible.

> We are astonished to hear it pretended, that if a woman speaks at an anti-slavery meeting, the responsibility is not her own, but rests upon every man in the assembly;—a guilt from which he cannot absolve himself by protesting against it, but only by breaking up the whole anti-slavery organization![42]

The next act in the predictable scenario was staged at the annual meeting of the Massachusetts Anti-Slavery Society in January 1839, where a small minority led by Torrey attempted in vain to deprive women of the right to take part in the meeting.[43] That faction had already determined to withdraw from the society and found their own newspaper, *The*

Massachusetts Abolitionist. A few months later the Rev. Amos A. Phelps resigned his positions as corresponding secretary and member of the board of managers of the Massachusetts Society, averring that "The Society is no longer an *Anti-Slavery* Society *simply*, but in its principles and modes of action, has become a *women's-rights, non-government Anti-Slavery Society.*"[44]

Phelps retained his membership in the society, however, and at the New England convention in May he offered a resolution that only men be permitted to participate in the proceedings. The reasons he listed were all technical: that only men had participated in the first two New England conventions; that the first had unanimously resolved that conventions be held annually thereafter and that the board of managers of the Massachusetts Society were to be a standing committee to plan such conventions; that the third New England convention was the first of the series held according to this arrangement; and that the basis of organization of that convention ought therefore to be regarded as the basis upon which all future conventions were to be conducted—that is, men only. Phelps's resolution was defeated, and a large majority approved Wendell Phillips's motion to invite all abolitionists present to participate. The minority thereupon withdrew and on May 27 organized the Massachusetts Abolition Society.[45] The first organizational split had occurred. The Essex County (Massachusetts) Anti-Slavery Society divided immediately afterward, with the seceders, led by the Revs. Charles T. Torrey, Alanson St. Clair, and Daniel Wise, forming a new organization auxiliary to the Massachusetts Abolition Society.[46] Other splits took place, including an unusually bitter one in the Boston Female Anti-Slavery Society.[47]

At about the same time the fight officially spread beyond New England, when the national society at its annual meeting in New York had a test vote on seating the women. The Rev. Nathaniel Colver moved that the roll of delegates be made up of men only, but the convention approved the Garrisonian Ellis Gray Loring's amendment to the resolution, recognizing "all persons, male and female, who are delegates from any auxiliary society, or members of this Society," as members of the convention.[48] After much wrangling and voting, James G. Birney presented a protest on behalf of 123 delegates "against the principle, assumed by a majority of persons representing said Society at its present meeting, that women have the right of originating, debating, and voting on questions which come before said Society, and are eligible to its various offices," on the following grounds. First, the action was contrary to the intent of the society's constitution when originally written. Second, it was contrary to the interpretation of the constitution and the custom of the society since its founding. Third, "it is repugnant to the wishes, the wisdom, or the moral sense of many of the early and present members of said Society, and devoted friends of the cause for which that Society was organized." Fourth, although the majority at the convention favored the participation of women, most abolitionists, male and female, throughout the country did not. Fifth, "it is rather the expression of local and sectarian feelings, of recent origin, than of those broad sentiments which existed among friends of our great enterprise at its beginning." Sixth, the founders of the society recommended separate clubs for women. And seventh, regardless of the dissidents' opinions on women's rights, this action would "bring *unnecessary* reproach and embarrassment to the cause of the enslaved," because it was contrary to custom. However, added the protest, if such action were a necessary part of the fight to end slavery, the signers would disregard such reproach.[49] The following year, when the national convention voted to appoint Abby Kelley to the business committee, the final division occurred, and the minority founded the American and Foreign Anti-Slavery Society (A & F).[50] The A & F's constitution provided for separate women's societies which were to be represented at conventions by male delegates.

IT SHOULD BE noted that the uproar did not start within the movement; the Pastoral Letter and sermons such as Winslow's on woman's place were the work of nonabolitionists, and the other protests and appeals before 1839 were written by clergymen who were local antislavery leaders or on the periphery of the movement or had only recently joined.[51] In the early stages of the controversy, even the conservative Lewis Tappan could write, "Let Mr Garrison conduct his paper, in his own way, untrammelled," provided there was no official connection between it and any antislavery society, and "Let it be understood that our friends Grimke 'go a warfare at their own charges,' as they in fact do & are not connected with any Anti Slavery Society."[52]

But the woman-question controversy quickly became involved in the religious and political disputes that were to tear the association apart in 1840, and its usefulness as a weapon in those other factional struggles was revealed quite early. The second clerical protest[53] declared that Garrison had done more than encourage women to leave their appointed sphere; he had also denounced certain clergymen for refusing to read notices of abolitionist meetings from their pulpits, had repudiated the institution of the Sabbath, had preached the heresy of "perfectionism," and was working for the overthrow of all organized society. "The great body of abolitionists," continued the protest,

> . . . deplore the evils of which we complain. . . . It is but a few only who sanction them. And, in fact, these few are not *properly abolitionists*. . . . That class of men amongst us, whose abolition involves the abolition of the Sabbath and the Christian ministry, are *radicals*. They ought to be designated by this title. Let them go out from amongst us, for they are not of us. They are the prolific fountain of all the evils which retard and injure the cause of abolition.[54]

This statement represented an ominous innovation, for here for the first time some abolitionists laid down an ideological test of membership that would exclude many of their co-workers.

What in fact were the Garrisonians charged with? It is important to note that they were not accused of using official abolitionist platforms or society publications to preach that women ought to have the right to go to the polls, to enter professions, to be admitted to colleges. No paid agent of the society was accused of mixing up "extraneous" topics with his lectures on antislavery, except the extreme radical Henry C. Wright, and his appointment was not renewed.[55] *The Liberator*, which ran articles on both sides of the issue (with no pretense of neutrality, of course), was never, after 1832, the organ of any society. In 1837 it was financially supported by the Massachusetts Anti-Slavery Society, but even then the agreement made it clear that the paper spoke, not for the society, but only for its editor.[56] Discussions at conventions only occasionally and briefly touched on women's rights in general; the advocates of this cause usually refused to become embroiled in debates on the issue in society meetings, and their policy was the same in regard to all the other heresies Garrison was charged with.[57]

What their opponents were really objecting to, then, was that advocates of women's rights and the other eccentric causes belonged to antislavery societies at all. The conservatives' philosophy of abolitionism required the American Society and its auxiliaries to be *officially* orthodox on all subjects besides antislavery, explicitly repudiating what were then called "ultraisms." Their aim was to show white Northerners that antislavery was respectable and perfectly compatible with conventional views on all other questions. Since they themselves held conventional views on those other questions, they were, from their point of view, fighting to prevent abolition from being publicly portrayed in a false light and from being used as a cover for the propagation of false doctrines. The Garrisonians were developing a theory of abolitionist organization that required complete toleration within the society of members with all sorts of views and therefore a very minimal platform on which all abolitionists could stand regardless of their opinions on other issues and their activities outside the organization. In insisting that women who wanted to participate in antislavery meetings be allowed to do so, they did not suggest that the conservatives resign. The conservatives, on the other hand, tried to read the radicals out of the movement. They had no choice, since the public insisted on

considering Garrison and *The Liberator* spokesmen for abolitionism, despite repeated disclaimers by both sides in the
controversy. A Garrisonian-type movement could thus include the conservatives, but the conservatives' type of movement could not include the "ultraists." Before the final split
in 1840, the Garrisonians fought for resolutions that represented the least common denominator of abolitionist thinking;
the conservatives fought for resolutions that represented the
least common denominator of their own group's thinking and
would have excluded the women's-rights advocates, nonresistants, and nonvoters.[58]

The Second Clerical Protest had argued frankly for a platform so constructed as to accommodate only those who
believed in the divinity of the Sabbath and the Christian ministry, and to exclude "radicals." It did not matter that the
"radicals" preached their doctrines only in their own organs
and from their own platforms, or that the "radicals" themselves endorsed the formula enunciated in the protest—that
they were "associated together *as abolitionists*, for no other
object," and would therefore have preferred that the common
object be the only test of membership. [The test-of-member-
ship issue was only a surface indication that two profoundly
divergent conceptions of abolitionism itself had developed and
with them two mutually exclusive attitudes toward organization, strategy, and tactics.]

In the 1839 annual report of the Massachusetts Anti-Slavery
Society, Garrison argued that freedom of discussion was an
essential condition for unity. Discussing the movement then
under way to form a new antislavery society that would refuse
equal status to women and exclude those male abolitionists
whose beliefs did not permit them to vote, the report argued
that if any test other than principle were set up—that is, if
"modes of action" were made tests of membership—the movement would be divided, "and a house divided against itself
cannot stand." Such tests, Garrison continued, would lead to
rivalries and jealousies; other members would propose new
tests, and the abolitionist platform would be narrowed further.[59]

The antislavery movement, he wrote, desired to achieve its goal of abolition by preaching, that is, by means of free speech. Was it "introducing a foreign topic" to allow free speech on the subject of slavery to anyone in the society's meetings? Should the society constitute itself a judge of any person's right to speak for God and humanity? Certainly not, replied Garrison to his own rhetorical question; let each society by majority vote decide who might join and participate, and let the minority in each case abide by the decision and not withdraw.[60] Two things should be noted in this argument. First, freedom of speech was demanded for anyone discussing *the subject of slavery*, not women's rights, perfectionism, or any of the other "extraneous" topics which the seceders from the 1839 convention accused the radicals of dragging in. That is, Garrison and his supporters would encourage untrammeled discussion of all questions as they related to the struggle against slavery, not the merits of those questions in their own right, and they insisted that such freedom of discussion could be guaranteed only if all understood that no one who was otherwise eligible for membership would be read out of the organization for any position he took on those other questions. And obviously, freedom of discussion *on all questions* implied freedom of discussion *for all persons:* a limitation of free speech to certain members would itself have been the adoption of an official position on a mooted question, it would have deprived the meeting of the thoughts of some individuals who might have made valuable contributions, and it would have created an authoritarian atmosphere hostile to the spirit of free exchange of ideas for which Garrison and his friends were contending. The second thing that should be noted is that the last sentence of Garrison's statement paraphrased above urges the dissident minority to remain; Garrison was proposing an antislavery platform broad enough to accommodate those whose quarrels with him on the "extraneous issues" and on political action induced them to declare his abolitionism spurious.

Some of the dissidents felt that Garrison's pleas for unity were as spurious as his abolitionism: they believed he had con-

structed an antislavery platform too narrow for them to stand
on side by side with his faction and then publicly deplored
their departure! Others, who never doubted his sincerity,
found his platform proscriptive in effect, despite his verbal
welcome to all who accepted the basic tenets of the movement: the sinfulness of slavery and the obligation of immediate
and unconditional emancipation. The New-York City Anti-
Slavery Society, in an "Address to Abolitionists" justifying the
1840 secession, pointed out that many people, identifying the
abolitionist movement with a minority of its members, had
been deterred from joining, and members considered resigning, to the great joy of the friends of slavery. The society's
enemies no longer dreaded an organization that was "resolved
into a Quixotic crusade of knights-errant valorously battling
for the *rights of women!*" It would be better for the enterprise to dissolve than that its object be "made subservient to
paltry disputes for a worthless pre-eminence, or personal
partialities for particular theories." The movement must discard all foreign questions. Let all abolitionists leave their
favorite doctrines at home and meet as abolitionists, the address proposed; in so doing they would show their diversity on
other subjects to be a pledge of the movement's strength.
Elizur Wright, Jr., summed up the thesis thus: "It is down-
right nonsense to suppose that the Anti-Slavery cause can be
carried forward with forty incongruous things tacked on to it.
You can't drive a three tined fork through a hay mow," but
turn it around, he said, and "you can drive in the handle."[61]

Here was a delightful irony: each side accused the other of
"sectarianism"! Each side claimed its proposed platform was
the "broad" one, on which the greater number of abolitionists could stand united. The conservatives called the
AASS sectarian for letting its abolitionism be identified in the
public mind with other causes approved by only a small "sect"
centered in New England (with some supporters elsewhere,
particularly in eastern Pennsylvania)—causes like women's
rights, nonresistance, anticlericalism, antisabbatarianism, and
nonvoting. The AASS would reply that antislavery was one
aspect of a broad struggle for human rights; as such it in-

evitably brought some women into public activity. Those who wanted to silence them were the sectarians; that is, they tried to have the struggle against slavery conducted according to religious and conventional principles not approved by all abolitionists. In doing so they made those principles issues in the societies.[62] An antislavery society that officially endorsed Saint Paul would be free to take official positions on infant baptism, temperance, and so on indefinitely. The Garrisonians insisted that the antislavery platform must be broad enough to include an abolitionist who agreed with Saint Paul and one who did not. They could work together for the slave only so long as neither attempted to impose his opinions on the other.[63] In effect, then, "sectarianism" meant to the conservatives the belief in false doctrines; it meant to the Garrisonians the refusal to work in a movement with believers in false doctrines.

GILBERT H. BARNES considers Garrison a hypocrite for not pushing his female disciples onto the lecture platform.[64] But Garrison was not a champion of women's rights per se. He championed freedom of speech as a corollary of his broad commitment to human rights; freedom for women to follow the dictates of their own consciences was a further corollary that he gladly accepted. If a woman asked to speak or was willing to serve on a committee he was prepared to defend her right to do so, and he was prepared to vote for her if he considered her, as an individual, qualified for the post she sought. His policy in his own bailiwick was thus perfectly consistent with his tenets.

I think another instance of the same misunderstanding is John L. Thomas's statement:

> All of Garrison's reform interests suffered from his inability to bring to them a coherent philosophy. His concern with woman's rights was at best sporadic. He supported the Seneca Falls Convention in 1848 and attended the first woman's rights convention in Massachusetts in Worcester in 1850. His nonvoting perfectionism, how-

ever, made him something less than an enthusiastic supporter of the franchise for women. "I want the women
to have the right to vote, and I call upon them to demand
it perseveringly until they possess it. When they have
obtained it, it will be for them to say whether they will
exercise it or not."[65]

There is no contradiction between his approval of woman
suffrage and his nonvoting principle.[66] Garrison did have a
coherent philosophy that encompassed both. Its core was an
insistence that every human being was equally, strictly, individually responsible to God to do his will as revealed in the
New Testament. It repudiated governments based on force
because force was incompatible with this equality, violated
what Garrison interpreted as Christ's prohibition of coercion
of any sort, and substituted human for divine authority. He
stressed the gospel injunction to be perfectly free of sin as an
ideal toward which every individual must strive, each account-
able to God for his own sins. An obvious corollary of this
philosophy was absolute equality of all mankind, including
women and Negroes.[67] He therefore opposed a law that prevented women from deciding whether or not they would vote,
just as he opposed laws excluding Negroes from militias, even
though he abhorred armies on principle. "We want impartial
liberty to prevail," he explained, "and then every one must
'give account of himself to God' for the manner in which he
uses it."[68] His view of woman suffrage was thus purely negative; it was the eradication of a positive denial of equality,
freedom, and responsibility he was after, not woman suffrage
as a good in itself.[69]

Abolitionists who agreed on the question of principle could
still, and did, ask Garrison whether tacking a historically
premature reform onto one that had a better chance of success
did not impede the progress of both. Garrison believed that
this challenge begged the question. He and his followers were
certain that all good causes helped each other.[70] This would of
course follow from a commitment to broad human rights that
encompassed all the reforms regardless of their relative "ripe-

ness," especially if conceived in terms of a single divine Truth with many aspects. Real conversion to one was a step toward conversion to that larger commitment. Garrison's experience might be illustrated by a metaphor that pictured the white American of his day as in a dark room. Someone lit a small candle, and in the dim light he could now see where another unlit candle was. Each successive candle he lit would throw more light on everything else in the room, including the candles themselves—the full light being, of course, God's single, all-encompassing Truth, and the candles being the small parts of it that each reform represented.[71] Garrison himself had gone through that experience, since abolitionism had led him to his wider commitment.

Birney, the Tappans, Phelps, and the other antifeminist abolitionists had the simplest conceivable reply: abolitionism, temperance, and certain other reforms were part of God's Truth, but the equality of the sexes was most assuredly not. They could tolerate the vagaries of that lunatic fringe that every movement for change attracts, so long as the public clearly understood that those vagaries were not part of the movement proper. But if the activities of the fringe succeeded in identifying its idiosyncratic demands with the cause, it must be repudiated so that potential recruits would not be frightened away or the nature of the movement itself distorted.[72]

In addition to the Garrisonian and the antifeminist positions on the woman question, there was a third position, that of abolitionists who favored sex equality but believed that issue ought to be played down so as to enable the movement to recruit the many people who were ready for abolitionism but not yet enlightened enough to accept women's rights. Once those people had become active in the slave's behalf, that activity would help prepare them for the next step toward the wider cause of human rights. This was the view of Theodore D. Weld. A champion of absolute equality of the sexes, he repeatedly encouraged the Grimké sisters to lecture publicly to "promiscuous assemblies," stressing that as Southerners they could do ten times more for the cause of the slave than any Northern woman, but that

Any women of your powers will produce as much effect as you on the north in advocating the rights of *free* women (I mean in contradistinction to *slave* women). . . . Now can't you leave the *less* work to others who can do it *better* than you, and devote, consecrate your whole bodies, souls and spirits to the *greater* work which you can do far better and to far better purpose than any body else. Again, the abolition question is most powerfully preparative and introductory to the *other* question. By pushing the former with all our might we are most effectually advancing the latter. By absorbing the public mind in the greatest of all violations of rights, we are purging its vision to detect other violations.[73]

Therefore he urged them to stress in their lectures the fundamental principle of human rights, secure in the knowledge that they would be helping to advance the cause of women's rights without explicitly advocating it. Further, the public's prejudices against women's lecturing would be dissipated more effectively and quickly by repeated exposures to the practice than by polemics on the theory of sex equality. Weld's difference with Garrison on this issue was thus only tactical.

This was not so in the cases of the Quaker poet John Greenleaf Whittier, of Massachusetts, and Elizur Wright, Jr., corresponding secretary of the AASS. Neither could see the larger issue involved. Whittier, an active abolitionist, wrote both private and public letters pleading with Garrison, the Grimkés, and others not to intrude the "irrelevant" and relatively minor grievances of white women into the struggle against the greater crime of slavery.[74] Wright refused to take the argument seriously: "I think the tom-turkies ought to do the gobbling, I am opposed to hens' crowing, and surely, as a general rule, to female-preaching." But, he added, if some women insisted on acting the part of men they should be permitted to do so; nature would assert itself in the end.[75] Whittier and Wright were among those anti-Garrisonians who founded the A & F, which segregated its women members. Weld refused for that reason to join.[76]

But what about the Birneys, Tappans, and Phelpses, those

abolitionists whose attitudes toward women were undistin-
guishable from those of most nonabolitionists? Both the Garrison faction and those who shared Weld's sentiments would
have preferred that a formula be found whereby all could
work together in the AASS despite their differences. But the
conservatives were no more willing to accept Weld's than
Garrison's solution, for Weld and Garrison agreed that
women must be accorded equal status in the organization.
Garrison, for his part, never considered relinquishing that
demand. The very experiences that the abolition movement
had undergone by late 1837, when the issue arose, provided
him with a cogent reason: abolitionists had had to fight constantly for the freedom to advocate their cause, and in the
course of the battle had learned, and proclaimed, that free
speech and slavery could not coexist for long in any society;
one must sooner or later destroy the other, and the spirit that
would cut off free speech *was* the spirit of slavery.[77] Garrison
saw his task within the organization as parallel to the task of
the abolitionists in American society—to liberate thought, to
create an atmosphere in which all issues could be discussed
freely.[78] He tried to keep the subject of women's rights out of
the society's meetings but insisted on his right to discuss it in
his paper, and he was convinced that his opponents could conscientiously accept (though not approve of) women's equal
status in the organization as a technically correct interpretation of the constitution. When they refused to make that
minimum concession, he was certain their action was part of a
larger plot to discredit him. The history of the later disputes
over religious questions and political action, with which the
women's rights issue became entangled, suggests the plot did
not exist solely in his imagination.

NOTES

[1] Rayford W. Logan, *The Negro in American Life and Thought:
The Nadir, 1877–1901* (New York, 1954).

[2] See Aileen S. Kraditor, *The Ideas of the Woman Suffrage Movement, 1890–1920* (New York, 1965), Ch. 7.

³ I do not mean to imply that the two movements were comparable in all respects or that a struggle for the vote can be equated with a struggle for freedom.

⁴ Keith E. Melder, "The Beginnings of the Women's Rights Movement in the United States, 1800–1840," Ph.D. dissertation, Yale University, 1964, has an extremely detailed and perceptive discussion of the relation of the woman question to abolitionism, especially in Chs. 2 through 6. I read this work after I completed this chapter, but made no substantive changes because his sources coincide almost exactly with mine and our generalizations concur on all but a few minor points. Melder's dissertation deals with the events within the abolitionist movement involving the woman question in far greater detail than is appropriate here. My discussion will recount those events only insofar as they throw light on abolitionist thinking on the goals, strategy, and tactics of abolitionism.

⁵ The Grimké sisters, Angelina Emily (1805–1879) and Sarah Moore (1792–1873), were born in Charleston to a famous slaveholding family. Their father's distinguished career included membership in his state's constitutional ratifying convention and the posts of senior associate justice of the state and speaker of the South Carolina house of representatives. Their maternal grandfather had been governor of North Carolina, and their two brothers also attained fame, one as a philanthropist and the other as a jurist in Ohio. In 1819 Sarah became a Quaker and eventually converted Angelina, and the sisters moved to Philadelphia. Angelina became an abolitionist in 1834 and two years later converted Sarah to the cause. In 1837 they traveled about New England lecturing for abolition, at their own expense; they were not official agents of the AASS. In 1838 Angelina married Theodore Dwight Weld, and both women retired from public activity, Sarah living thereafter with her sister's family.

⁶ The "Address of the American and Foreign Anti-Slavery Society" (the anti-Garrisonian "new organization" formed in 1840 by seceders from the AASS), published in *The Liberator*, June 19, 1840, emphasized that the women had asked permission to speak, and it argued that that showed they had not been considered regular members. See also William Goodell, *Slavery and Anti-Slavery*, p. 453; [Wendell P. Garrison and Francis J. Garrison], *William Lloyd Garrison, 1805–1879: The Story of His Life Told by His Children* (hereafter referred to as Garrisons, *Garrison*), I (1805–1835) (New York, 1885), 413. It should not be inferred that the issue of women's rights had never arisen before this time. In fact, at the 1836 convention of the Massachusetts Anti-Slavery Society, Dr. Charles Follen made an eloquent plea for equality of the sexes. See *Fourth Annual Report of the Board of Managers of the New-England Anti-Slavery Society* (Boston, 1836), pp. 52–53. The report does not indicate that any dissent was made. After the controversy arose the following year, however, most proponents of women's rights refrained from making such speeches at society meetings.

⁷ An excellent account of the episode is in Eleanor Flexner, *Century of Struggle: The Woman's Rights Movement in the United States* (Cambridge, Mass., 1959), pp. 45–50.

⁸ They mention their shyness in several letters, one of which is

Angelina E. Grimké to Amos A. Phelps, August 17, [1837], Phelps Papers, BPL.

⁹ This and other details about the lectures can be found in a series of letters from Angelina Grimké to Jane Smith throughout 1837, in the Weld Papers, UM; they constitute a sort of diary, with summaries of the lectures, the reactions and sizes of the audiences, and the sisters' thoughts concerning their mission. Only one of these letters is in the published *Weld-Grimké Letters*.

¹⁰ *The Liberator*, August 11, 1837.

¹¹ They express this conviction in many letters. An unusually interesting one is Sarah M. Grimké to Amos A. Phelps, August 3, 1837, Phelps Papers, BPL. See also Sarah M. Grimké to Henry C. Wright, August 27, 1837, Anti-Slavery Letters, BPL.

¹² Garrison published them all. See "Appeal of Clerical Abolitionists on Anti-Slavery Measures," *The Liberator*, August 11, 1837; "Appeal of Abolitionists of the [Andover] Theological Seminary," *ibid.*, August 25, 1837; "Protest of Clerical Abolitionists, No. 2," *ibid.*, September 8, 1837; "Abolition Women," a lecture by the Rev. Albert A. Folsom of Hingham, *ibid.*, September 22, 1837. From this time on, through 1840, *The Liberator* frequently printed letters on all sides of the woman question. The Andover Appeal and the Protest No. 2 berated Garrison and his supporters mainly for perfectionism and anti-institutionalism. Women's-rightsism was included simply as one of his heresies.

¹³ Mrs. Child (1802–1880) had been a successful novelist before her conversion to abolitionism, when she sacrificed her lucrative career to publish the pamphlet *An Appeal in Favor of That Class of Americans Called Africans* (1833). After the anti-Garrisonians withdrew from the AASS in 1840, taking the official organ, *The Emancipator*, with them, the society founded a new paper, *The National Anti-Slavery Standard*, and from 1841 to 1842 Mrs. Child was its editor.

¹⁴ "Letter from Mrs. Child, on the Present State of the Anti-Slavery Cause," *The Liberator*, September 6, 1839. See also "Speaking in the Church," *ibid.*, July 23, 1841. This editorial by Mrs. Child is reprinted from *The National Anti-Slavery Standard*.

¹⁵ Wright (1797–1870), a former hatmaker and Congregational preacher, joined the New-England Anti-Slavery Society in 1835 and became a traveling agent for the AASS. When the Grimkés began their lecture tour he made himself their unofficial booking agent. His alleged incompetence and undisputed radicalism caused the society to transfer him to Pennsylvania and then drop him from its roster of agents. He was an even more uncompromising pacifist than Garrison and provoked the ire of the conservatives by his numerous heretical articles in *The Liberator*.

¹⁶ Angelina E. Grimké to Theodore D. Weld and John G. Whittier, August 20, 1837, Gilbert H. Barnes and Dwight L. Dumond, eds., *The Letters of Theodore Dwight Weld, Angelina Grimké and Sarah Grimké* (Magnolia, Mass., 1965), I, 428. See also Anne Warren Weston to Lucia Weston, n.d., but evidently in September 1840, Weston Papers, BPL: commenting on a lecture tour in Connecticut by Abby Kelley, a Quaker abolitionist from Massachusetts, Miss Weston wrote that one minister

had "preached a sermon at her from the text 'Notwithstanding I have a few things against thee because thou sufferest that woman Jezebel *which calleth herself a prophetess*, to teach, & to seduce my servants to commit fornication.' He called her by name applying this verse to her, said every thing he could to attack her character: that 'she was travelling up & down by night & by day, always with men & never with women—' Not a woman in the town but was afraid to speak to her tho' they had known her well."

17 The abolitionist ministers probably were particularly anxious to show that abolitionism did not imply women's-rightsism, in view of such statements as that of the Rev. Albert A. Folsom, that neglect of her domestic duties was an inevitable result of a woman's conversion to abolitionism (the speech is in *The Liberator*, September 22, 1837). Statements such as Folsom's were also calculated to reduce the size of the Grimkés' audiences and no doubt provided an additional motive for the Grimkés, Garrison, and other abolitionists who favored women's rights, to use the podium and the printing press to show not only that female abolitionists did not neglect their duties but also that public work in behalf of the slave was itself a duty of a Christian woman.

18 1 Cor. 14:34-35; Ephesians 5:22-24. Other favorite New Testament verses were 1 Timothy 2:11-12 and 1 Peter 3:1.

19 See, for example, letter to the editor from Henry C. Wright, *The Liberator*, May 22, 1840. Wright contended that the spirit that said women should work separately in their own societies was the same spirit that would send Negroes to Liberia. He quoted Lewis Tappan to the effect that it was "contrary to the usages of civilized society" for women to act in organizations with men, and he cited the opinions of the Revs. Amos A. Phelps and C. W. Denison that such integration would be contrary to the gospel. Wright observed that both arguments were used to keep Negroes in slavery or segregated. The same arguments appear in an editorial by Oliver Johnson immediately preceding Wright's letter, and in "Address of the Executive Committee of the American Anti-Slavery Society to the Abolitionists of the United States," *ibid.*, July 31, 1840.

20 Caroline L. Shanks, "The Biblical Anti-Slavery Argument of the Decade 1830-1840," *Journal of Negro History*, XVI (April 1931), 150.

21 *The Liberator*, May 24, 1839.

22 Phelps (1805-1847), after graduation from Yale, was a Congregationalist minister in Massachusetts until 1834, when he became general agent of the New-England Anti-Slavery Society. From 1835 he held the same post in the Massachusetts Anti-Slavery Society. He became corresponding secretary of that organization in 1838 but resigned the following year. Phelps broke with Garrison during the controversy over the status of women in the AASS. In 1839 he returned to preaching, although for a short time a few years later he edited *The Abolitionist*, the organ of the anti-Garrisonian Massachusetts Abolition Society.

23 *The Liberator*, February 26, 1841. In 1837 Phelps, always a conservative on religious and social questions, had criticized the clerical remonstrants for causing unnecessary dissension within the movement (see his letter as general agent of the Massachusetts Society, *ibid.*, Au-

gust 18, 1837, and his letter to John G. Whittier, August 17, 1837, Phelps Papers, BPL). But later, when the controversy over the woman question became involved in the general factionalism, he made his conservative views public and joined the anti-Garrison group.

24 Sarah Douglass to Charles K. Whipple, April 26, 1841, Anti-Slavery Letters, BPL.

25 *The Liberator,* October 6, 1837, reprinted from *The New England Spectator.* A long excerpt from this document is reprinted in Aileen S. Kraditor, ed., *Up from the Pedestal: Selected Writings in the History of American Feminism* (Chicago, 1968).

26 "Letters to Catherine E. Beecher, No. XII," *The Liberator,* October 13, 1837. See Kraditor, ed., *Up from the Pedestal.*

27 See, for example, the protest of those members of the AASS national convention of 1839 who withdrew because women were permitted equal status with men in the convention and on its committees (*Sixth Annual Report of the Executive Committee of the American Anti-Slavery Society* [New York, 1839], pp. 44–47).

28 James Mott (husband of Lucretia Mott, the pioneer feminist) to Anne Warren Weston, June 7, 1838, Weston Papers, BPL. See also resolution passed by the Providence Ladies' Anti-Slavery Society at its quarterly meeting in October 1837, in which the ladies expressed their gratitude, as women, to the pioneers in the cause of emancipation, in Europe and America, for helping them discern their own rights "by means of the full light which their benevolent efforts have shed on the equality of the rights of man" (*The Liberator,* November 3, 1837).

29 See, for example, Oliver Johnson's editorial, *ibid.,* August 11, 1837 (Johnson was editor pro tem. in Garrison's absence), and a resolution of the Bristol County Anti-Slavery Society at its annual meeting in New Bedford, Mass., as reported *ibid.,* October 27, 1837.

30 Maria Weston Chapman, *Right and Wrong in Massachusetts* (Boston, 1839), pp. 12–13. Mrs. Chapman (1806–1885) was Garrison's chief female supporter, a nonresistant and feminist, leader in the Boston Female Anti-Slavery Society, and writer of its reports entitled *Right and Wrong in Boston.* After the 1840 split in the AASS she became a member of the executive committee of the national organization. Upon David Lee Child's resignation as editor of the *Standard,* in 1844, Mrs. Chapman was one of the editorial committee of three that replaced him (the others were Edmund Quincy and Sidney Howard Gay).

31 For this reason the remark by Gilbert H. Barnes in *The Anti-Slavery Impulse, 1830–1844* (New York, 1933), p. 158, is debatable: "The net result of the woman's rights controversy was to reduce the antislavery influence of the Grimké sisters' agency and to retard materially the actual progress of woman's emancipation." But numerous letters in *The Liberator* show that many people were stimulated to think about the question for the first time, that many women abolitionists who had already harbored forbidden thoughts of female emancipation were emboldened to pursue those thoughts further than they would have dared to otherwise, and that some male abolitionists pondered the analogies that had been suggested between Negro rights and women's rights. The exclusion

of women from membership at the 1840 World's Anti-Slavery Convention in London was, as is well known, the incident that induced Elizabeth Cady Stanton and Lucretia Mott to organize the first women's-rights convention, and the effort to seat them at the London convention was a direct outgrowth of the controversy.

32 Lydia Maria Child, in *The National Anti-Slavery Standard,* as reprinted in *The Liberator,* July 23, 1841.

33 *First Annual Report of the American Anti-Slavery Society,* back cover.

34 For the antifeminists' construction of the constitution, see Lewis Tappan to Theodore D. Weld, May 26, 1840, Tappan Papers, LC; protest of 123 members of the 1839 national convention, printed in *Sixth Annual Report of the Executive Committee of the American Anti-Slavery Society,* pp. 44–47, especially points 1 and 2 on p. 45; "Address of the American and Foreign Anti-Slavery Society," *The Liberator,* June 19, 1840.

35 One is reminded of the debate over Lincoln's constitutional powers during the Civil War; of course the Constitution did not anticipate a civil war, and so both sides were in a sense right—and wrong.

36 "To the Public," signed by Elizur Wright, Jr., corresponding secretary, in behalf of the executive committee, reprinted from *The Emancipator,* official organ of the AASS, in *The Liberator,* September 1, 1837.

37 Both statements are *ibid.*

38 Torrey (1813–1846) was a Yale graduate, Massachusetts pastor, lecturer for the Massachusetts Anti-Slavery Society, and corresponding secretary of the Andover Anti-Slavery Society when it was formed in 1835. In 1844 he was arrested in Baltimore for having helped some fugitive slaves escape, and was sentenced to six years in prison, where he died of tuberculosis.

39 *The Liberator,* June 8, 1838.

40 *Ibid.,* July 6, 1838. See also ninth resolution passed at the 1839 annual meeting of the Essex County Anti-Slavery Society, reported *ibid.,* June 21, 1839; and "Address to the Abolitionists of Massachusetts," signed by Francis Jackson and Garrison, president and secretary respectively of the Massachusetts Anti-Slavery Society, *ibid.,* July 19, 1839. One Garrisonian who was certainly guilty of the conservatives' charges was Maria Weston Chapman. Her most serious breach of the principle asserted by the "Member of the Convention" was in the annual report of the Boston Female Anti-Slavery Society for 1837, which she wrote. It includes a long argument for sex equality, including biblical citations. Unlike the Grimkés' articles, this was an official antislavery-society document. Five leaders of Mrs. Chapman's organization recorded their dissent from "some portions" of the report. See *Right and Wrong in Boston, No. 3* (Boston, 1837), pp. 3, 74–75. This incident was exceptional, however.

41 See, for example, Oliver Johnson, *The Liberator,* July 27, 1838.

42 *Ninth Annual Report of the Board of Managers of the Mass. Anti-Slavery Society* (Boston, 1841), p. 16. Italics in original. On this one

point, the violently anti-Garrisonian Joshua Leavitt, editor of *The Emancipator*, agreed. See "The Woman Question," *The Emancipator*, May 23, 1839.

43 *The Liberator*, February 1, 1839.

44 *Ibid.*, May 3, 1839. The copy of the original letter, dated April 30, 1839, in Phelps Papers, BPL, differs slightly in punctuation.

45 Letter to the editor from Phelps, now recording secretary of the new society, *The Liberator*, June 14, 1839. Since Phelps was one of those who had strong objections, on religious and physiological grounds, to women's public activity (see his letter *ibid.*, February 26, 1841), the purely technical arguments in his resolution provoke speculation whether his action was not a tacit admission that if he had given his real reasons he would have dragged into the meeting an extraneous issue which had not been introduced by his opponents. Phelps's manuscript letters reveal a hot temper and impulsiveness. Certainly if the women's-rights issue itself had come before the meeting he would have fought it out on its own terms.

46 *Ibid.*, June 21, 28, and July 5, 1839.

47 *Ibid.*, November 1, 5, 22, and December 6, 1839; *Address of the Massachusetts Female Emancipation Society to the Women of Massachusetts*, a circular with a letter written on the same sheet: M. V. Ball to the English abolitionist Elizabeth Pease, May 6, 1840, in Anti-Slavery Letters, BPL. Miss Ball presents the anti-Garrison version of what happened. The other side is presented in Maria Weston Chapman to Elizabeth Pease, April 20, 1840, in the same collection. See Henry B. Stanton to Elizur Wright, Jr., April 11, 1839, Wright Papers, LC: "The Boston Female Soc. had a meeting yesterday, to fight a new edition of the Quarterly meeting of the Mass. Soc. Mrs. Chapman roared like a *female bull!* A motion was made to pledge $500 to the *Am.* Soc.—She moved to amend by pledging, $1000 to the *Mass.* Soc.—'The debate took a wide range'—caps, ribbons, tapes, needles, curls & flounces flew at each other most furiously. Mrs. Shipley moved to amend the amendment by striking out *Mass.* & inserting *Amer.* Mrs. Chapman fired a whole broadside of non-resistance into this proposition." And more. Stanton (1805–1887) deserves to be better known in his own right rather than merely as the husband of the leading feminist Elizabeth Cady Stanton. He was one of the "Lane Rebels," the group of students at Lane Theological Seminary in Cincinnati who under the leadership of Theodore Weld engaged in a series of revival-debates on slavery in 1834 that resulted in the conversion of most of the students to abolitionism, and withdrew en masse from Lane when the trustees attempted to prevent their antislavery activities. Stanton was AASS agent for Rhode Island, 1834–1836, and organized the state antislavery society. He was one of the most articulate anti-Garrisonians from the late 1830s on, and later became active in the Massachusetts Liberty party.

48 Barnes, on p. 159 of *The Anti-Slavery Impulse*, states: "Among the regularly constituted delegates a majority was against the measure; but the women insisted upon casting their ballots for the resolution in advance of their right to do so, and their votes gave it a majority." The reference to "regularly constituted delegates" is misleading; the constitu-

tion gave rank-and-file members the right to attend and vote at conventions, and such members had done so in all previous conventions. The phrase "in advance of their right to do so" prejudges the issue. Colver's and Loring's motions could be regarded as attempts to clarify the constitution, and according to the Garrisonians, women members had always had the right that Loring's motion merely stated explicitly. Or, the vote could be interpreted as a referendum of all constitutionally defined members to decide which of those members were to act in the society's meetings. By stating that woman had no right to vote on the issue, Barnes transforms into the constitutional ground of the vote the issue that the vote was to decide! Admittedly, I am doing the same when I say the women did have the right to vote. The point is, of course, that the issue could not be settled this way.

⁴⁹ *Sixth Annual Report of the Executive Committee of the American Anti-Slavery Society*, pp. 27-30, 44-47.

⁵⁰ This was the convention that Garrison "packed" with his boatload of disciples from New England. Barnes discusses Garrison's stratagem on pp. 169-70 of *The Anti-Slavery Impulse*, but his animus against Garrison causes him to distort what happened. He devotes most of three paragraphs to the chartering of a boat, the fact that in Lewis Tappan's words, "a large part of the town of Lynn" responded to Garrison's appeal for passengers, and the consequent vote by which the convention confirmed Miss Kelley's appointment to the business committee. He dismisses in one sentence the efforts of the Tappan faction to rig the convention its way. But see Henry B. Stanton to Amos A. Phelps, dated "Saturday," and written on the blank pages of a circular from the British and Foreign Anti-Slavery Society dated February 15, 1840, Phelps Papers, BPL. See also comment by Lydia Maria Child in letter to Ellis Gray Loring, May 17, [1840], Child Papers, NYPL, concerning "a *very* extensive and active agitation on the part of the Ex. Committee. The degree of diligence and tact manifested would exceed your belief. No opportunity . . . has been omitted in this region [central Massachusetts], to preoccupy the minds of the people against the Massachusetts Board. *Every* minister, influential deacon, or active sectarian, for miles and miles and miles around, has been furnished with the N. York side of the case, without any chance of hearing the Mass. side. Private letters *innumerable* have been written in every direction, especially by Phelps. . . . Nothing is more observable in all these transactions than the efforts at secrecy [*sic*]." Cf. Barnes's statement (p. 279, n. 22) that the Executive Committee restricted its activities to general appeals to attend the convention to secure a majority. Perhaps this statement reflects the inadequacy of his research into manuscript materials. For private efforts to rig other conventions, see C. T. Torrey to Edwin F. Clarke, March 7, 1840, Miscellaneous Slavery Collection, NYHS, and A. St. Clair to Phelps, March 30, 1839, Phelps Papers, BPL, among others. The Garrisonians' activities were well publicized. *The Liberator*, April 24, 1840, reprinted from *The Emancipator* a letter from Garrisonian James S. Gibbons to Joshua Leavitt, editor of *The Emancipator*, urging "all abolitionists" to come to the New York convention to help save the society. An anti-Garrisonian appeal for a large turnout appeared in a Connecti-

cut paper and was reprinted in *The Liberator*, May 1, 1840. The May 8 issue had an article describing the special travel arrangements; it said that in view of the many statements proposing dissolution of the society or change of the constitution to eliminate the clause permitting rank-and-file members to vote at conventions, the friends of the old organization ought to go en masse, for if they did not, it would be understood by all that the cause was languishing.

51 Leaders like Birney and the Tappans seem to have been embarrassed by the furious attacks of the clerics. Certainly Elizur Wright and Henry B. Stanton were. Birney and the Tappans, and other leaders who were conservative on the woman question, found ample opportunities for public attacks on Garrison on other questions, although once the innovations in women's activities had evoked the public outcry, they were willing to use them or countenance their use in their factional struggles with Garrison. The nonresistance and nonvoting issues, to be discussed in later chapters, were more important to them. Arthur Tappan signed a statement by the A & F that the same abolitionists who favored women's rights were those who denied the obligation to yield obedience to civil government; Birney at the London Convention used the same tactic in his effort to prevent the seating of women delegates, although the "no human government" theory had no bearing on the question at issue (*The Liberator*, June 19, July 24, 1840).

52 Tappan to Amos A. Phelps, August 22, 1837, Phelps Papers, BPL. Lewis Tappan (1788–1873), along with his partner and older brother, Arthur, was a wealthy New York merchant, a Presbyterian, and an active worker for benevolent and religious causes. When Garrison was jailed for libeling a proslavery merchant in Baltimore in 1829, it was Arthur Tappan who paid his fine. But Lewis was the more active abolitionist of the two, one of the leaders of the conservative "New York group," and broke with Garrison over the latter's various heresies in the late 1830s. After the AASS schism in 1840, Tappan became active in the A & F.

53 See footnote 12 above.

54 *The Liberator*, September 8, 1837.

55 Lewis Tappan to Amos A. Phelps, August 22, 1837, and Elizur Wright, Jr., to Phelps, September 12, 1837, Phelps Papers, BPL; Charles C. Burleigh to James M. McKim, November 13, 1837, Anti-Slavery Letters, BPL.

56 Garrison to Anna E. Benson, February 4, 1837, Garrison Letters, BPL; "To the Public," signed by Francis Jackson and Nathaniel Southard, president and recording secretary respectively of the Massachusetts Anti-Slavery Society, *The Liberator*, September 8, 1837; "Our Cause," *ibid.*, November 3, 1837; *Fifth Annual Report of the Board of Managers of the Massachusetts Anti-Slavery Society* (Boston, 1837), p. xxxvi.

57 It need hardly be pointed out that they energetically used other media to propagate their views. Sarah Grimké advocated women's rights in some of her public lectures (see Angelina E. Grimké to Jane Smith, July 27, [1837], Weld Papers, UM). She wrote fifteen "Letters on the Equality of the Sexes, and the Condition of Woman. Addressed to Mary S. Parker, President of the Boston Female Anti-Slavery Society"; *The*

Liberator serialized them in the issues of January 5, 12, 26, February 2, 9, 16, 1838. Starting in the issue of June 23, 1837, *The Liberator* printed Angelina Grimké's "Letters to Catherine Beecher," some of which dealt with the woman question; see letters 11 and 12, issues of September 29 and October 13, 1837. See also letter by Sarah Grimké in *The New England Spectator* (a religious paper violently hostile to Garrison and women's rights, and the paper which originally published many of the clerical assaults on Garrison) as reprinted in *The Liberator*, October 6, 1837, under the title "Province of Woman. The Pastoral Letter." Selections from these essays by both Grimkés may be found in Kraditor, ed., *Up from the Pedestal.*

58 See pages 124, 129–30 below.

59 "Extracts from the Seventh Annual Report of the Massachusetts Anti-Slavery Society," *The Liberator*, February 1, 1839. This part of the report dealt mainly with the question of political tests and only incidentally with the woman question and religion. It will therefore be discussed at greater length in Chapter 5. Garrison's prediction came true. The impotence of the Massachusetts Abolition Society and the A & F was due to several circumstances one of which was internal dissension, especially over political action. As for religious sectarianism, see St. Clair to Phelps, June 21, 1839, Phelps Papers, BPL: discussing the proposed leadership of the Massachusetts Abolition Society, St. Clair marked this section *"Confidential":* "Dont have any more congregationalists on the Executive Committee. There are already jealousies among some of the Baptists who are with us, on account of the preponderating *number!* of that denomination. I think it best by all means to wait till we know what Baptists will go with us, before filling the vacancies in the Committee. It will be extremely injurious to have any suspicion a particular denomination has a controling [sic] influence entertained by any other sect."

Published announcements of newly formed executive committees, lists of sponsors of mass meetings, and such must be interpreted with caution; often the lists were published before the individuals on them had been asked if they would serve. The Phelps Papers, BPL, for example, contain several letters written in summer 1839 by men who had seen their names listed as officers of the new society and who wrote to Phelps to decline the honor.

60 "The 'Woman Question,'" *The Liberator*, February 1, 1839. This article was a continuation of the extracts from the report.

61 "Address to Abolitionists from the New-York City Anti-Slavery Society," signed by John Jay, chairman of the executive committee, May 8, 1840, Chapman Papers, BPL; Elizur Wright, Jr., to Amos A. Phelps, September 5, 1837, Phelps Papers, BPL. Wright (1804–1885) was a Connecticut-born Yale graduate who was teaching mathematics at Western Reserve College when he became converted to abolitionism. He was a corresponding secretary of the AASS from 1833 to 1839 and then became editor of the newly founded organ of the Massachusetts Abolition Society, *The Abolitionist.* In the 1840s he was active in support of the Liberty party, although poverty and the needs of a large family forced him to devote much time to efforts to sell copies of his translation of La Fontaine's fables. In 1845 Wright started a life insur-

ance company for teetotalers, and between that time and 1850 he edited his own paper, the Boston *Chronotype*.

62 Lydia Maria Child, who thought it preferable for women to do their abolitionist duty and not talk about women's rights, wrote that the advocates of women's rights had *not* forced the issue into society meetings; on the contrary, even *The Liberator* had not entered the controversy except when Garrison felt he had to defend the Grimkés against the attacks. If a clergyman thought it wrong for a woman to speak in public, he had a right to his opinion, she said. "I should agree with the Massachusetts Society that it would be a monstrous violation of freedom to request or advise him to withdraw from the society because some of his views seemed likely to retard the progress of the cause." She went on to say that those on the other side insisted on introducing a foreign topic when they objected, in the meetings, to women's participation, and that the society very properly replied that it did not meddle with that subject and would take no action on it. Women, she wrote, had been regular dues-paying members from the start, and the society did not prescribe their mode of action any more than that of other members ("Letter from Mrs. Child, on the Present State of the Anti-Slavery Cause," *The Liberator*, September 6, 1839). The fight over the propriety of prescribing modes of action turned out to be a preliminary skirmish for the more important battle on political action which, when it came, was fought in exactly the same way.

63 Although the Garrisonians tried to follow this policy before the organizational split, they tended more and more to relax it as time went on. Supporters of Garrison, especially those whose opinions were more "ultra" than his, did mix up extraneous issues with abolitionism after it had become clear that there was no chance of keeping the AASS platform broad (by their definition of the term).

64 *The Anti-Slavery Impulse*, p. 160: Garrison and his followers "consistently opposed the enlistment of New England women in the public agitation." Barnes offers no evidence, and I know of none, to support this statement. It is true that Garrison did not encourage such enlistment; he accepted the women's own convictions of their duty. Barnes's evidence is doubtful in several places, on this topic. On p. 156 he mentions Angelina Grimké's asking the Boston abolitionists to have her name added to the list of speakers at a hearing of a Massachusetts legislative committee in early 1838. Barnes: " 'They all flinched,' wrote Angelina, 'except F. Jackson.' Scorning to deal further with 'Abolitionists who were only right in the *abstract* on Woman's rights and duties,' Angelina applied to the chairman of the legislative committee herself, who courteously appointed a time for her to speak. After it was arranged that she should appear, the Boston abolitionists decided to approve it." Barnes's footnote on p. 271 cites Angelina to Weld, February 11, 1838. The relevant portion is in Barnes and Dumond, eds., *Weld-Grimké Letters*, II, 538–39, where she writes that she asked S. Philbrick (with whose family the sisters were boarding) to tell the abolitionists, when he went into Boston, that she was willing to speak. Then, after the comment on abolitionists who favored women's rights only in the abstract: "they all flinched as I understand except F. Jackson. . . ."

Barnes presents hearsay as direct testimony and does not indicate by
ellipsis the omission of "as I understand." The footnote adds that "the
tardy approval by the Boston abolitionists" is in Sarah Grimké to Gerrit
Smith, February 16, 1838. The only relevant part of that letter is a
paragraph on p. 551, *ibid.*, in which Sarah states that they had written to
the chairman asking permission to testify, had received it, and rejoiced
that God had found them worthy to plead for the slave. There is not a
word on the Boston abolitionists in the letter. In any case, we are not
given the Bostonians' own reasons for their hesitation. Barnes gives
Henry B. Stanton credit for first suggesting, half in earnest and half in
jest, that Angelina testify, and accurately cites the letter in which she
reports the suggestion (Angelina to Weld, February 11, 1838). His footnote praises Stanton at length as a champion of women's rights. He does
not, however, mention the letter Sarah wrote the very next day, complaining of Stanton's having left Boston before the hearing: "Brother
Stanton we think is deserting in a time of need. . . . Somehow he seems
not to give his cordial approbation to Angelina's having an opportunity
to address the Committee . . ." (*ibid*, p. 541).

65 *The Liberator: William Lloyd Garrison* (Boston, 1963), pp. 372-73.
66 Lucretia Mott, for one, explicitly linked them: "Far be it from me
to encourage women to vote, or to take an active part in politics in the
present state of our government. Her right to the elective franchise,
however, is the same, and should be yielded to her, whether she exercise
that right or not. Would that man, too, would have no participation in a
government recognizing the life-taking principle. . . . But when, in the
diffusion of light and intelligence, a convention shall be called to make
regulations for self-government on Christian principles, I can see no
good reason why women should not participate in such assemblage,
taking part equally with man." "Discourses by Lucretia Mott. Discourse
on Woman, Delivered Twelfth Month 17th, 1849," in Anna D. Hal-
lowell, ed., *James and Lucretia Mott, Life and Letters* (Boston, 1884), p.
500. Garrison would have agreed with this entire statement.
67 See his statement at a women's rights convention in New York in
1853, as quoted in Elizabeth Cady Stanton and others, eds., *The History
of Woman Suffrage* (New York, 1881), I, 549: "I have been derisively
called a '*Woman's Rights Man*.' I know no such distinction. I claim to be
a HUMAN RIGHTS MAN, and wherever there is a human being, I see God-
given rights inherent in that being whatever may be the sex or com-
plexion."
68 Editorial commenting on "Right of Suffrage to Women," reprinted from *The New York Tribune* in *The Liberator*, January 11,
1850. The *Tribune* had expressed the same opinion as Thomas and had
coyly suggested that Garrison, Phillips, and their friends were not asking
women to vote; they were asking that women "have the right to *refuse
to vote*." In his reply, Garrison pointed out that the editor of the
Tribune was a Whig; "yet, anxious as he is to have that party in the
ascendant, we presume he would protest against the exclusion of
Democrats from the ballot-box . . . because it would be a blow struck at
human freedom and equality."
69 This may be inferred from the wording, for instance, of two

resolutions he offered at the 1842 Non-Resistance Society convention, as
reported in *The Liberator*, October 28, 1842: first, that the federal and
state constitutions were "based on usurpation, inasmuch as they proscribe
one half of the people, on account of their sex, from the exercise and
enjoyment of what are called civil and political rights"; and second, that
"friends of human rights" ought to petition their state legislatures to
abolish "all those laws which make any distinction, in regard to rights
and immunities, on account of sex." (Incidentally, this call for woman
suffrage appeared almost six years before the Seneca Falls convention.
Garrison was, of course, wrong in believing the U.S. Constitution
prevented women from voting. It never did. Even the word "male" did
not appear in it until the Fourteenth Amendment was added in 1868.)
The suffragist Alice Stone Blackwell was perhaps reflecting her New
England abolitionist heritage when she explained, a generation later, that
although she opposed any property test for voting, she would welcome a
law to give the vote to all taxpayers regardless of sex rather than the law
then in force that specifically barred women. Such a change would
remove a positive discrimination against one part of the population.
(*Woman's Journal*, May 21, 1903)

70 A few expressions of this conviction among his followers are:
Angelina E. Grimké's note at the end of Sarah M. Grimké to Henry C.
Wright, August 27, 1837, Anti-Slavery Letters, BPL; Sarah M. Grimké
to Amos A. Phelps, August 3, 1837, Phelps Papers, BPL; Abby Kelley to
Garrison, October 20, 1837, as quoted in Garrisons, *Garrison*, II, 174n;
and especially Henry C. Wright's letter in *The Liberator*, October 13,
1837. Cf. Elizur Wright, Jr., to Garrison, November 6, 1837, in Garrisons, *Garrison*, II, 179: "You say, 'Truth is *one*, and not conflictive or
multitudinous.' True; but the *people* are conflictive, and moreover they
cannot receive and unitedly act upon more than one great truth at
once." Lest it be inferred that only the Garrisonians believed all truths
helped one another and that all non-Garrisonians favored tactical pref-
erences among them, cf. James G. Birney to Gerrit Smith, June 1, 1846,
Dumond, ed., *Birney Letters*, II, 1021–22. Arguing in favor of the
Liberty party's broadening its platform to include many reform planks
and disagreeing with Smith's assertion that inclusion of the other planks
would be "premature," Birney wrote that abolitionists should not fear to
tell all the truths they knew; each one supported the others. He asked:
When, reading the Bible, we learn a truth we have not understood
before, does it weaken or strengthen those we did know before? "So, of
emancipation. Does a republican, economical, and free government . . .
conflict with emancipation?" Of course not. (For further discussion of
the Liberty party platform, see Chapter 5 below.) The issue between
Garrisonians and other abolitionists would seem, then, to be not abolition
alone versus universal reform but different notions of what universal
reform entailed.

71 This metaphor is my own. See Garrison's own explanations in
"The Grandeur of our Cause," *The Liberator*, May 23, 1845; "Our New
Volume," *ibid.*, January 2, 1846; "The Annual Meeting at New-York,"
ibid., April 22, 1842; "The Second Reformation—'Come-Outerism'—The
Clergy and the Church," *ibid.*, December 22, 1843.

72 Louis Filler, in *The Crusade against Slavery*, p. 130, remarks: "In assessing the harm Garrison and his associates may or may not have done the antislavery movement, it must be recalled that their opponents in the antislavery societies also offended elements of the public with irrelevant opinions. The Tappans, for example, with their rigid sabbatarian principles and anti-Catholic bias, outraged as many citizens as did Garrison—in some cases, many more." It need hardly be noted that a demonstration that the Tappans outraged public opinion does not help one to assess the harm that Garrison may have done the movement. More important, however, is that Filler in my opinion misses the point: I strongly doubt if the Tappans' irrelevant opinions outraged nearly as many *potential abolitionists* as did Garrison's antisabbatarianism and defense of women's rights. Anti-Catholicism and sabbatarianism were quite respectable with the evangelical Protestants among whom the abolitionists exerted their main efforts at conversion. (On p. 132 Filler does remark that the Tappan school of abolitionists had a more "conventional" sort of antislavery movement in mind.) To Garrison's opponents the main task of the movement was to win as many recruits as possible as soon as possible, and this could be done only by leaving those recruits in undisturbed possession of all their other beliefs. The task was certainly agreeable to those abolitionists who shared those other beliefs. To the Garrisonians, that brand of abolitionism was worthless, even to the slave; such recruits would betray their abolitionism when it conflicted with their selfish interests and especially with their political loyalties. The task of the movement was, therefore, to free the public mind of its ideological shackles and bring about, as far as possible, a deep commitment to all human rights. That commitment would ensure the individual's fidelity to principle, for any prejudices incompatible with it would be dropped, and the individual would not be tempted to betray the cause in any test situations. Therefore I question Filler's judgment that the reason the Tappans' prejudices "did not breach antislavery unity" was that those prejudices "were peripheral" whereas Garrison's advocacy of women's participation was not. From Garrison's viewpoint (the viewpoint of which Filler is a champion), the Tappans' sabbatarianism was not a peripheral issue; it was in fact part of an authoritarian philosophy that fostered the proslavery spirit in the nation at large and the proscriptive spirit in the antislavery movement.

73 Weld to Sarah and Angelina Grimké, August 15, 1837, *Weld-Grimké Letters*, I, 426–27. See also Weld to Sarah and Angelina Grimké, August 26, 1837, *ibid.*, p. 434.

74 Whittier to Abby Kelley, March 8, 1841, Stephen S. and Abby Kelley Foster Papers, AAS; Whittier to Sarah and Angelina Grimké, August 14, 1839, *Weld-Grimké Letters*, I, 424; "Rights of Women in Anti-Slavery Conventions—The Question Fairly Stated," a letter to the editor from "A Member of the Convention," *The Liberator*, July 6, 1838, quoting and discussing a letter from Whittier in *The Pennsylvania Freeman*; "Woman's Rights," *The Liberator*, July 27, 1838 (the last third of this article, in the "Miscellaneous" section of the paper, is a reprint from *The Pennsylvania Freeman* of a Whittier article in which he rejected the argument that the admission of women to equal status in

antislavery meetings involved the free-speech issue, and he declared that abolitionists should not turn away from their main task "to discuss irrelevant matters of minor importance" or "to turn universal reformers, and with the abolition banner floating over our heads, '*run a muck*' at every thing which we may conceive to be erroneous in religion, morals, and politics." As time went on Whittier's language became more bitter and sarcastic. In a letter printed in *The Pennsylvania Freeman* and copied into *The Liberator*, November 27, 1840, he commented on those American abolitionists who had tried to have women recognized as delegates to the London Anti-Slavery Convention. He ridiculed, among other things, "our '*platform*' on which men and women lose their distinctive character, and become 'souls without sex,' " and later in the article referred scornfully to "our Yankee doctrines of equality, or sexless democracy."

75 The letter continues, "I have no sympathy with the *terrors* of certain *male women* who quote Paul at the top of their lungs, as if our friend Theodore's wife [Angelina Grimké Weld] or Abby Kelly [*sic*] were about to wrest from them their diploma of manhood forever & aye—but I have just no doubt at all that Paul & propriety are both on their side in the *argument*. Paul, if I understand him, however, did no less than hint that his instructions for the regulation of women might without much danger have been left to *nature herself*. And whatever was the confidence of the Apostle in the correctness of his views of propriety, I think he must have been too much of a gentleman to choke a woman with authority, as well as too *wise a man*." (Elizur Wright, Jr., to Amos A. Phelps, July 11, 1838, Phelps Papers, BPL; a copy is in Wright Papers, LC.) William Goodell was another prominent abolitionist who thought the innovation "harmless and unimportant" (letter to the editor, *The Liberator*, July 17, 1840).

76 See Barnes, *The Anti-Slavery Impulse*, pp. 160, 176, and 274n. Barnes's quotations from Whittier give the impression that Whittier's position was similar to Weld's. The passages cited in note 74 above, however, prove that he did not endorse full equality of the sexes. (The Wright Papers, LC, and the Phelps Papers, BPL, which contain the letters cited in note 75, are not among the few manuscript collections listed in Barnes's bibliography.) I do not contend that Whittier, Wright, or others such as Stanton and Leavitt whom Barnes links with them, were as hostile to women's rights as Birney, Tappan, and Phelps. But the question may legitimately be asked whether one who sincerely believes a certain reform desirable will support an organization that actively exerts its influence against it. Weld's advice to the Grimkés was calculated to advance the cause of women's rights, but Whittier's advice was to ignore it as unimportant, and Wright's view was that the exercise of those rights was a harmless deviation from scripture and nature. Their respective positions were, I think, accurately reflected in their attitudes toward the A & F. Nevertheless, Barnes lumps all these men together in his effort to demonstrate that the sincere advocates of sex equality were not in the Garrison camp.

77 See Russel B. Nye, *Fettered Freedom: Civil Liberties and the Slavery Controversy 1830–1860* (East Lansing, Mich., 1949), *passim*.

78 Cf. Henry B. Stanton to Elizur Wright, Jr., February 9, 1839, Wright Papers, LC. Stanton thanked Wright for some articles sent to *The Massachusetts Abolitionist* (the anti-Garrison paper recently founded), but explained that the editors had deleted part of one of them because it would provoke a reply by Garrison, which "we could not publish; & then the cry of 'proscription'—'gagism'" would be raised. "We understand the game. They mean to embarrass us. The plan is to send us articles about non-government, womens rights, perfection, &c, &c, &c, & then, if we excluded them cry out, 'ay, *you are opposed* [*sic*] *to free discussion, are you!*' Bah. As tho. I was obliged to stand all day & hear a man talk nonsense. Ours is not a free discussionist, but an abolitionist journal." On Stanton's own position on the woman question the evidence is ambiguous. See documents cited in note 64 above. The evidence on his vote on admitting women at the London Convention is conflicting. See Garrison to his wife, June 29, 1840, Garrison Letters, BPL, and Wendell Phillips to Oliver Johnson, in *The Liberator*, July 24, 1840; both say Stanton voted to admit the women. But "Mr. Stanton and the Woman Question," *ibid.*, December 4, 1840, reprinted from *The National Anti-Slavery Standard*, cites both Birney and Stanton as denying he so voted. See also Stanton to Elizur Wright, Jr., [December 2 (?), 1839], Wright Papers, LC: Stanton wrote that he did not split with the AASS on the woman question, that on that issue the AASS was in the right, and that he deplored the A & F's having "made everything to turn" on that question.

4

RELIGION AND THE GOOD SOCIETY

IN THE FIGHT over the woman question the anti-Garrisonian abolitionists showed their concern with what today would be called the movement's "public image." This is particularly evident from the fact that the assault on the innovations in women's public activity originated with clergymen outside or on the periphery of the movement and only later was joined by conservative abolitionist leaders. Both radicals and conservatives recognized the crucial importance of ministers in molding public opinion, and this recognition accounts both for the attempts to discredit the clergy and for the efforts to conciliate it. Both principle and expediency dictated a switch toward a more conciliatory policy on the part of some of those conservatives at the same time as Garrison and some of his supporters were adopting more and more heretical views on religion.

That development represented a divergence from a common starting point; both the conservative and the radical factions had accepted the principles stated in the AASS constitution that slavery was a "heinous crime in the sight of God" and immediate emancipation a duty. Certain corollaries of those principles were not spelled out but were accepted by all the early abolitionists: that the guilt of slaveowning and the obligation to repent were individual, not collective, responsibilities; and that the aim of abolitionist agitation was to induce innumerable individual conversions very similar to those that the religious evangelists were inducing.

Neither faction ever dropped those principles. Those abolitionists, such as John A. Collins, who adopted collectivistic social philosophies, and others, such as Henry B. Stanton, whose activity became primarily political, drifted out of the organized antislavery movement. To those who remained within it, albeit in rival organizations, the duty of immediate emancipation remained a normative principle and never a prediction or program of action. As a normative principle, however, it was susceptible to quite contrary applications. To the conservatives it remained compatible with a social philosophy that accepted conventional religious and political institutions and beliefs. It led certain others to increasingly radical attitudes toward those institutions and beliefs. The controversy over the woman question exposed the incipient differences and caused them to become more explicit and more fully thought out, till the woman question was pushed into the background and the factional fight centered on the religious issue itself.

THE DEVELOPMENT of Garrison's thinking can be traced in the pages of *The Liberator*. One can see the embryo of his later nonresistance in an editorial at the end of 1835 in which he condemned all penal enactments as essentially retaliatory and contrary to the principle of reliance on God. Followers of Christ, said Garrison, "ought never to trust in an arm of flesh for protection, but should wholly 'cease from man'—ought never to prosecute, or imprison, or put to death, for any injury done to them by their enemies."[1] Seven months later he contended that the Sabbath was not authorized in the New Testament. He did not oppose Sabbath observance, but he argued that exaggeration of the importance of outward ceremonies fostered neglect of "weightier matters"; and he especially opposed attempts to force its observance. The following month, he inveighed against defensive war, and here he used the term *non-resistance*. Two issues later he denounced a Vermont paper for justifying the mobbing of Fanny Wright. Society could not, he proclaimed, protect itself by cutting off free speech, and he asked whether truth must use weapons such as fines and prisons to defeat error.[2] It will be noted that two themes run through all these editorials: reliance on divine rather than human defenses against evil, and an exaltation of freedom of speech for everyone including those on the side of error.[3]

Henry C. Wright too was combining these themes into a single religious principle at the same time as Garrison, although their formulations differed somewhat in emphasis and considerably in practical application. Wright's received full exposition in his debate with "Alethea" in the columns of *The Liberator* in the middle of 1837.[4] "Alethea" wrote protesting Wright's lesson to children that God had given man no dominion over man, and he inferred that Wright's doctrine would abolish all human government. Wright replied that the Bible was his only lawbook; whatever human laws a man was obliged to obey derived their authority from God, not from human legislatures. He would, therefore, not abolish any human government based on gospel principles.

Garrison entered the debate in the issue of June 23. He argued that human governments were the result of defiance of God's commands. They were, however, to be preferred over anarchy, in the same way as a hailstorm was preferable to an earthquake. He obviously knew that his advocacy of the abolition of coercive government would not make that government disappear in the foreseeable future; his statement of the principle, like the abolitionists' statement of the principle that immediate emancipation was obligatory, was the promulgation of a truth, a normative doctrine, and not the advocacy of a program of action. This is clear from his statement that to ask whether society must not restrain criminals was to beg the question:

It is assuming that a government of men may sin econo-
mically for individuals. It is simply a choice between two
evils, both of which the gospel is designed to remedy. It
is asking, whether men who are resolved to be intemperate, had not better be persuaded to drink wine, instead
of whiskey.

To the objection that the alternative to coercive government
was anarchy, he replied:

Wicked men must and will have laws to control one
another. They will not forgive each other's trespasses.
. . . So that it is idle to talk of a government ceasing to
exist over a sinful people; for their very disobedience
renders it necessary, until they are willing to submit to
Christ. What then? Shall we, *as Christians*, applaud and
do homage to human government? Or shall we not rather
lay the axe at the root of the tree, and attempt to destroy
both cause and consequence, together?

Those who, like Birney,[5] later announced that Garrison would
make their wives and daughters the undefended prey of every
rapist had already been refuted: an integral part of Garrison's
doctrine was the tenet that coercion of criminals would not
disappear until crime itself did, since both forms of coercion,
that of the government and that of the criminal, went together
as two forms of one sin. He never thought that his preaching
would weaken the vigilance of the constabulary. Its object was
to destroy the illusion that coercive government was consistent with gospel principles, for that illusion helped to prevent men from seeing the cause of the crime that coercive
government was intended to prevent.

Less than two months later the clerical protests over
women's public activity began to appear and with them the
question of the relation of Garrison's religious radicalism to
the abolitionist movement. Clerical Protest No. 2, signed by
the Revs. Charles Fitch and Joseph H. Towne, who claimed to
speak for nine tenths of New England abolitionists, stated that
The Liberator was the organ of the Massachusetts Anti-Slavery Society. In the same issue two officials of the society ad-

dressed a letter to the public, pointing out that *The Liberator*, although supported by the society, was not its organ and that Fitch, a member of the board, should have sought redress from the board if he thought it was endorsing Garrison's opinions as expressed in the paper. He had, however, never complained before this.[6] Clerical Protest No. 3 followed soon after, as did a plea from John Greenleaf Whittier for mutual love, and another blast at the clergy by Henry C. Wright.[7] Wright, like Garrison, denied that he had ever denounced the clerical office itself. That office, he asserted, had been created by Christ, but most men who now occupied it were unfit for it, because they endorsed the use of force.[8]

Recent scholarly works have contended that once Garrison had adopted nonresistance and other radical causes he insisted on preaching their tenets from antislavery platforms and tried to transform the abolitionist societies into nonresistance and universal reform societies.[9] The Elijah Lovejoy episode shows this is not so. By the time of the riot in November 1837, when Lovejoy, an abolitionist editor in Alton, Illinois, was shot down by a proslavery mob, many prominent New England abolitionists had decided that all force was un-Christian, and they were, accordingly, as shocked at Lovejoy's having defended his press and his life as they were by his murder. The Unitarian minister Samuel J. May, for one, criticized *The Emancipator*, organ of the AASS, for not having condemned Lovejoy's resort to force.[10] One reason, which May later offered, why the society should disavow Lovejoy's action deserves special note:

> Now that we have become a numerous body, and of great consequence, by reason of our numbers, in the estimation of the political parties,—now let us be especially careful in our adherence to our principles. Else shall we find men rushing into our ranks who have not put on Christ—men who have not considered or do not understand the reasons by which he purposes to overthrow the empire of sin; and such fellow-laborers will soon involve our country in servile and civil war.[11]

Garrison defended *The Emancipator*. He was as much a non-resistant as was his friend May, but he had a clearer conception of the tactical needs of the abolitionist movement. He pointed out that most members of the society approved of self-defense and that *The Emancipator* was their organ as well as that of the nonresistant members. He further argued that it was not the province of the leadership of the association to condemn Lovejoy for having fought.[12] Here the leader of the alleged scheme to transform the antislavery societies into nonresistance societies was trying to convince his own supporter that the organization must remain neutral on the question of nonresistance.

This episode suggests that Garrison would make a sharp distinction between the antislavery organization and a movement that would work for what he felt were the other reforms required by a true reading of the Christian message. He would have been the last to suggest that abolition of slavery was not intimately related to peace, equality of the sexes, and the abolition of forms and ceremonies that had, he believed, been illegitimately imposed on Christian worship. On the contrary, to him these were all parts of the single divine Truth, and abolition of slavery was only one step toward universal brotherhood. But precisely because the changes he favored were so sweeping and so unpopular, he insisted on an *organizational* distinction between abolitionism and his other causes, and he continued trying to keep them separate as long as there remained any chance of unity between the radicals and the more conservative abolitionists.[13]

At the same time *The New England Spectator*, which on several occasions took positions that conservative abolitionists adopted later, resorted to a tactic that anti-Garrisonians within the societies did not yet adopt. In its editorial "Errors of Influential Men," which Garrison reprinted in his "Refuge of Oppression" column, the department reserved for "proslavery" material, *The Spectator* deplored the recent falling off of church attendance by Boston Negroes and thought it had found the reason:

One who has shown himself the ardent and untiring friend of the colored man, sets lightly by the Sabbath, the house of God, and the divine ambassadors of the Prince of Peace. One day with him is as good as another. He neglects the house of God on that sacred day, and does his own pleasure, by attending to avocations which belong to other days, and not exclusively to the worship of God. . . . He has no reverence for the ministerial office, but holds that one has as good a right to preach as another. . . . Christian friends, is it not time for something to be done, not to destroy this man's influence in favor of the oppressed, but to counteract the influence of his errors which go to ruin souls?

Garrison reprinted the reply he had sent to *The Spectator*. He said, among other things, that *The Spectator* had known his views for a long time and that his attitude toward the Sabbath was the same as that of Calvin and other religious reformers as well as the Quakers. Yet it had said nothing till recently. He inferred that its "new-born zeal for the Sabbath" was personal hostility and the desire to suppress *The Liberator*. He insisted that he now complained not of this

affected regard for the Sabbath. I complain of your holy impertinence and pharisaical proscription being manifested upon abolition ground. I complain of you for attempting to introduce sectarian tenets and denominational strifes into the cause of bleeding humanity.— Again, see that you apprehend my meaning. I do not say that, because you are professedly engaged in the anti-slavery enterprise, you are obligated to suppress your sentiments on other subjects. No. Vindicate the Sabbath, if you will; extol the "Christian ordinances," and eulogize the clergy, as often as you desire. But do so in your character as an orthodox congregationalist, not as an abolitionist. You are false to the agreement which binds us together as friends of immediate emancipation, and which makes us all ONE in the cause of liberty, notwithstanding our religious and political differences, in pointing the finger of sectarian reproach at a brother.

He then recounted a recent incident in which a clerical abolitionist, speaking at a meeting of the Massachusetts Anti-Slavery Society in Worcester, had announced that Garrison had
never publicly professed his religious creed and habitually
neglected Christian ordinances. He, for one, would not work
with those who did not go for the Sabbath and the ministry.
Garrison now wrote that if he had retorted on that occasion
that *he* would not work with a man who thought only one of
the seven days ought to be kept holy, humanity would have
charged him with having abandoned her sacred cause. After a
long exposition of what he did believe in regard to the Sabbath, the ministry, and the church, Garrison demanded to
know by what espionage *The Spectator* had learned how often
he neglected public worship; who kept tally? Later in his
letter he wrote that he might have ignored this libel but for
the fact that it libeled his Negro friends as well. He believed a
larger proportion of them went to church than formerly, but
he had not inquired. Furthermore, very few of them knew his
views on the Sabbath, and he had not discussed such questions
with any of them; nor were they influenced by his opinions on
that subject. *The Spectator* insulted them by implying that
they could not tell who their friends were. For many years
many ministers had told them the American Colonization Society was worthy of their support, but they had known
better.[14]

The beginning of 1838 saw the end of the Massachusetts
Society's subsidy of *The Liberator*, and the paper, now un-
ambiguously Garrison's personal organ, was free to discuss all
the implications of his philosophy.[15] In the issue of December
15, 1837 (and again in later issues), he published the "Prospec-
tus of THE LIBERATOR. Volume VIII." "In entering upon
our eighth volume," he wrote,

> the abolition of slavery will still be the grand object of
> our labors, though not, perhaps, so exclusively as hereto-
> fore. There are other topics, which, in our opinion, are
> intimately connected with the great doctrine of inalien-
> able human rights; and which, while they conflict with

no religious sect, or political party, as such, are pregnant with momentous consequences to the freedom, equality and happiness of mankind. These we shall discuss as time and opportunity may permit.

In addition to the paper's old motto, "Our country is the world—our countrymen are all mankind," he would offer a new one: "Universal Emancipation."

> Up to this time, we have limited its application to those who are held in this country . . . as marketable commodities. . . . Henceforth, we shall use it in its widest latitude: the emancipation of our whole race from the dominion of man, from the thraldom of self, from the government of brute force, from the bondage of sin—and bringing them under the dominion of God, the control of an inward spirit, the government of the law of love, and into the obedience and liberty of Christ. . . .
>
> Next to the overthrow of slavery, the cause of PEACE will command our attention. . . . If a nation may not redress its wrongs by physical force—if it may not repel or punish a foreign enemy who comes to plunder, enslave or murder its inhabitants—then it may not resort to arms to quell an insurrection, or send to prison or suspend upon a gibbet any transgressors upon its soil. If the slaves of the South have not an undoubted right to resist their masters in the last resort, then no man, or body of men, may appeal to the law of violence in self-defence—for none have ever suffered, or can suffer, more than they. . . .
>
> As to the governments of this world, . . . we shall endeavor to prove, that, in their essential elements, and as at present administered, they are all Anti-Christ; that they can never, by human wisdom, be brought into conformity to the will of God; that they cannot be maintained, except by naval and military power; that all their penal enactments being a dead letter without an army to carry them into effect, are virtually written in human blood; and that the followers of Jesus should instinctively shun their stations of honor, power and emolument—at the same time "submitting to every ordi-

nance of man, for the Lord's sake," and offering no *physical* resistance to any of their mandates, however unjust or tyrannical. . . .

If the Lord's Prayer is not a mockery, he asked, and his will is to be done on earth and there is to be no statute book but the Bible, then must not Christians come out and be separate from the kingdoms of this world, which are all based on violence? How can the wickedness of men be overcome? By loving one's enemies and resisting not evil, by ceasing to look to man for redress of grievance. If, as all abolitionists agreed, the slaves were not justified in appealing to force, how could anyone be, unless the distinction were founded on difference of color?[16] Universal emancipation, he added, implied the emancipation of woman, and therefore *The Liberator* would support "the RIGHTS OF WOMAN to their utmost extent." Garrison added that readers who disagreed with these principles were welcome to use *The Liberator*'s columns for their replies, and he stressed that the abolitionist movement was not to be held answerable for his opinions.

The technical independence of *The Liberator* was, however, a subtlety that many people could not, and quite a few would not, grasp. When later in the year one of his supporters wrote to Garrison that as an adherent of both the abolitionist and nonresistance movements she would like to see the latter have its own journal, he concurred.[17] *The Liberator* of February 1, 1839, announced publication of the first number of *The Non-Resistant*.

A few months earlier the New England Non-Resistance Society was founded at a three-day convention that according to Garrison would be

destined to become more memorable in history, than the famous "three days in Paris." They will constitute an important chapter in the annals of Christianity. Mankind shall hail the TWENTIETH OF SEPTEMBER with more exultation and gratitude, than Americans now do the FOURTH OF JULY. This may now be regarded as solemn bombast, but it is prophetical, and shall not fail to be fulfilled.[18]

Garrison was sometimes a perceptive prophet, but in this instance he was only half right.

Garrison kept his promise; *The Liberator* freely discussed the peace question, as well as other controversial issues, in the ensuing years. As always he welcomed letters arguing positions contrary to his own, and as a result the paper in those years is a fascinating archive of sources on the religious and social speculations of the antebellum generation. One topic of continuing debate was the so-called no-human-government theory. Garrison provoked this argument with an editorial recounting his recent visit to the local circuit court. The proceedings opened with a prayer by a minister, and Garrison commented that that act represented a union of church and state. Every Christian present, he added, was bound by his religious profession to forgive trespasses; yet here were all varieties of government officials, convened for the purpose of inflicting death or imprisonment on their fellow men.

> A people wholly redeemed from iniquity would need no police, no penal code, no dungeon, no gibbet. Hence, nothing but rebellion against God, on their part, can make such a system of government necessary; for, that it is necessary while they remain slaves to their own lusts, we are ready to concede. What then? Will they plead their own disobedience, their pertinacious and malignant rebellion against the government of the Most High, as justifying the erection of their own bloody tribunals? What! rebels against God undertaking to establish justice, and to extend the kingdom of the Redeemer, by pains and penalties, by parks of artillery and regiments of soldiers?[19]

In the following week's issue of *The Liberator*, the Rev. Orange Scott resorted to the *reductio ad absurdum* method to refute Garrison's argument. Garrison's theory, he suggested, would imply that a parent must not spank his child and that a woman must not resist an attacker or cause him to be arrested. "Are lions to be converted into lambs, by letting them out of their cages?" he asked. "You reply that you trust in God."

As well might you trust God to edit and print your paper, without any human agency. . . . If your perse-cutors were to put you in a den of lions as they did Daniel, you might trust in God as he did; but if you were voluntarily to let a den of lions loose upon yourself, you would not find it so easy to trust in God. The *presump-tuous* have no reason to expect the protection of God.

As for human governments, Jehovah himself had instituted them, and nowhere in the Bible had he abrogated them.[20]

Scott's assertion of the divine ordination of human govern-ments was seconded in a letter to Henry C. Wright from Henry Grew, printed in *The Liberator* seven months later. Grew explained that God had in his wisdom and benevolence appointed such governments as a means to restrain selfishness, and abuse of authority did not justify nonallegiance. Wright had contended that to acknowledge allegiance to human gov-ernment was to obey the will of man as the supreme law of life, and "We cannot obey God and man." Grew replied, "Then the Word of God requires an impossibility, for it cer-tainly requires obedience to both. . . . [C]hristians are com-manded to 'OBEY MAGISTRATES.' Titus 3.1." By inference the magistrate had the right to compel obedience; this constituted an exception to the commandment, Thou shalt not kill. Grew approved advocacy of the principles of meekness, patience, and love. But in the present state of the world, the physical barriers to evil must not be removed.[21]

The "practical" objections by Scott and Grew to the repudiation of forceful government were easily enough met by Garrison's repeated explanation that the physical barriers to evil would not be removed before the need for them had been eliminated by means of the propagation of nonresistance principles. Not so easy to deal with were practical questions concerning the proper behavior of nonresistants in specific cir-cumstances. When Charles Stearns, a young pacifist and Garri-sonian abolitionist, was jailed in Hartford in 1841 for refusing to report for militia duty, a friend of his wrote to Garrison asking if a nonresistant ought to pay the fine to avoid prison. Nonresistants did not refuse to pay ordinary taxes, but should they regard as a tax a fine imposed for refusal to violate their consciences? Garrison replied:

> Formerly, when we occupied *Quaker* ground in regard to war and civil government, we argued as they now do against the propriety of paying a militia tax; but since we have been led to perceive that they are contending, in essence, for a "distinction without a difference," we have come to a different conclusion. Still, we are not wholly satisfied as to the correctness of our present views; and in our letter to C. Stearns, we expressed a hope that the subject would be freely discussed on every side.[22]

On the essential point, however, Garrison was wholly satisfied: that it was one thing to admit that unregenerate men needed physical restraint in the form of governments and another thing to justify such governments as divinely ordained. To justify violent governments was essentially to justify the wickedness that made them necessary, but preaching the principles of nonresistance was the first step toward creating the conditions for the kingdom of God on earth. The other side of his nonresistance was his perfectionism, and in an unsigned editorial entitled "Perfection," he reiterated this crucial distinction between the Christian's duty and what was immediately realizable, a distinction identical to that which all abolitionists made between the duty of immediate emancipation and the form that emancipation would actually assume once the duty had been universally accepted. He began the editorial by noting that a dispute was in progress in orthodox churches concerning the doctrine of perfectionism.

> Now, what is the point in controversy? Not, who is a Christian, or whether this or that individual has attained to a state of "sinless perfection"; but whether human beings, in this life, may and ought to serve God with all their mind and strength, and to love their neighbor as themselves! Whether "total abstinence" from *all* sin is not as obligatory as it is from any one sin! . . . The argument is clear. If men cannot be wholly free from sin at any time in this life, then they are not responsible for their sinful acts.

He cited a statement published by a presbytery in upstate New York that the doctrine of total abstinence from sin was contrary to the teachings of the Bible and "utterly destructive to the life and growth of true holiness." And he sarcastically commented:

> True holiness will be perilled by inculcating the duty that men ought to be and may be holy and unblameable! True holiness will grow and thrive in exact proportion as sin is made a component part of it! . . . [T]hese ecclesiastical bodies are determined to make a christian life compatible with a military profession, with killing enemies, with enslaving a portion of mankind, with the robbing of the poor, with worldliness and ambition, with a participation in all popular iniquities. Hence, when abolition declares that no man can love God who enslaves another, they deny it, and assert that man-stealing and Christianity may co-exist in the same character. . . .
>
> Instead, therefore, of assailing the *doctrine*, "Be ye perfect, even as your Father in heaven is perfect," let us all aim to establish it, not merely as theoretically right, but as practically attainable; and if we are conscious that we are not wholly clean, not yet entirely reconciled to God, not yet filled with perfect love, let us, instead of resisting the light and the truth, and denying that freedom from sin is a christian's duty and privilege, confess and forsake our sins—give no quarter to unrighteousness—put on the whole armor of God, that we may be able to stand against the wiles of the devil. . . .[23]

Another issue warmly debated in the columns of *The Liberator* was the proper attitude toward the Bible. It has been seen that Garrison and Wright based their theories regarding government and perfection on scriptural commands, insisting that a human ordinance, to be lawful, must be consistent with the sacred texts. In time, however, their position subtly changed. In the course of so many polemics in defense of principles deduced from the Bible they began to defend those principles independently of the Bible. Those polemics evoked replies by their adversaries, who cited contrary texts from the same authority, and the contradictions could not always be eliminated by reinterpretation. Inevitably Garrison and Wright were led to repudiate certain texts as contrary to God's true intent and to decide that not all of the Bible was inspired. By what criterion must one discriminate between the true and the false? Neither man claimed to have received direct revelations. The only alternative was to discard the arbitrary will of God as the determinant of true principles set forth in the Bible, and in its place to hypostatize those principles themselves. These two, who had begun by judging the world by Truth and Right as revealed in the scriptures, ended by judging the scriptures by Truth and Right as revealed by their own reason.

As late as 1842 Garrison was still relying on scriptural authority for truth; in the issue of August 19 he offered $1,000 to anyone who proved that the Sabbath was authorized in the New Testament.[24] By the beginning of 1843, however, he was writing that the Bible must be read discriminatingly. Discussing the Millerite craze, he first deplored the false teaching that the Second Advent was in the future rather than 1,900 years in the past. Furthermore, it was, he contended, a

> ridiculous notion, that this magnificent creation of God, —the heavens which declare his glory, and the earth "which endureth forever,"—are to be consumed by material fire. . . . To the highly figurative language of scripture, a literal interpretation has been given; and what is strictly literal has been tortured into a tropical form of speech.[25]

Yet even when he rejected one passage of scripture it was on the basis of another; his evidence that the Second Advent was not scheduled for the period between March 21, 1843, and March 21, 1844, as the Millerites predicted, was the text, "Verily, I say unto you, *This generation* shall not pass away, till ALL BE FULFILLED."[26]

Then in 1845 he discovered Thomas Paine. In the issue of November 21 he explained that until a few days before, he had never read a paragraph of Paine, having been brought up to regard that notorious infidel as "a monster of iniquity." Now

Garrison realized that Paine was a sincere, intelligent, and powerful writer, with reason his only guide. Garrison then presented his own views. The Bible ought to be examined in the light of reason. One could not expect to understand everything in it, but then, no one knew how the sun gave light or the acorn grew into an oak. However, anything in it that was absurd or monstrous should be rejected. It was ridiculous to assert that everything in the Bible was divinely inspired. The reader must "search the scriptures" and decide what was true and what false, "what is the letter that killeth, and what the spirit that maketh alive." No one knew who wrote the various books, but that did not matter, since the Bible must stand or fall on its merits, "by its reasonableness and utility, by the probabilities of the case, by historical confirmation, by human experience and observation, by the facts of science, by the intuition of the spirit. Truth is older than any parchment."[27]

Garrison retained these views for the rest of the period covered by this study. In the spring of 1847, for example, he wrote: "If religion be not a sensible thing, it must be a very foolish thing. If it is supernatural, it is not natural; and therefore, though it may possibly answer for another world, it clearly can be of no advantage for the present."[28]

It remained for Henry C. Wright to state the corollary heresy of Garrison's demotion of the Bible. In "The Bible, if Opposed to Self-Evident Truth, Is Self-Evident Falsehood," he announced that at every step he had taken in the past ten years to oppose injustice and oppression, he had encountered the Bible as his sternest foe. Hence, he had ceased to look to the Bible as the authority for the wrong of slavery and war. Slavery and war were self-evident wrongs, and no Bible could prove them right.[29]

An even more shocking heresy was proclaimed by Charles B. Stearns. In the issue of October 10, 1845, he opened what came to be known as "The Rights of God" controversy, when he announced that the Old Testament should be laid aside; that God had no right to take a human life because life was his gift to men and inviolable; and that God never punished sinners. The two latter propositions, he argued, must be true unless one was prepared to assert that it was wrong for men to imitate God. In the ensuing months the last page of *The Liberator* was filled with angry rejoinders, but Garrison did not enter the dispute till the end of January 1846, and then only indirectly. He first defended the right—rather, the duty—of his paper to open its columns to views of all sorts, in the interest of "the cause of bleeding humanity," and he expressed his faith in the weakness of Error and the invincibility of Truth in free discussion. Truth, he wrote, always encouraged freedom of thought, was never afraid of scrutiny. But how was Truth to be discovered?

> I know of no safer, higher, or better way, than to leave the human mind perfectly untrammelled to contend for unlimited investigation, to vindicate the supremacy of reason, to plead for unfettered speech, to argue from analogy, to decide upon evidence, to be governed by facts, to disclaim infallibility, to believe in eternal growth and progress, to repudiate all arbitrary authority, to make no man or body of men oracular, to learn from the teachings of history, to see with our own eyes and hear with our own ears. . . . [W]ho shall dogmatically assume to decide what is heresy . . . ?

He who was ready to take on all comers was not thereby proved right, said Garrison, but he who would silence or scorn opponents was either a coward, a ruffian, or a fanatic.

> On the other hand, he who forms his opinions from the dictates of enlightened reason, and sincerely desires to be led into all truth, dreads nothing so much as the suppression of free inquiry. . . . We have too little, instead of too much dissent among us. . . . Even if we assent to what is true, merely because it is fashionable to do so, we are not true believers, but only echoes.

Garrison then quoted from a subscriber, hitherto a friend, who had forbidden his family to read Stearns's letter and who felt obliged to terminate his subscription to a paper that gave publicity to such ideas. Garrison denied that *The Liberator* had endorsed Stearns's views; Stearns and the other letter writers spoke only for themselves. But had he not, Garrison asked, been shocked by the many proslavery articles that *The Liberator* had since its founding reprinted in the "Refuge of Oppression" column? As a nonresistant, had he not been horrified by the letters the paper had printed from advocates of defensive war? Garrison suggested that the subscriber felt confident in his vews on slavery and war, but not so certain in his opinions on "the rights of God." And was it wise of him, asked the editor, to assume "an absolute control over the reason and conscience of his family"? Should they not have the right to test all truths? "A forcible suppression of error is no aid to the cause of truth. . . ." He (Garrison) would want his children to consider no subject too sacred to investigate, since he was not infallible. Then he implied that he sided with Stearns on the doctrinal issue.[30]

GARRISON'S RELIGIOUS OPINIONS certainly grew more radical in the years after the outbreak of factionalism in the AASS in 1837, but his defense of freedom of thought and speech remained constant. Perhaps his orthodox opponents had good cause, then, from their own standpoint, to discredit his free-speech doctrine before it could be used to justify the propagation of heresy. A few of the conservatives at first said that if the Massachusetts Society's subsidization of *The Liberator* were to be ended at the close of 1837 they would not complain of the paper's contents thereafter.[31] But after the subsidy arrangement was terminated and they could no longer complain of a financial connection between the journal and the abolitionist movement, their efforts to disavow its ideological connection increased.

Even before the end of the society's support of *The Liberator* the first steps had been taken to drum the heretics out of the movement. Owing to the Garrisonians' strength in the Massachusetts Society, this could be done only by the founding of a new society. By the fall of 1837, Phelps was writing that he could "not *yet* go with" those who were planning such a step, but he wished success to their efforts.[32] In January 1839 Lewis Tappan wrote to Phelps about the meeting that had recently founded an "Evangelical Union Anti Slavery

Society" for New York City and asked why "the christians in Boston" had not done the same. But the Massachusetts men had their own plans. The Rev. Orange Scott, in a letter of the same date, told Phelps he thought perhaps a new paper should be founded in Boston. Unfortunately, a large majority of those who would attend the approaching meeting of the Massachusetts Society, he said, would be Garrisonians; hence it would be impossible to have the new paper adopted as the society's official organ. Let *The Liberator* and the new journal therefore both be independent for the coming year, so that Massachusetts abolitionists "will see that somebody besides *Garrison, can* make an anti-slavery *paper*."[33] By the following month Phelps had received many letters, almost all from clergymen, advocating the formation of a new society.[34]

Those closer to the national leadership had been wrestling with the same problems for some time. Almost a year and a half earlier, James G. Birney had written, "I have no expectation that G[arrison] can be reduced to moderation, and I am not prepared to say, that his departure from us may not be the best thing he could do for the cause of Emancipation."[35] In the summer of 1838 Henry B. Stanton, writing to Birney about the dispute between the national office in New York and the Massachusetts Society over the latter's refusal to pay a large sum that the New York office claimed was owed it, suggested that if the Bostonians were required "to fulfill their part of the arrangement to the letter," they might in anger withdraw their society from the AASS; that "will do no hurt. Would it not do good?" Stanton asked Birney to keep the letter private.[36]

Inevitably, however, the plans came to light, and by the beginning of 1839 Garrison had become convinced of the existence of a clerical plot against him and his paper. In the issue of January 11, *The Liberator* carried his editorial "Watchman, What of the Night?" in which he warned those who planned to attend the annual meeting of the Massachusetts Society, scheduled to begin January 23, of "a deep scheme laid by individuals, at present somewhat conspicuous as zealous and active abolitionists, to put the control of the anti-slavery movements in this Commonwealth into other hands. This scheme, of course, is of clerical origin. . . ." In the next issue, Garrison spelled out the details of the plot, named the Rev. Charles T. Torrey of Salem as the ringleader, and predicted that *The Liberator*'s discussion of the peace question would be the ostensible reason for the proposal to start a new paper.[37]

The private correspondence among the "plotters" merits extensive quotation, as it is far less familiar to modern students of the abolitionist movement than are Garrison's accusations. Torrey, for example, wrote to Phelps concerning the coming quarterly meeting of the Massachusetts Society:

> . . . now as to the course of the meeting next week—a word or two—I think of making a proposition at the opening of the meeting, to refer the whole controversy to a large committee from both parties in equal numbers, with instructions to report, if possible, some measure of conciliation. If it is voted down, as it probably will be, we have them *on the hip* at once— If it is accepted they will have to yield something, and we may place them in a position in which they will be compelled to make the division, if one comes, on the true ground. For we must not permit them to have the chance of making the split on the point of difference with the American Society. We must force them on the horns of perfectionism non resistance and recreancy about political action.
>
> What say you brother plotter?[38]

In regard to an approaching county convention, the Rev. Alanson St. Clair wrote to Phelps:

> How the abolitionists stand, I do not know, but so far as I have learned the Methodist Clergymen are right to a man. . . .
>
> Dont fail to write to every orthodox clergyman on the cape, who is an abolitionist, to be on hand. Has Scott written his brethren?
>
> Have an eye to Bristol Co. If they notify a meeting for week after next, send in a good stock of agents to drum up.

St. Clair then listed people to contact in the various towns, and he added, "Dont fail to have Scott in New Bedford, & Colver in Fall River beforehand to pick open the eyes of the Methodists & Baptists."[39]

A "Circular sent out by Scott & Phelps," dated April 16 and addressed to "Dear Sir," stated that there were special reasons why the friends of the cause, who were anxious that its original principles be maintained, should attend the annual meeting of the AASS to be held in New York in three weeks. The writers explained how those principles were to be threatened at the convention. "A source" that the readers were assured was reliable had revealed that "certain individuals in this city & State" intended to move to amend the AASS constitution by deleting the following clauses (as quoted in the letter):

> "While it (the Society) admits that each State in which Slavery exists has, by the constitution of the United States, the exclusive right to *legislate* in regard to its [Slavery's] abolition in the States &c"— "The Society will also endeavour in a constitutional way to influence Congress to put an end to the domestic Slave-trade, and to abolish Slavery in all those portions of our common country, which come under its control, especially in the District of Columbia, and likewise to prevent the extension of it to any State that may be hereafter admitted to the Union."

If the convention defeated the attempt to strike out these clauses, the letter continued, the "certain individuals" would then propose that the following clause be deleted: "The Society will never, in any way, countenance the oppressed in vindicating their rights by resorting to physical force."

If the first plan succeeded, explained Scott and Phelps, the society would become a "no-government" association. If it failed, and the second plan succeeded, "it would be to withdraw the guarantee solemnly given at the outset, that we would not excite or countenance insurrection among the slaves."

We will not stop to speak of the motives which may and probably do influence the movers in this matter, but will simply state, that, should they succeed in either of these attempts, it would result in the speedy destruction of the Anti-Slavery *Society*, if not of the Anti Slavery *cause*. Should the constitution be altered in either of these fundamental points, it will destroy the confidence of the community in our integrity and stability, and will assuredly result in driving from the Society all such men as Arthur Tappan, Wm. Jay, J. Leavitt, J. G. Whittier, Wm. Goodell, J. G. Birney[,] LaRoy Sunderland, Alvan Stewart, T. D. Weld,—in short, every man who beleives [*sic*] in the propriety of governmental action for the removal of Slavery and the necessity of a pacific assurance to the community that the Society will not countenance insurrections. In a word the Anti-Slavery association will be in peices [*sic*].

We do not say that the bringing forward of these propositions has been *finally* & *absolutely* determined on. On this point we are not distinctly advised. We only know that it has been matter of deliberation—*that one* prominent individual at least has said that they would be brought forward, &, we have reason to believe, that another individual is now visiting different parts of the country to secure the attendance of persons at the Annual Meeting, who will favor these or similar projects, that nothing will prevent the bringing forward of such propositions and the success of one or the other, but the prompt and general attendance of those who are satisfied with our constitution, and wish it to remain substantially as it is. Such should let no small consideration prevent their attendance on the occasion alluded to. Indeed should the attempts to which we have adverted not be made, we have no doubt from recent movements in this State that questions will come up whose decision will decide the fate of our present organizations. We see not under existing circumstances how this can be avoided. We trust you will not fail to be present, and to urge others who are determined to maintain the integrity of the cause to accompany you. Does not the crisis demand it? Do you not owe it to the slave?

The signatures of Orange Scott and Amos A. Phelps appear at this point, followed by: "P.S. The Board of the state society have appointed several women as delegates. That will bring up the woman question."[40]

The disclaimer in the last paragraph was wise, since the "plan" of the no-government faction described here is a complete fabrication. Not only is there no evidence for it; it is diametrically opposed to that faction's thinking in general and the plans for the meeting.

One more private letter may be cited to show that Garrison's charges of a "plot" were not without substance. Nine months after the anti-Garrisonians had withdrawn from the Massachusetts Anti-Slavery Society and founded the Massachusetts Abolition Society, Henry B. Stanton, an agent of the AASS, wrote to Phelps, a leader of the new organization. His letter was a confidential suggestion that Phelps's executive committee invite Stanton to come to Massachusetts to "help raise, among your auxiliaries & friends, the $1250 apportioned to the State Abolition Society, by the Am. Soc., at its special meeting." Do not breathe a word of this to anyone, he urged; pretend it is your own idea. Later Stanton expressed hope that "all the friends of good old constitutional abolitionism in your state" would go to the next annual meeting of the AASS "& save the cause & the Society from being wrecked on the shoals of licentiousness & fanaticism."[41]

We have noted, in Chapter 3, the conventions in 1839 and 1840 at which the ostensible cause of the splits was the woman question, and we shall have occasion, in Chapter 5, to discuss them again to see how the question of political action was one of the important causes. It is appropriate here to point out that the disputes over religion involved the issues of the proper status of women and of political action. In addition, the religious conservatives were deeply concerned lest religious heresy deprive the abolitionist movement of public influence. Garrison's efforts to distinguish between the religious radicalism that he preached as an individual and the principles of abolitionism on the basis of which adherents of all religions could work together in the AASS did not satisfy the conservatives. The founding of the New England Non-Resistance Society, rather than confirming that distinction, only incensed the conservatives more, because the leaders of the Non-Resistance Society were well-known abolitionists. Nor did it matter that Garrison refused, at an antislavery convention in Albany, to defend nonresistance after it had been attacked on the floor by several "new organizationists" from the Bay State.[42] What brought about the division was not the nonresistants' having tried to make their radical doctrines the official position of the society, but the evangelical abolitionists' attempts to make the society officially repudiate the radical religious doctrines. One of the more important such attempts was the statement by James G. Birney, in the official organ of the AASS, that

> the "no-Government" doctrines . . . seem to strike at the root of the social structure; and tend . . . to throw society into entire confusion, and to renew, under the sanction of religion, scenes of anarchy and license that have generally heretofore been the offspring of the rankest infidelity and irreligion.

He hastened to add that the "moral deportment" of the adherents of these doctrines had been perfectly proper. Nevertheless, the only honorable course would be for them to resign from the society. But "These Sectarians have not as yet separated themselves from the American Society. Far from it. They insist that their views are altogether harmonious with what is required for membership by the constitution." He admitted that the society had no board of inspectors to look into individuals' qualifications; nor could the society expel a person who lacked the qualifications for membership. Since there was no selfish purpose to be served in joining, it was assumed that anyone who joined honestly considered himself qualified. But if later he found he had "become disqualified, as several have, by materially changing their opinions," the same integrity that would then prevent him from joining ought to persuade him to resign. An equally honorable course, he suggested, would be for the "no-government men" to move for an alteration in the society's constitution.

Two things should be noted: first, Birney was clearly calling the nonresistants dishonorable, a point that should be stated explicitly in view of the contrary impression conveyed by most scholarly discussions of the controversy; and second, his suggestion that they should try to change the constitution so as to make it consistent with their membership contradicts the allegation by Phelps and Scott (see page 98 above) that the nonresistants *were* planning to try to change the constitution. In fact they were perfectly content with the constitution as it was.[43]

Garrison, in reply, protested *The Emancipator*'s publication of Birney's article:

> It is as much out of place in the Emancipator, as would be an essay in favor of infant sprinkling, or the claims of the "holy mother church." It is a bold attack upon the pacific views entertained by a portion of the abolitionists. . . . If this attack be allowable, so must a defence: hence, it opens the whole question of non-resistance, (so much dreaded by many,) for discussion and settlement in the organ of the American Anti-Slavery Society!

He insisted that nonresistants had "carefully avoided promulgating" their views "as connected with the objects" of the AASS. They had advocated those views as men, and would continue to do so, but not as abolitionists.[44] In this dispute, as in the controversy over the status of women, it was the conservatives who tried to mold the society in their own image.

PERHAPS IT WOULD be more accurate to say that they wished to mold the antislavery movement in their image of American society as it would be if purged of its imperfections. The factional differences grew out of divergent theories of the good society. To the anti-Garrisonians slavery was an anomaly in an otherwise fairly satisfactory society. To be sure, all of them believed their fellow Americans' drinking habits were scandalous. Some of them thought the suffrage laws needed revision, either to broaden or to restrict the right to vote.[45] Most of them were involved in one or more of the various reform crusades. But by and large nineteenth-century America was to them a sound society in need of improvement. Slavery was its worst sin and its abolition would eradicate the worst deviation from its fundamentally acceptable social structure. These abolitionists, in a word, were reformers, not radicals. To the nonresistants, slavery was a symptom of a basic flaw pervading the entire society, the worst example of the nation's reliance on force rather than on love. Other examples were the coercive United States government itself, economic competition, and inequality of races and sexes. The abolition of slavery would be only one step toward the fundamental regeneration of American society, which would require a profound ideological reorientation and ultimately abolish the government. That government, which to the conservative abolitionists was the administrator of justice, was to the nonresistants inherently unjust because coercive. To nonresistants there were other slaves to free besides the Negro—slaves to a false religion and to a corrupting social order—and those slaves included white abolitionists. The nonresistants, in a word, were radicals, not reformers. Paradoxically the reformist abolitionists were more radical than they realized; or rather, their demand for the abolition of slavery linked with the establishment of political and civil equality of the races would require an alteration in American society more drastic than they thought or were by temperament prepared for. And the nonresistants were less radical than they imagined, for they had no profound understanding of the nature of power and the conditions for its overthrow.

The nonresistants' radical vision of the good society was, in turn, based on their radical conception of man. When Garrison intoned, Be ye perfect, even as your Father in heaven is perfect, he was in effect repudiating the doctrine of original sin, a doctrine that most of his conservative opponents accepted and that underlay their approval of most contemporary American institutions including coercive government. Garrison was, in other words, a nonresistant because he was a perfectionist, believing that men were capable of obeying divine commands to be free of all sin and that when the time came when they were willing to follow Christ's example, social relations would be based on love, not on force. It is in the light of this tenet that Garrison's insistence on freedom of discussion within the antislavery movement must be seen. The principle of freedom of speech and advocacy rested on his belief that the only alternative to it was imposed conformity, a form of coercion. To the nonresistants, then, that freedom was an aspect of their long-range goal as well as an indispensable means for achieving it. The conservatives agreed with them that it might pave the way for religious radicalism, and since their conception of freedom was in theory narrower than that of the nonresistants, they could weigh the question of freedom of advocacy within the abolitionist movement in terms of its effect on the movement's public image and other questions of sheer expediency.

That freedom to dissent, and not nonresistance itself, was the crucial issue is evidenced in the fact that the Garrisonian faction included many who were not nonresistants or perfectionists but who for other reasons opposed efforts to have the AASS officially endorse any faction's religious or political principles and disavow others. Thomas F. Harwood, in a recent study of the abolitionist movement, expresses succinctly the widespread view that the Garrisonian faction is identifiable by its common acceptance of radical religious doctrines. He suggests that the group was typified by Henry C. Wright, Nathaniel P. Rogers, and Parker Pillsbury, and he notes what he calls the "surprising" adherence

> of intellectually respectable individuals like Ellis Gray Loring, Edmund Quincy, Wendell Phillips, and the two Samuel J. Mays, and, later, Theodore Parker. Perhaps their continued adherence is to be explained by an affinity between Garrison's uneducated but very romantic egotism and the intensely individualistic romanticism that characterized the intellectual ethos of New England at the time.[46]

Their adherence would not be surprising, however, without the prior definition of the group in terms of religious radicalism, and the rather strained effort to find a solution to the problem would not be necessary, for there would be no problem. Quincy and the elder May were in fact nonresistants. But Loring, Phillips, the younger May, and Parker were not. Nor were the political abolitionists Samuel Sewall and George Bradburn, who adhered to the Garrison faction throughout the controversies over religion and broke with Garrison only later, when he repudiated the Constitution and hoisted the disunionist flag. Francis Jackson, president of the Massachusetts Anti-Slavery Society during the factional fight, was never a nonresistant; and the list could be extended.[47] On the other hand, the anti-Garrisonians included individuals who were nonresistants, such as Charles T. Torrey, a principal leader of the "clerical plotters"![48] The theory that the Garrisonian faction can be identified by common acceptance of specific doctrines breaks down even further when it is recalled that several members of the peace convention in September 1838 walked out when women were allowed to participate, and that several anti-Garrisonians within the AASS held rather liberal views on the woman question, one of the alleged common doctrines of the faction.

It could be argued with almost equal cogency that Garrisonism ought to be identified with "intellectually respectable individuals" like Phillips and Jackson and that the adherence of the ultraists was "surprising." Garrison disapproved of the church-disrupting activities of Pillsbury and Foster,[49] although it is undeniable that his views were closer to theirs than to the views of Phillips and Jackson.

Nearer to the truth would be the assertion that neither definition of the faction in terms of specific doctrines is correct. The intellectually respectable individuals supported Garrison because they supported freedom of discussion and believed that the attempts by the other faction to persuade the organization to repudiate any members' religious or political doctrines would hurt the cause of antislavery. The extreme ultraists supported Garrison because only his conception of the antislavery platform made room for them. Although the key to Garrison's ideology is perfectionism, the key to the Garrisonian faction and its activities within the AASS is freedom of advocacy. To Garrison, universal reform was a means to universal freedom, and freedom of discussion was a means to universal reform. Freedom was thus both a means and an end, in his view, and therefore he must support freedom of advocacy for erroneous as well as correct opinions. Once the basis for the unity of his faction is understood, it is not "surprising" that people of very different beliefs could belong to it.[50]

After the schism of 1840, that faction became more homogeneous in doctrines; one of the practical incentives to breadth of principles had been removed. It was not until after the schism that the AASS and its affiliates began to pass resolutions that smacked of nonresistance.[51] Historians who argue that the 1840 split resulted from Garrison's having turned the association into a universal reform society are thus predating that transformation and possibly reversing cause and effect.

Garrison's attitude toward the various reforms he espoused seems to have changed upon his conversion to perfectionism. Those he supported before 1837 he regarded as goods in themselves, or at any rate independently of his support for abolitionism, as did his conservative opponents throughout the period dealt with here. The reforms he added after 1837 he tended to subsume under the perfectionist rubric rather than to see them as good in their own right. Thus, he could say of one cause he had supported from the start, "Absorbed as we are in our advocacy of the anti-slavery enterprise, we nevertheless feel a strong and quenchless interest in the cause of temperance."[52] He does not seem to have given much thought to the connection between temperance and his over-all philosophy; he simply assumed that it was a reform that all good people ought to favor. Those causes he adopted after 1837, however, he saw as corollaries of his new religious creed; it was in that way only that he defended sex equality and the abolition of capital punishment.

His conservative opponents supported some of the same causes[53] as well as the same basic principles of abolitionism as defined in the constitution of the AASS. The underlying issue in the clash was not the definition of abolitionism or support for other causes; it was the relation between abolitionism and other causes, principally those of a religious nature. The same abolitionist principles could be worked into very different religious frameworks, and the conservatives feared that continued alliance with the radicals would help the latter promulgate heresy and that such alliance would prevent religious and social conservatives from joining the movement. Hence the question was never whether the antislavery societies should tolerate "extraneous" causes, but whether they should tolerate or repudiate *unpopular* "extraneous" causes,[54] for the repudiation of religious heresy was the endorsement of religious orthodoxy, and *The Emancipator* under the editorship of the anti-Garrisonian Joshua Leavitt occasionally editorialized on subjects other than antislavery.[55]

The conservatives' repudiation of ultraism and their organization of a respectable national society in 1840 did not, however, bring the anticipated thousands of new recruits flocking to their standard. It was the A & F's misfortune to be born during a nationwide depression, and even the contributions of passive supporters were pitifully scanty. A more important reason for the new organization's poor showing may be that the A & F did not challenge accustomed modes of thought and living. By being careful to show that abolitionism did not require a drastic change in values and behavior, the conservative leaders may also have inadvertently demonstrated that their brand of abolitionism was not vitally necessary to the Christian life. Why should a person who was indifferent to abolitionism espouse it if it was presented to him as something that need not change his life in a fundamental way? He could, to be sure, be induced to contribute money that he would not have given to the AASS. But a reform portrayed as compatible with his conventional beliefs and activities could not at the same time be seen as requiring him to alter them—for example, to give up his white-supremacist assumptions and to brave odium by trying to convert his fellow parishioners. Abolitionism itself was, after all, nearly as unpopular in the 1830s and 1840s as the various ultraisms. It was not until the passage of the Fugitive Slave Law in 1850 that the threat of slavery to Northerners made abolitionism respectable. Prior to that time, the persistence of most Northerners in thinking it radical and a threat to their way of life and their values manifested, I suspect, a sound instinct for consistency among the various tenets that made up their world view. Perhaps it was the conservative abolitionists, insisting that the principles of the AASS constitution were not radical, who were inconsistent and unrealistic.

NOTES

¹ "Sentence of the Rev. Geo. B. Cheever," *The Liberator*, December 12, 1835.

² *Ibid.*, July 23, August 6, and August 20, 1836. In the August 6 editorial, *The Vermont Chronicle* is quoted as saying that Garrison's opposition to gag laws was "a denial of the right of society to protect itself by law against libelous, licentious and blasphemous publications." Garrison replied: "Cannot purity grapple successfully in an open field with licentiousness, without the aid of a constable? If men or women blaspheme, shall we not rather pray for them, than extort money from their pockets, or incarcerate their bodies?" Two observations may be made. Fines and prison terms were at that period imposed for more "offenses" than is the case today, including "offenses" that now are considered matters of private opinion. Second, Garrison was not denying the community's right to protect itself; he was denying that physical penalties did protect it. His denunciation of "carnal means" was therefore not a demand that the community give criminals a free hand; it was a propaganda technique to teach the community the true nature of the dangers that threatened it and the only defense that he believed could be effective.

³ *The Liberator*, July 4, December 2, 1835; July 23, August 6, August 20, 1836. See also issue of August 27, 1836, and others in the same period. Lydia Maria Child was another who favored nonresistance prior to the women's rights controversy (*ibid.*, April 2, 1836). Violence in any case, she argued, was opposed to the spirit of the gospel. If it were ever justified it would be justified for the slave. In the issue of August 27, Garrison wrote that he had received many letters commenting on his discussion of the Sabbath. He assured his readers that he had not intended to make his paper the arena of controversy over a topic foreign to its main object. But doubtless he would in the future advance sentiments, on various topics, that some readers would disapprove. He assured them that his columns were always open to those who wished to refute him. *The Liberator*, as a paper patronized by abolitionists of many sects, ought not to attack specifically sectarian tenets, he added; but the Sabbath question was general, not sectarian.

⁴ *Ibid.*, May 26, June 9, June 23, July 7, July 21, 1837.

⁵ James G. Birney, "View of the Constitution of the Am. A. S. Society as Connected with the 'No-Government' Question," *The Emancipator*, May 2, 1839.

⁶ *The Liberator*, September 8, 1837. See *ibid.*, January 24, 1840, for letter to Garrison from Fitch, who had been converted to the movement that preached the imminent coming of the Day of Judgment. Fitch wrote that he had been recalling his past life and wondering how he would view past feelings and acts if he beheld Christ coming to judge the world. He found he had much to be ashamed of; that in many instances he had been moved by the "desire to please men, for the sake of their good opinion"; and that that desire had been his only object in the part he had played in the clerical protests, although at that time he had not been as conscious as he now was of his true motive. He sent this letter to Garrison not, he said, to win applause but because his conscience and heart impelled him to and because truth and the spirit of God required him to. Garrison was free to do what he chose with the letter; if good could be done thereby, Garrison could make it as public as the sin had been. Garrison prefaced the letter with a brief comment, rejoicing at the recantation, forgiving Fitch, and hoping the other clerical appellants would follow his example. The recantation is also in *Eighth Annual Report of the Board of Managers of the Mass. Anti-Slavery Soc.* (Boston, 1840), pp. 7–8. Fitch's confession that he had been motivated by selfish considerations receives some support in letter from A[lanson] St. C[lair] to Amos A. Phelps, August 17, 1837, Phelps Papers, BPL (both St. Clair and Phelps later broke with Garrison): "At what you say Fitch & co are about, I am astonished— Though I believe there was some call for advice to moderation in point of epithets &c. (had it been given in the right way & place) yet I am grieved to the heart, that, for personal considerations, any man should attempt to break the ranks and divide against themselves, the persecuted Abolitionists."

⁷ Protest No. 3 was also by Fitch and Towne and was actually a letter to the editor of *The New England Spectator*, reprinted in *The Liberator*, September 29, 1837. Whittier's letter (*ibid.*, September 22, 1837) said that all sides had erred. Wright's letter to Garrison (*ibid.*, October 13, 1837) was entitled "Clerical Appeals, Protests, &c. &c." Another letter from Whittier appears in the issue of October 27, 1837. All issues in this period contain small news items reporting resolutions passed by anti-slavery societies, mostly in support of Garrison and *The Liberator*.

⁸ Garrison made the same point in "Reply to Dr. Osgood," *ibid.*, August 2, 1839. By February 10, 1843, however, he had repudiated the "clergy and other ecclesiastical usurpers." See "The Second Advent. No. I," in *The Liberator* of that date; also, "Letter of Dr. Brisbane," *ibid.*, March 1, 1844.

⁹ See, for example, John L. Thomas, "Romantic Reform in America, 1815–1865," *American Quarterly*, XVII (Winter 1965), 661; and Timothy L. Smith, *Revivalism and Social Reform* (New York, 1965; first published in 1957), pp. 181, 183, 187. Walter M. Merrill, in *Against Wind and Tide: A Biography of William Lloyd Garrison* (Cambridge, Mass., 1963), pp. 136–37, asserts: "Just as abolitionism leveled society, so it ought to be concerned with all good causes, Garrison thought." And the

author asks, "How could the abolitionists retain a unity of opinion sufficient to accomplish their main purpose if they must support every current reform?" Garrison never said they must. But he insisted that the antislavery *societies* must not *oppose* any current reform either.

10 May to Garrison, December 18, 1837, and December 26, 1837, both in Anti-Slavery Letters, BPL. See also Sarah M. Grimké to Anne Warren Weston, December 7, 1837, Weston Papers, BPL; letter to the editor from Henry C. Wright, *The Liberator*, December 8, 1837; letter to the editor from S[arah] M. G[rimké], *ibid.*, January 5, 1838. For various reactions to Lovejoy's action, see articles in issues of November 24 and December 1, 8, 22, 29, 1837; January 5, 12, 1838; February 16, 1838.

11 May to Beriah Green, *ibid.*, January 5, 1838, reprinted from *The Emancipator*.

12 Garrison to May, December 30, 1837, Garrison Papers, BPL; and editorial note in *The Liberator*, January 5, 1838. Garrison's position became the official position of the Massachusetts Anti-Slavery Society. See *Sixth Annual Report of the Board of Managers of the Massachusetts Anti-Slavery Society* (Boston, 1838), pp. 37-38, third and fourth resolutions.

13 A good statement of this theory of organization, by a moderate Garrisonian (who later broke with Garrison on the ground that he had deviated from it), is "Letter from Mrs. Child, on the Present State of the Anti-Slavery Cause," *The Liberator*, September 6, 1839. Lewis Tappan, whose other causes were more respectable, adopted the same tactical line at the time of the discussion of Lovejoy. See his letter to the editor (*ibid.*, January 5, 1838) in which he explains that most signers of· the AASS's Declaration of Sentiments, adopted at the founding of the organization, were "non-combatants" on principle, but that the minority who were not were permitted to sign, understanding that the society was pledging nonviolence only in regard to the cause which it was organized to further: abolition of slavery. These members were not pledging to eschew forcible defense of their own lives and property. Tappan went on to assert that some nonresistant members seemed to think, erroneously, that the Declaration was a pledge of thorough nonresistance. He for one believed force always anti-Christian as well as inexpedient, but he wished everyone to be clear that this doctrine was not a principle of the AASS. He suggested that a full discussion be held in *The Liberator* of "the Peace question," with abolitionists on both sides contributing their views.

14 *Ibid.*, October 27, 1837. Apropos of Garrison's attitude toward his Negro supporters, it should be noted that Merrill has distorted an important piece of documentary evidence. On pp. 147-48 of *Against Wind and Tide*, discussing the clerical plot against Garrison, Merrill writes: "When the plotters tried to convert some of the free colored to their views, Garrison congratulated himself that they were so loyal to him that if he went to hell, they would follow." Merrill cites a letter from Garrison to George Benson, January 14, 1839, Garrison Letters, BPL, but he does not quote it. The following is what Garrison actually wrote to

George W. Benson on that date: John E. Fuller had visited him recently to discuss the controversy and the projected new anti-Garrison paper. Fuller had switched sides and now favored the paper. "He is trying to influence our colored friends to think well of the new project; but he finds they are true as steel, and therefore angrily tells them that he believes that if Garrison should go to hell, they would go with him."

15 For general analyses of the nonresistance philosophy, see Merle Curti, "Non-Resistance in New England," *New England Quarterly*, II (January 1929), 34–57, and John Demos, "The Antislavery Movement and the Problem of Violent 'Means,'" *ibid.*, XXXVII (December 1964), 501–26. Both articles cover the post-1850 period as well as the period covered in the present study.

16 This was a favorite argument of nonresistants. Henry C. Wright, for example, argued that if Lovejoy and "the men of Bunker Hill" had been justified in fighting, so would the slaves. But the Bunker Hill casualties on both sides were murdered. He added that abolitionists who counseled the slaves to peace but lauded Lovejoy for fighting were hypocrites, and so were those who cheered the Founding Fathers every Fourth of July; every patriotic speech about the colonists fighting for liberty was a speech to the slaves telling them they had the right to butcher their masters for freedom (*The Liberator*, December 22, 1837). See also Garrison, *ibid.*, February 11, 1842. The Massachusetts Anti-Slavery Society's board of managers declared that those who applauded the patriots of '76, yet deplored Lovejoy's emulation of them, were hypocrites (*Sixth Annual Report of the Board of Managers of the Massachusetts Anti-Slavery Society*, p. 37). Garrisons, *Garrison*, II, 190, state that that resolution was evidently written by Garrison.

17 Anne Warren Weston to Garrison, November 11, 1838, Anti-Slavery Letters, BPL. See also George Bourne to Garrison, October 1, 1838, and March 2, 1839, in the same collection.

18 *The Liberator*, September 28, 1838. The officers of the new society are listed *ibid.*, October 12, 1838.

19 "U. S. Circuit Court," *ibid.*, October 19, 1838.

20 "The No Human Government Theory," letter from Orange Scott, *ibid.*, October 26, 1838. Several important articles in this issue, which were polemics in the factional struggle in the AASS, will be omitted from consideration here, to be cited later in this chapter in the discussion of that struggle.

21 *Ibid.*, May 24, 1839; see also Grew's article, *ibid.*, January 3, 1840.

22 *Ibid.*, September 17, 1841. See also "Governmental Taxes and Military Fines," *ibid.*, September 24, 1841.

23 *Ibid.*, October 15, 1841. See also "Absolutism, Monarchy, Republicanism, To Be Superseded," *ibid.*, March 3, 1848.

24 A Rhode Islander claimed the reward (*ibid.*, September 30, 1842); Garrison refuted the "proof" furnished and therefore declined to pay.

25 "The Second Advent. No. I," *ibid.*, February 10, 1843.

26 "The Second Advent. No. II," *ibid.*, February 17, 1843. The emphases are Garrison's. He followed the quotation with two exclamation points.

27 "Thomas Paine," *ibid.*, November 21, 1845. He added that Paine, in calling the Bible a pious imposture, was as wrong as the fundamentalists at the other extreme.

28 "Mystical Religion," *ibid.*, April 9, 1847.

29 *Ibid.*, August 11, 1848. The article evoked a heated dispute. See Wright's "The Bible a Self-Evident Falsehood if Opposed to Self-Evident Truth," *ibid.*, September 22, 1848, and "Is God Unjust and Changeable, or Men, the Writers of the Old Testament, in Some Things Mistaken?" *ibid.*, November 10, 1848; other Wright articles with similar titles, *ibid.*, November 17, 24, 1848; William Goodell, "To Henry C. Wright," and Henry Grew, "Is the Bible a Lie, or Is Henry C. Wright Mistaken?" *ibid.*, December 22, 1848; and several other articles on both sides in the issues of December 1, 8, 1848; January 12, February 3, March 9, 16, 23, 1849, and occasionally thereafter. In "Woman's Rights Convention," *ibid.*, May 3, 1850, Wright wrote that if the Bible preached male superiority, it was "thus far *null and void,* simply because it is opposed to nature." When a neighbor reproached Nathaniel P. Rogers, a Garrisonian, for preaching abolition and said that Jesus never did, Rogers replied that the Golden Rule, if put into practice, would abolish slavery immediately. But suppose Jesus did not preach abolition: "then, I say, *he didn't do his duty*" (Robert Adams, "Nathaniel Peabody Rogers: 1794–1846," *New England Quarterly,* XX [September 1947], 369). For an interesting parallel, see David Brion Davis, *The Problem of Slavery in Western Culture,* pp. 378–79, discussing a book written between 1749 and 1752 by James Foster, "a famous dissenting preacher" in England: "By that time latitudinarian religion had become so infused with nature and reason that the Bible could be treated as a useful supplement." Foster wrote, "if the *Gospel,* instead of confirming, had abrogated the common ties of human nature, it would be both impiety, and inhumanity, to embrace it."

30 " 'The Rights of God'—Free Discussion—Freedom of the Press," *The Liberator,* January 30, 1846. The editorial also discussed a letter Garrison had received from a Quaker woman who had been shocked at Stearns's "blasphemous" letter, averring that it was calculated to arouse the worst side of human nature. Garrison asked why she had not been so disturbed at other articles in the same issue, including proslavery material in the "Refuge of Oppression." Were they not as blasphemous? See also issues of March 27, April 3, and April 10, 1846, for further contributions to the dispute.

31 Lewis Tappan to Amos A. Phelps, August 22, 1837, Phelps Papers, BPL: "We all know that our friend Garrison has always refused putting the Liberator under the control of any Society or association. . . . Let Mr Garrison conduct his paper, in his own way, untrammelled. This will satisfy many who do not like his paper, in all respects, & who feel unwilling that it shall be considered the organ of the Ms. Soc." See also Phelps to John G. Whittier, August 17, 1837, and Whittier to Phelps, August 21, 1837, both in Phelps Papers, BPL.

32 Amos A. Phelps to Professor [William] Smyth, October 24, 1837, Phelps Papers, BPL. Seven months later, however, Phelps accepted re-

appointment as general agent of the Massachusetts Society. See Phelps to the Board of Managers, May 29, 1838, Phelps Papers, BPL.

33 Tappan to Phelps, January 15, 1839, and Scott to Phelps, January 15, 1839, both in Phelps Papers, BPL.

34 A typical one is that from the Rev. J. N. Parsons, February 1, 1839, Phelps Papers, BPL: "Could not something like the 'Union Evangelical Ant. S. Soc. of New York City,' be formed, which will draw the Evang-l strength of the State? The cause of truth is certainly in awful jeopardy from the endless innovations which he [Garrison] is making, & there is imminent danger that he will *infinitely more than undo* the good he has accomplished."

35 Birney to Lewis Tappan, September 14, 1837, in Dumond, ed., *Birney Letters*, I, 425.

36 Stanton to Birney, August 11, 1838, *ibid.*, p. 465. In a letter to Birney on August 17, Stanton spoke more moderately: he now thought "it will all blow over" (*ibid.*, p. 466). His optimism did not last long. See his account to Birney, January 26, 1839, of the "stormy" annual meeting, just concluded, of the Massachusetts Society. "The split is wide," he observed, "and can never be closed up. . . . A very large corps of Methodists were present, and went right and with their whole hearts, almost to a man. Scott told me that the Methodists generally in the State would go against all these distracting *isms*. Our cause in this State is ruined unless we can seperate [*sic*] the A. S. Society from everything which does not belong to it. I am for meeting it here, now, on the spot where the evil exists. . . . Nil desperandum etc.

"We have resolved upon a new paper. . . . 2200 subscribers are pledged. We have got a Committee and are going ahead. We want an Editor. We have set our eyes upon bro. E. Wright Jr." (*ibid.*, pp. 481–82).

37 "Annual Meeting," *The Liberator*, January 18, 1839. See also various letters in the same issue, concerning the "plot," and a great deal of material, on both sides, in the inside pages of the issue of January 25.

38 Torrey to Phelps, March 21, [1839], Phelps Papers, BPL. In a letter to Phelps on March 30 (same collection), Torrey calls Garrison's paper "the Lyingberator."

39 St. Clair to [Phelps], March 30, 1839, Phelps Papers, BPL.

40 This document, in the Phelps Papers, BPL, is evidently a draft; it contains many corrections, some in Phelps's handwriting, although the bulk of the writing is in another hand. All emphases and the bracketed interpolation in the first quotation are in the original. The circular actually sent out was evidently dated April 20, as is clear from acknowledgments by recipients; several such acknowledgments are in the collection.

41 Stanton to Phelps, February 20, 1840, Phelps Papers, BPL. Barnes, *Anti-Slavery Impulse*, p. 168, states that Garrison's organization "of course" refused to raise money to help the national committee in New York to pay its debts, but that "the Massachusetts Abolition Society, which also claimed jurisdiction over Massachusetts territory, invited Stanton to tour the State." Barnes does not mention Stanton's letter and

hence does not show that the invitation to Stanton came in response to a confidential letter from Stanton himself. The Phelps collection, which contains this letter and is the richest source on the anti-Garrisonian movement, was not one of the manuscript collections Barnes consulted. The same collection contains a printed circular from the British and Foreign Anti-Slavery Society, dated February 15, 1840, on the blank pages of which is a private letter from Stanton to Phelps, dated "Saturday." In it is the following passage: "As to the annual meeting. We are preparing for it. We shall generally go for dissolution, unless we can open the whole feild [*sic*] as it used to be, & bring things on to their original basis. A.T.—L.T.—J.G.B.—S.E.C.—S.S.J. & H.B.S.—are fully for this—L.R.S.—T.S.W—pretty much so—J.S. verging towards it—J.S.G dead against.— If someone (will St. Clair be the man?) can come on here & drum up cautiously we can dissolve the concern the very afternoon of the public meeting! *Inter nos,* some one *must* come on here & get out the voters, & the thing is done— 'A word to the wise' &c. Be *careful* who comes." The initials stand for Arthur Tappan, Lewis Tappan, James G. Birney, Samuel E. Cornish, Simeon S. Jocelyn, Henry B. Stanton, LaRoy Sunderland, Theodore S. Wright, Joshua Leavitt, James S. Gibbons. Stanton's predictions proved accurate. Gibbons was the only Garrisonian on the AASS executive committee.

⁴² Garrison, "National Anti-Slavery Convention," *The Liberator,* August 9, 1839: "A strenuous attempt was made to get a resolution adopted of a proscriptive and binding character; but it was rejected by an overwhelming majority. To the attacks made upon non-resisting abolitionists, I made no reply, as a matter of principle, for, as I have never intruded my views of peace and government upon any anti-slavery meeting, so I will not stand up in their defence at any such meeting, however unjustly they may be assailed." See also proceedings of that convention reported in *The Emancipator,* August 15, 1839. For another instance of Garrison's efforts to keep nonresistance out of abolitionist meetings, see Edmund Quincy to Henry C. Wright, December 31, 1838, in Garrisons, *Garrison,* II, 254. An exchange of letters in the Phelps Papers, BPL, is revealing in regard to Garrison's desire to avoid mutual denunciations if possible. On July 8, 1839, Phelps wrote him a letter headed "Important Information." He stated that he had received a letter from a man who had a friend who had attended the recent quarterly meeting of the Worcester North Division Anti-Slavery Society at Templeton, Massachusetts, and who had told Phelps's informant that after the meeting about half a dozen Garrisonians had surrounded him and warned him to beware of Phelps, Daniel Wise, Orange Scott, Alanson St. Clair, Elizur Wright, Jr., and others, saying they were traitors, colonizationists, and bad men. Phelps guessed that the Garrisonians referred to included John A. Collins and Oliver Johnson and was now writing to ask Garrison to publish in *The Liberator* a warning notice to the public to beware of Phelps, Wise, and the others, because if they *were* all those things it was important that the public know it. Garrison replied on July 9, sending Phelps's note back to him, "because I am not willing to make you appear ridiculous, by publishing it in the Liberator. If you wish to know what was said of your course at Templeton, by

Messrs. Collins and Johnson, just apply to them, and I doubt not they will frankly tell you. But do not show yourself to be unduly sensitive and weakly credulous, by giving heed to any such statements as have been made to you by one who was not at the meeting, and who undertakes to report what was said in private conversation, as stated to him by 'a young man.' " He signed the letter, "Yours, as in auld lang syne." Garrison's letter was addressed to "Bro. Phelps"; Phelps's began, "Mr. Garrison."

43 Most of Birney's article dealt with the political-action dispute and will therefore be discussed in Chapter 5.

44 Birney, "View of the Constitution of the American A. S. Society as Connected with the 'No-Government' Question," *The Emancipator*, May 2, 1839, reprinted in *The Liberator*, June 28, 1839; Garrison, "Reply to James G. Birney," *ibid.*

45 James G. Birney and Beriah Green favored restriction of the right to vote. See Birney to Gamaliel Bailey, April 16, 1843; and Green to Birney, April 23, 1847, both in *Birney Letters*, II, 732–34, 1066–67.

46 Thomas Franklin Harwood, "Great Britain and American Anti-slavery," unpublished Ph.D. dissertation, University of Texas, 1959, pp. 368, 370.

47 The Massachusetts Anti-Slavery Society and almost all its auxiliaries consistently supported Garrison throughout the factional fight; only a small minority seceded in 1839 to form the Massachusetts Abolition Society. Yet only a small minority of the old society's members were nonresistants. See Executive Committee of the New-England Non-Resistance Society to Arthur Tappan, *The Liberator*, July 31, 1840; and Ellis Gray Loring to editor of *The Emancipator*, *The Liberator*, May 8, 1840.

48 See letter to editor from Torrey, *The Liberator*, November 1, 1839: "And while I retain my present views of the utter wickedness of 'self-defence by physical force,' and 'lawsuits in defence of personal character,' such assaults may pass, with perfect impunity, till we meet in the presence of the 'Great God, and our Savior, Jesus Christ.' " Perhaps, however, Torrey's views should be discounted, in view of a letter to Phelps from Torrey's widow, September 15, 1846, Phelps Papers, BPL, in which she states that her husband had been "partially insane upon some subjects."

49 Stephen S. Foster and Parker Pillsbury were the most notorious of the "Come-Outers," those who believed that the churches were incorrigibly corrupt and that the abolitionists were morally obligated to "come out" from them. The notoriety of these two men was earned by their practice of entering churches and loudly calling upon the congregation to leave. They were often ejected forcibly.

50 Hence his war on the churches and the ministry is explicable only secondarily in terms of doctrinal disagreements. Primarily it was motivated by his conviction that they closed off freedom of thought and imposed conformity, blind acceptance of doctrines on faith, and reverence for authority whose legitimacy could not be determined in the absence of liberty to question.

51 See Lydia Maria Child to Ellis Gray Loring, May 16, 1844, Child

Papers, NYPL; Edmund Quincy to Richard D. Webb, January 29, 1843, quoted in Garrisons, *Garrison*, III, 88; letter to editor from J. M. Aldrich and Garrison's comment on it, *The Liberator*, September 19, 1844 (discussing resolution on religion offered but not acted upon at an antislavery society meeting in New Bedford, Mass.). It may be argued that the official condemnation of the U.S. Constitution and therefore of all voting, by Garrison-dominated societies after 1842 (to be discussed in Chapter 7 below), also represented a departure from the earlier policy of leaving "modes of action" up to individual members. But even then the Garrisonians insisted that those who did not accept the new doctrine could be bona fide abolitionists and should not resign from the society. The letter of Mrs. Child cited above contains this passage: "I am thankful that you have entered a protest against the wild spirit of ultraism, which is driving one of the best of causes to its ruin. I have long felt that the judicious and moderately conservative among us gave up the reins too much to these Jehus. The effect is, to make our money and abilities serve to advance things which we do not in our consciences approve. If they go on with their favorite work of sifting out all but the Simon Pures, they will soon sift down the society to N. P. Rogers, Abigail Folsom, and S. S. Foster." Later she wrote that it was that spirit which had caused her to resign as editor of *The National Anti-Slavery Standard*, the official weekly of the AASS after the 1840 schism. "Between you and I [sic]," she observed, "Mrs. Chapman was *determined* that the popularity of the Standard should be *forced* to sustain the come-outerisms of church and state." (The Abigail Folsom referred to above was an emotionally unbalanced woman who attended all radical conventions in Boston and spoke interminably from the floor before being carried out of the hall, still speaking.)

52 "The Licence Law—Political Action," *The Liberator*, February 21, 1840.

53 In 1844 Garrison and Phillips were active in the campaign to have capital punishment abolished in Massachusetts. After they had testified before a legislative committee, a petition was presented to the committee asking that capital punishment be retained. It was signed by seven ministers, three deacons, and three laymen. Among the group were Phelps, Nathaniel Colver, J. C. Lovejoy, Joshua Leavitt, and Hiram Cummings, all "new organizationists" and bitter foes of Garrison. Another was the publishing agent of *The Emancipator*, now in the hands of the A & F. To drive home what he believed was the logical connection between their motives for splitting the abolitionist movement and their support for the death penalty, Garrison entitled an editorial "A New Development—New Organization in the field in defence of the Gallows—The Advocates for gagging Women, in favor of strangling Men," *The Liberator*, February 23, 1844.

54 Garrison explicitly made this accusation in his editorial *ibid.*, March 8, 1839 (the plot, he wrote, was to supplant *The Liberator* with "a paper . . . less offensive to the clergy, and less free in its spirit, and that will not dare to utter a word upon any other question of reform—*unless it be popular!*"), and in his "Remarks" on a letter from James G. Birney, *ibid.*, April 5, 1839. Italics in original.

[55] See, for example, William Jay to Executive Committee of the AASS, June 3, 1837, Elizur Wright, Jr., Papers, LC. Jay asserted that "while the American Anti Slavery Society inflexibly & fearlessly adheres to its avowed principles, it should maintain an honest & scrupulous neutrality in respect to those religious doctrines on which its members are known to differ, & which have no connection whatever with the subject of abolition." He believed the editor of *The Emancipator* had, in the May 11 issue, departed from that rule in an editorial in which he advised every abolitionist family to buy and study Charles G. Finney's *Lectures to Professing Christians*. The paper was published by the society, and its editor was appointed by the executive committee and paid by the society, Jay added. "Hence the paper is supposed to exhibit, not the peculiar theological views of its Editor, but the sentiments held in common by the members of the Society"; it was not at liberty to propagate sentiments that many members opposed. If an Episcopalian (Jay was one) should become editor, would the executive committee tolerate a recommendation of a treatise defending "the apostolic institution of Episcopacy"? LaRoy Sunderland had the right to attack Finney's views in his *Watchman*, Phelps to preach them in his pulpit, and Leavitt to print them in his *Evangelist*, "but the Ex. committee have no right through their official journal to express any opinion about them, or to advise people to buy the volume in which they are set forth." Jay went on to say he was eager to have the society's journals avoid "the appearance of sectarian influence" and exclude "from them controverted matters not connected with the avowed principles & objects of the Society, & having a tendency to create dissentions among its members." That did not, he insisted, infringe freedom of expression, for abolitionists could use other media—"*unofficial* journals."

5

POLITICS

WHEN THE AASS began to split, in the late 1830s, in part over political tactics, the struggle was neither between political and antipolitical abolitionists, nor between those who considered the United States government morally defensible and nonresistants who rejected all forcible government. Nor did the struggle focus on the expediency of the third-party tactic. Throughout the internecine battles in the AASS Garrison had the support of many abolitionists who believed in voting; among his prominent associates were the Whig David Lee Child and the Libertyman Samuel E. Sewall. In the opposing faction were anti-third-party men like Lewis Tappan, who did not go over to the Liberty party till 1843, as well as charter members of that party like Birney. Whereas a nonresistant would clearly be unable to support the Birney-Tappan faction, non-nonresistants like Wendell Phillips and Francis Jackson rejected voting for either Liberty party or major-party candidates and championed Garrison's cause within the society. As in the fight over religious questions, the common ground of the anti-Garrisonians was their conviction that they must show the public that radical doctrines were incompatible with abolitionism, and the common ground of the Garrisonians was the belief that the antislavery platform must be kept broad enough to hold abolitionists of all varieties so long as they agreed that slavery was sinful and must be immediately abandoned.

In the early years of the AASS its members gave little thought to the political implications of their movement and simply assumed that an abolitionist who could vote should prefer antislavery candidates. The society's constitution pledged abolitionists "to endeavor, in a constitutional way," to influence Congress to abolish the interstate slave trade and to end slavery in the District of Columbia and the territories. It did not spell out how this was to be done. As long as the movement consisted of a handful of zealots motivated by religious principles and totally without prestige and influence, they were not forced to examine their assumption that moral suasion, to which the society's constitution committed them, precluded organized political action. Like others of their class they took it for granted that politics was sordid and corrupting and that to engage in it was in effect to confess that "moral means" had failed.[1]

What were "moral means"? An examination of numerous resolutions and other official statements reveals that political influence was exerted "morally" by an abolitionist who petitioned a legislative body or testified before a legislative committee or interrogated candidates concerning their views on slavery and published the replies. Such activities could be carried on by abolitionists as individuals or by antislavery societies. An abolitionist exerted "moral" influence also by voting for an antislavery candidate running against a proslavery candidate, or, where both candidates were unacceptable, by "scattering" (casting a write-in vote); but in this case the abolitionist's action should be performed as an individual. The automatic revulsion, in the early years, from organized political action most often expressed itself as fear that abolitionists would lose what little respect they enjoyed in the community, for that respect was based on the obvious fact that they had nothing to gain personally from their crusade. If they were to form their own party or party faction, however, some people would accuse them of coveting the spoils of power or office.[2]

By the late 1830s the AASS had so grown in numbers and

potential political influence that it became imperative to define its relation to the political process more precisely. This development was accelerated by the growing conviction of many leaders that the customary modes of exerting influence on government had yielded inadequate results. Now the assumption that politics was sordid and dirty provided a rationale for reversing the traditional attitude toward organized political action: some leaders began to argue that politics was sordid because moral men left it to the politicians. Politics would not corrupt abolitionists, they discovered; the abolitionists could regenerate politics.[3] To accomplish this miraculous reformation, they would have to build their political strength quickly, and for this two things were desirable. The first was to attract the support of the thousands of antislavery voters who did not belong to the AASS and were generally conservative on political and religious issues. The second was to make the AASS itself the nucleus of the new political pressure group. Obviously neither change could be effected until the nonresistants were separated from the society.[4]

After a few preliminary bouts the main event took place at a meeting of the Massachusetts Anti-Slavery Society in January 1839, when Henry B. Stanton and James G. Birney tried to force the society to choose between nonresistance and political action. The society, in backing Garrison, did not choose nonresistance; it strenuously denied that an antislavery society should or could make that choice.

Various societies had in fact been passing resolutions stating that it was an abolitionist's duty to use all the political power he possessed for the good of the cause. In June 1838 the New England Anti-Slavery Convention adopted "with great unanimity" two resolutions offered by Alvan Stewart: first, that it was every abolitionist's duty to use political influence to elect to Congress men who would use their power to abolish slavery wherever Congress's jurisdiction extended; and second, that any attempt to form a third party was to be deplored, but that it was an abolitionist's duty to vote, irrespective of party, for such men, and such only, as would promote abolition.[5] The annual meeting of the Ohio Anti-Slavery Society resolved that its devotion to solely spiritual weapons was not meant to discourage abolitionists from voting; that it approved of inter-rogation of candidates; that abolitionists who believed in the lawfulness of existing governments were bound by their prin-ciples to promote the election of and vote for good men; and that for various reasons the organization of a third party should be condemned.[6] Such resolutions became standard, and nonresistants joined with others in voting for them.

The position that Garrison and his supporters took on politi-cal action was spelled out in a letter to abolitionists of Massachusetts by Francis Jackson and Amos A. Phelps in be-half of the board of managers of the Massachusetts Anti-Slavery Society. They began by saying they disagreed with those who opposed any form of political action as polluting their religious cause. Politics was a branch of morals, and if it had been degraded they were not therefore justified in giving it up to bad men. They went on to say that they valued politics chiefly as a means of agitating the subject of slavery. All they needed to win was to gain the ear of the nation; that meant agitation, and the most effective agitation was in a legis-lature, with the whole nation the audience. That did not mean they would make abolition a political question, they insisted; no, it was a moral question. A third party would be unwise because it would make abolition mainly a political issue, with every member having to vote for its candidates regardless of his interest in other issues besides abolition. But petitioning legislatures and questioning candidates were approved modes of political action. As to voting, the address told abolitionists that their duties as voters were mainly negative: do not vote for any candidate who is unwilling to give the right answers to your questions; and vote not as a bloc but as individuals. Where all candidates are unacceptable, adopt the "scattering" policy. Aim at becoming the balance of power so that the parties will come to *you*; do not ally with *them*. The funda-mental principles of both parties were fine, but their leaders had betrayed those principles. At the end of the document, in *The Liberator*, an editorial note by editor pro tem. Oliver Johnson, a nonresistant, endorsed it.[7]

note as *indis* for Abolitionists

Various leaders of the later third-party movement were arguing along the same lines in this period, although with certain subsidiary tenets that Garrison would not endorse. For example, William Goodell, whose principal distinction was his penchant for writing interminable manifestoes in his *Friend of Man* (Utica), organ of the New-York State Anti-Slavery Society, produced a book-length series of articles that *The Liberator* dutifully reprinted in full in the summer of 1838.[8] In the main they argued against the organization of a third party, although, along with Garrison, Goodell insisted that abolitionists had the right to organize one if the major parties failed to yield to abolitionist pressure. Among the reasons why a third party should be avoided if possible was that the abolitionists in the major parties acted as a leaven which a third party would remove. The scattering policy was better; it would teach candidates a lesson. To say that engaging in political action is dabbling in dirty waters, wrote Goodell, is to say that government is a device of the devil and not an ordinance of God. Abolition of slavery was no more and no less than the repeal of the laws that established it. Hence abolitionists must work for repeal of those laws; the only alternative was bloodshed.[9]

The coming dissension was augured in a debate during a convention at Lockport, New York, at which Henry B. Stanton argued that political action was the practical application of moral power and that abolitionists could not throw off their responsibilities without adopting the no-government theory. This time the political resolutions, though passed, met with some opposition.[10] What was new in this debate was the effort to label the views of some members incompatible with abolitionism. Previously, nonresistants had willingly acquiesced when majorities at meetings had passed resolutions that recommended voting. In later years, after the schism, they themselves passed resolutions reflecting the new majority opinions. But at neither period would they countenance any effort to make acceptance of majority policy a test of membership. Thus when the showdown came, at the beginning of 1839, the issue was not whether abolitionists must or must not vote; it was whether the organization could condemn as spurious abolitionists those members who had religious scruples against voting. And when the proscriptive purpose of the Stanton-Birney faction became clear, both sides had to scrutinize the wording of all resolutions presented, and picayune amendments became important factional weapons. A provoting resolution that a nonresistant might have accepted earlier now provoked dissension if under the circumstances its passage would imply condemnation of nonvoters.

It was at the annual meeting of the Massachusetts Anti-Slavery Society in January 1839 that Stanton's famous challenge to Garrison took place: Stanton demanded that Garrison state publicly whether he considered voting a sin. Garrison replied, "Sin for me!" and refused to assert that what was a sin for one abolitionist was a sin for all.[11] Abstracted from its context, this reply would seem to raise the philosophical question whether an abolitionist's actions should be based on what was objectively right or on what he *thought* was right—or as some would put it, on divine law or his own conscience—and in fact this problem was the subject of some subsequent debate.[12] In its context, however, Garrison's reply was the only possible one, given his conviction that the antislavery societies must not pass on any *moral* questions but the sinfulness of slavery and the duty of immediate emancipation; they must not, in abolitionist terminology, "coerce the consciences" of members. If he had answered Stanton's question, "Yes, voting is a sin," he would have condemned the majority of members and taken a position, on an abolitionist platform, on a principle not in the society's constitution. If he had replied "No," he would have condemned his own philosophy. Everyone understood that the question was a "Have you stopped beating your wife?" trap.

Stanton's challenge represented an attempt to force Garrison to equate nonresistance with true abolitionism at an official antislavery meeting, something Garrison had never done and would continue refusing to do. There was always a distinction between what he would say in *The Liberator* as a nonresistant and what he thought proper to say as an abolitionist in an antislavery society meeting. When he replied that voting was a sin *for him*, he was saying in effect that one did not have to be a nonresistant to be a bona fide abolitionist. Stanton's aim was to get official endorsement for the proposition that a real abolitionist could not be a nonresistant. He was, as the Garrisonians proclaimed in later editorials, dragging in an "extraneous question."

The meeting eventually passed Garrison's resolution:

> That those abolitionists who feel themselves called upon, by a sense of duty, to go to the polls whenever an opportunity is presented to vote for a friend of the slave—or [Garrison obviously meant *and*] who, when there, follow their party predilections to the abandonment of their abolition principles—are recreant to their high professions, and unworthy of the name they assume.[13]

Stanton promptly labeled this "a genuine non-resistant resolution," apparently because it failed to state that all male abolitionists must vote.[14]

Birney was less devious; at a meeting of the Massachusetts Society two months later, he proclaimed it the duty of all abolitionists who had the right to vote to do so, and that those with religious scruples against voting ought to resign from the society. A letter he wrote shortly thereafter, to clarify the views he had expressed at that meeting, was printed in *The Liberator* of April 5, 1839. Birney contended that the AASS constitution imposed the duty of voting; hence anyone whose conscientious scruples led him to repudiate use of the elective franchise did not qualify for membership. Birney would not expel any such member; "yet, I thought it an unworthy attempt in any *new* sect, which might spring up among the abolitionists, to bend the constitution to suit their peculiar tenets—tenets which were wholly unthought of at the time of its adoption." The cause had been retarded in New England for the past year or two, he added,

> because it has had to move under the weight of other questions not necessarily connected with it. FROM EVERY ONE OF THESE—without pronouncing at this time as to

their merits or demerits—it must BE WHOLLY RELIEVED;— so that EMANCIPATION shall stand out before the community SINGLE and ALONE.

He closed by stating that at the meeting he had intimated that he would be inclined to support a change in the constitution to suit the views of those who refused to vote, if the amendment was duly submitted at the next annual meeting of the AASS; but now he held himself free to act on that occasion as the cause required.

Garrison's "Remarks" following the letter opened by repeating Birney's statement that those who could not vote were disqualified from membership and ought in fairness to resign; and he observed that it was not the nonresistants who were proscriptive. As to the statement that the nonresistants' peculiar tenets had not been thought of when the constitution was written:

> True, so far as a large majority of those who subscribed to that instrument were concerned,—but not true in regard to individual members. Nor do we believe that any one of the signers imagined that a person would be disqualified from remaining in the society, who should come to the conclusion that, as a follower of the Prince of Peace, he could not mingle in politics. . . .
>
> It seems, according to our friend, that, so long as slavery exists, abolitionists are bound to be strictly "men of one idea." If not, what is meant by the language, that "emancipation must stand out before the community, *single* and *alone*"? Does it mean that every attempt to coerce the consciences of abolitionists, by an arbitrary construction of the constitution, must be put down? If so, we say amen. What are those "other questions," from the weight of which the anti-slavery cause must be relieved, or it will never be fully accomplished? . . . What abolitionist, who writes on his own responsibility, is under an obligation not to divulge his thoughts, as a man and a christian, on any other subject (unless it be popular!) besides slavery? Is the discussion of the Peace question, by abolitionists, either foreign to their enterprise, or out of place in the columns of the Liberator?

Then what is implied in the following sentence contained in the constitution of the parent Society?—"This Society will NEVER, *in any way*, countenance the oppressed in vindicating their RIGHTS by resorting to physical force."

The same issue carried a letter from Stanton, who quoted at length from an article in *The Liberator* of December 20, 1834, in which Garrison had offered advice to Negro voters of Boston on the need for a Christian party in politics.[15] In his "Remarks" on Stanton's letter, Garrison explained:

The "need of a christian party in politics" was grounded upon the party subserviency which is manifested at every election, to the sacrifice of every principle of justice and humanity. So far as men are enabled to burst the degrading shackles of party, and vote as conscience and duty seem to them to require, so far we respect and honor them. Such men will be likely to go still further, and take a still higher stand, as light shall break in upon their minds.

The good men who thought they ought not to meddle in politics and to whom he had given that advice were not non-resistants but men who believed in the legitimacy of the government. "Their condemnation is, not only that they do not lay the axe at the root of the tree, but that they do not act up to their own principles." As to his advice to the Negro voters, it was, he conceded, written at a time when his vision was imperfect as to what voting men into governmental authority really involved. But, he added, he would much rather see Negroes using their political rights than "lost to all considerations of their equality with their white fellow-citizens." But it would be better still if they were nonresistants.

It is better that men should be sober than drunken; and more desirable that they should have even an arbitrary government, than that they should live in a state of anarchy.[16] But, to be in a sober condition is not spiritual redemption; neither is any government of man's device to be compared with the government of Christ.

Garrison added that he could not recall if he had stated, as Stanton said, in *The Liberator* in 1834 that he had voted, but if he had, he could only say that "whereas we were then blind, now we see; and greatly do we rejoice in the light." In any case, he asked, why the "parade of quotations" from my paper? It has never been the organ of any society, and the question is not what I think or have thought on the question of voting; the question is whether nonvoters are disqualified from membership.

Garrison spelled out his position in greater detail in "The Anti-Slavery Organization," in the same issue. The movement, he began, was founded on the basis of an agreement that slaveholding was sinful and ought immediately to be forsaken. This agreement provided common ground for people of all sects and parties and of no sect or party, and for five years all sorts of members cooperated in mutual love and without inquiry into each other's views. But recently dissension had torn the Massachusetts Society, allegedly because some members had departed from the old standard by refusing to vote. It was now asserted that anyone who refused to cooperate in upholding a government based on force was disqualified from belonging to an antislavery society. By that test Samuel J. May, Effingham L. Capron, George W. Benson, Edmund Quincy, Charles C. Burleigh, Amos Dresser, Isaac Winslow, Joshua V. Himes—all eminent abolitionists—and others had never been eligible to belong. But why were these passages from the constitution and the Declaration of Sentiments and *The Liberator*'s old issues not discovered before this? Garrison left the answer to his readers and went on to explain his conception of abolitionism.

> Abolition is not "the fulfilling of the law"—it is not christianity in its comprehensive signification, but only an adjunct of it. It may exist where there is no spiritual life, finding nourishment in the soil of human sympathy and natural humanity. Hence, it sits in judgment upon nothing but the guilt of the nation, in reducing one-sixth portion of the people to brutal servitude. It arraigns no

man for his religious creed or governmental opinions.
. . . In its official, organized form, it appeals to all sects
and parties for support, while it expresses no opinion as
to their distinctive character, or their lawful existence. It
takes men in masses just as it finds them:—talks of
cleansing every church in the land from the abomination
of slavery, just as earnestly as if it approved of every
such organization, though it has no authority to determine which is orthodox or which heterodox:—discourses
largely upon the duty and necessity of reforming the
government, so that there may be an abrogation of all
laws upholding slavery—just as freely as though there
was a perfect agreement among its members as to the
rightful supremacy of government. In this aspect, it is
not inconsistent, but tolerant; it recognizes only the fact,
that slavery is protected both by Church and State, and
therefore must, in the order of events, be overthrown by
influencing Church and State to cease from their oppression. In order that the Church may be purified, it does
not require abolitionists to be united with any such
organization; for such a requisition it has no right to
exact. In order that the State may be reformed, it ad-
dresses itself only to those who feel that they are bound
to participate in State affairs. . . . It simply condemns
men out of their own mouths—measures them by their
own acknowledged standard of action. . . . It predicates
the duty of ecclesiastical or political action, not upon the
inherent excellence of ecclesiastical or civil organizations,
but upon the fact of their existence . . . and upon the
views and professions of those who are allied to them by
choice.

One who joins the abolitionist movement, he added, is not
obliged to give up his religious or political views. If the society
should presume to enforce on all members the views of some,
it would violate the spirit of its constitution and demonstrate
that it did not, as it claimed, welcome the aid of all men
regardless of creed. "This distinction between the liberty of an
individual, and of an association composed of many elements,
is important, and essential as much to the harmony of the
whole body as it is to personal free agency."[17] He concluded

that the hue and cry about the duty to vote was evidently motivated by hatred of nonresistance rather than by concern for the slave, and he noted that those most "rampant" for political action were clergymen.

The struggle was renewed at the AASS annual meeting in New York in May 1839. The annual report, written by Lewis Tappan, which was presented to the convention, contained a thirty-page section openly aimed at forcing the society to choose between nonresistance and the theory that the movement must require its members to go to the polls. "It is the strange mistake," wrote Tappan,

> of even some of its professed friends, that it is no part of the business of the American Anti-Slavery Society to concern itself about the *application* of the power which it accumulates. . . . [I]n its Declaration of Sentiments and Constitution, the design of the society in regard to political action was very distinctly and unreservedly stated. The former document laid down the doctrine, as fundamental, that, "Every man has a right to his own body—to the products of his own labor—*to the protection of law,* and to the common advantages of society."— "That the slaves ought instantly to be set free, and brought under *the protection of law.*"

This right, he argued, implied the duty to protect it, and the duty was imposed not only on the lawmakers but also on those who elected the lawmakers. If public servants failed to do their duty, each voter was morally obligated to elect others who would not fail.

> The proposition, as it is laid down in our Declaration of Sentiments, and as, we believe, it is generally understood, seems to us to imply, that it is the duty of *some government* or other to do for the slaves what every government professes to do for its subjects—throw between them and all aggression upon their inalienable rights, the shield of an adequate *physical force;*—for, if the "protection of law" does not mean that, it means nothing.

At this point Tappan added, in a footnote, "By *law* here, we cannot suppose that any other than *human* law is intended,

which cannot exist without *penalties*, and of which the penalties are necessarily *physical*." Then, in the text:

> If, therefore, any of our citizens have been surprised or
> disappointed by our resort to the *ballot-box*, . . . the
> fault is their own:—and if any Abolitionists who possess
> the elective franchise have refused to *use* it to the best of
> their knowledge in behalf of the slave, it appears to us
> that they have either renounced the belief that the slaves
> have a right to "the protection of law,"—thus either
> adopting the principles of slavery, or rejecting those of
> law—or, they would exchange our republican for some
> other form of government.

There followed an exegesis of the AASS constitution's clause
that obligated members to endeavor "in a constitutional way"
to influence Congress to abolish slavery in all areas within its
jurisdiction; Tappan contended that this clause necessarily
implied the duty of voting.[18] (During later arguments over
the meaning of this phrase, Garrison said it meant "not in an
unconstitutional way.") The attempt to influence Congress by
petitioning had failed; therefore, said Tappan, "So far as practical means are concerned, if the ballot-box be given up, the
cause is given up with it."

Turning his attention explicitly to those members who were
conscientiously prevented from voting, Tappan noted their
contention that resolutions declaring voting a duty were attempts to coerce the consciences of members. He disposed of
this objection by asserting the majority's right to state its
principles in form of resolutions; to say it had no such right
was to say the minority could coerce the consciences of the
majority! The programs of the two groups, said Tappan, were
mutually exclusive, and the former harmony within the AASS
could no longer prevail "unless one party waives its right of
acting, or the other its right of limiting action according to its
own interpretation of the Constitution." He added the gratu-
itous observation that he could not see how a nonresistant
could encourage a voter to vote right, "unless it be right to
advise others to do evil that good may come, or to encourage
every man to walk in the sight of his eyes, whether his path be

right or wrong." He hoped that both factions would cease their bickering and, each in its own way, test their respective plans by actual experience. But he predicted dire consequences if the nonresistants converted many, for their converts would be friends of law and order, and if such men withdrew from politics in large numbers, "the legislation of the country will soon be left to the elements of the mob. Who can doubt that these men will then do universally by law, what they now attempt to do in spite of it?"[19]

The report caused angry debate on the floor of the convention. The climax came when Birney introduced a resolution declaring "that to maintain that the elective franchise ought not to be used by abolitionists to advance the cause of emancipation, is inconsistent with the duty of abolitionists under the constitution." This of course would have read the nonvoters out of the organization. Charles C. Burleigh offered a substitute carefully phrased so that all factions could concur: "That the abolitionist who regards it as his duty to use the elective franchise, and yet uses it against, or neglects to use it *for* the promotion of the cause of emancipation, is false to his own principles and clearly fails to do his duty." The political abolitionists won, although the resolution finally passed was somewhat milder than Birney's, and it fell a bit short of stating that nonvoters ought to resign.[20]

The wrangling at the 1839 convention was repeated at every important abolitionist convention in the East until the final break came at the anniversary meeting in New York in May 1840. The factions set forth their positions most clearly, however, in a war of articles printed in *The Emancipator* and *The Liberator*. The chief exchange was between Birney and Garrison. *The Emancipator* of May 2, 1839, published Birney's "View of the Constitution of the American A. S. Society as Connected with the 'No-Government' Question," and Garrison reprinted it in *The Liberator* of June 28, along with his reply. Birney began by listing what he believed were the fundamental principles in the AASS constitution that a person must accept to be qualified for membership: first, that each state had a constitutional right to legislate in regard to aboli-

tion within its own borders; second, that the society must
address arguments to the public to show that slaveholding was
a crime in the sight of God and to show the duty and safety of
emancipation without expatriation; third, that the society must
influence Congress in a constitutional way to end the domestic
slave trade; fourth, that slavery must be abolished in areas
under the jurisdiction of Congress; and fifth, that no new slave
states must be admitted. Birney then argued that *to address* the
public and *to influence* Congress implied two different modes
of action: influence implied the threat of removal, and that
could be accomplished only by voters. For years there had
been too few abolitionists to attempt organized voting pressure
on Congress. Nevertheless the editor of *The Liberator* had
himself defended the moral propriety of carrying antislavery
principles to the polls, and he had voted for an abolitionist and
encouraged others to do the same. Within the past twelve or
eighteen months, however, the society had grown large
enough for many abolitionists to begin thinking about affect-
ing elections, and some were even advocating formation of a
third party. But just at this time, and in that part of the nation
where political action had been most successful, a sect had
arisen whose members regarded it as a religious obligation to
refrain from voting. This tenet was part of a doctrine that
condemned all force and hence considered human governments unlawful; these sectarians logically would even withhold
from parents the power to chastise their children.

> In short, the "No-Government" doctrines, as they are
> believed now to be embraced, seem to strike at the root
> of the social structure; and tend . . . to throw society
> into entire confusion, and to renew, under the sanction
> of religion, scenes of anarchy and license that have
> generally heretofore been the offspring of the rankest
> infidelity and irreligion.

But in other respects the nonresistants were illogical, he argued, for they did not object to petitioning Congress. How
could they refuse on principle to help elect congressmen but
after the election consent to deal with them as congressmen?

Further, how could the nonresistants, who considered voting an endorsement of forceful government, advise voting abolitionists how to cast their ballots?

> The attempt to exercise influence, under such circumstances, would seem, at least, as much out of place, if not as physically absurd, as for the celestial angels to direct their "fallen" brethren how best they might make their *sinful* movements declare the glory of God and advance the cause of universal benevolence.

Clearly, said Birney, these individuals had ceased to consent to the society's principles, "are virtually no longer entitled to membership," and should resign. Justice to other members and to the slave as well as self-respect required that they do so. He closed by remarking that

> it is high time that something was done to bring this subject directly before the great body of the abolitionists, in order that they may relieve their cause from an incubus that has so mightily oppressed it in some parts of the country during the last year. It is in vain to think of succeeding in emancipation without the co-operation of the great mass of the intelligent mind of the nation. This can be attracted, only by the reasonableness, the *religion*, of our enterprise. To multiply causes of repulsion is but to drive it from us, and ensure our own defeat. . . .

Garrison's reply began with a protest that *The Emancipator*, organ of the AASS, had published Birney's attack on the nonresistants, with no comment by the editor, whereas it had printed Garrison's reply along with the editor's own attack on Garrison. Such partiality, he complained, violated "the spirit of our anti slavery compact" and was "as much out of place in the Emancipator, as would be an essay in favor of infant sprinkling, or the claims of the 'holy mother church.'" But if the attack be allowed, so must a defense, and hence the whole question of nonresistance was unfortunately opened for discussion and settlement in the official organ of the AASS.

Garrison took up Birney's contrast between *influencing* Congress and *addressing* the public; on that "philological distinction," he exclaimed, rested Birney's argument on the duty of members to vote! But petitions, remonstrances, facts, and arguments were means of influencing Congress, and therefore the constitution of the society did not require members to vote. Further, to influence Congress was not necessarily to recognize the rightfulness of its authority; one could petition His Holiness the Pope to stop granting indulgences without thereby recognizing his office; one could beg a military chieftain to spare a village without thereby "sanctioning his murderous vocation."[21] Birney, in his statement that the nonresistants ought to resign, had said that the AASS had, however, no board of inspectors to pass on members' qualifications. Garrison accused Birney of constituting himself just such a board. And incidentally, by what right did Birney, he asked, determine whether abolitionists might or might not spank their children? The nonresistants believed their views perfectly consistent with membership and had no intention of resigning; they believed, rather, that all varieties of abolitionists could work harmoniously together under the constitution, provided they thought of the slave first, and did "not attempt to make our individual views of religion or politics . . . the standard by which to measure the whole body." All members believed slavery a sin and immediate abolition a duty; why not allow each member to carry out those basic principles wherever he conscientiously could? I for one, said Garrison, am happy to join with all who accept those principles, regardless of sect or creed or party.

As to Birney's mention of Garrison's having voted, the editor of *The Liberator* replied in effect, what of it? When, he asked, did you become my disciple? Neither I nor *The Liberator* has ever prescribed rules for all abolitionists to follow. Further, nonresistants have never introduced their views of government into antislavery societies or tried to use the societies to spread those views.[22] It is the accusers who are the transgressors; they have used the official organ of the society, the abolition lecture platform, and the societies' meetings to war on the religious views of fellow members. Garrison named Birney, Stanton, Elizur Wright, Jr., Phelps, and Orange Scott among the culprits. As for the nonresistants, he added, we have advocated nonresistance as *men*, and shall continue to do so, "*but not as abolitionists.*" Garrison cautioned that he was not saying the signers of the Declaration of Sentiments and the constitution had intended to take the ground now occupied by the nonresistants. They had, he said, subscribed to all the principles of that philosophy, but they had not thought through all the implications of their pacifism. Nevertheless, in the constitution's clauses requiring only moral suasion by abolitionists and peaceful submission by slaves,

> *non-resistance is more explicitly enjoined upon abolitionists, than the duty of using the elective franchise.*
>
> Once more, I beg not to be misapprehended. I have always expected, I still expect, to see abolition at the ballot-box, renovating the political action of the country —dispelling the sorcery influences of party—breaking asunder the fetters of political servitude—stirring up the torpid consciences of voters—substituting anti-slavery for pro-slavery representatives in every legislative assembly—modifying and rescinding all laws which sanction slavery. But this political reformation is to be effected solely by a change in the moral vision of the people;— not by attempting to prove, that it is the duty of every abolitionist to be a voter, but that it is the duty of every voter to be an abolitionist. . . .

Birney certainly knew that no nonresistant had ever proposed a resolution that members of the AASS or any auxiliary society must *not* vote; nor had any society dominated by non-resistants passed any such resolution. It is significant that his faction considered technical ground for complaint the opposition of Garrisonians (who, it must be remembered, included voters) to resolutions stating that abolitionists *must* vote.[23] Or, to put the case another way, the anti-Garrisonians knew that their adversaries had never tried, nor would they try, to narrow the antislavery platform to exclude them. Garrison's own refusal on the official antislavery platform to condemn voting or third-partyism per se made it clear that he would not have tried to put the AASS on record as opposing a parallel political movement that did not war on the AASS. Nor could the Birney group have reasonably feared that the nonresistants would convert enough abolitionists to diminish antislavery influence on elections; on the contrary, the chronic complaint of all varieties of abolitionists—nonresistants, Libertymen, Liberty Leaguers, Whigs, and Democrats—was that antislavery society members were as addicted to the great national pastime as other Americans and repeatedly put aside their abolition principles "just this once" to vote their party ticket. Hence, when the anti-Garrisonians deliberately split the AASS they did not, as they alleged, do so to make political action possible; they did so to discredit the nonresistants and thereby demonstrate to the American people that abolitionism was respectable. As one student of political abolitionism (very unsympathetic to Garrison) has observed, Garrison won the 1839 argument with Birney on both fact and logic, but, she adds, the case for a third party was not *ipso facto* disproved.[24]

There were, in this dispute, two distinct issues: the nature of the AASS platform and the tactical expediency of concerted political action. Garrison was willing to discuss both but would not allow the latter to define the former. Since the efforts to concentrate the political power of abolitionists were, in both fact and logic, separate from the history of the antislavery societies, it is appropriate at this point to trace those efforts from 1839 to the end of the period under examination.[25]

NOTES

[1] This opposition of moral, peaceful means to political means suggests an interesting contrast between the abolitionists and the woman suffragists from the 1890s on. The latter argued that the progress of civilization had seen force give way to consent in government; in earlier periods fighting men had ruled society with bullets, but now all adults, including women and other noncombatants, must rule via ballots. Since government was no longer based on force, argued the suffragists, there was no logical reason to restrict the vote to men. Consent by the majority was contrasted to rule by arms. The *anti*suffragists often contended that governments were ultimately based on force and that to give the vote to citizens unable to back their ballots with bullets would be to

invite violence by the outvoted minority. (For a discussion of this debate see Kraditor, *Ideas of the Woman Suffrage Movement*, pp. 250–51.) Garrisonian nonresistants too believed that governments were ultimately based on force, that voting meant participation in such governments, and that majority balloting put into practice the principle that might makes right.

2 For a few examples of these views expressed by abolitionists who later supported the Liberty party, see: Gerrit Smith, speech on October 22, 1835, in Louis Ruchames, ed., *The Abolitionists*, pp. 116–17; Elizur Wright, Jr., to Theodore D. Weld, April 2, 1836, *Weld-Grimké Letters*, I, 292; Betty Fladeland, *James Gillespie Birney: Slaveholder to Abolitionist* (Ithaca, N.Y., 1955), p. 148; editorial (evidently by Elizur Wright, Jr., the editor), *Quarterly Anti-Slavery Magazine*, II (January 1837), 113–14; *Fourth Annual Report of the American Anti-Slavery Society*, pp. 113–14 (by Wright); Francis J. LeMoyne to Birney, December 10, 1839, *Birney Letters*, I, 512–14; "A Separate Political Organization," editorial evidently by the editor, Gamaliel Bailey, in *The Philanthropist*, reprinted in *The Liberator*, December 6, 1839; Lewis Tappan, "A Third Political Party," *The Emancipator*, November 14, 1839.

3 See especially William Goodell, "Political Action against Slavery," reprinted from *The Friend of Man* in *The Liberator*, August 31, 1838. A general discussion of this new argument is in Margaret L. Plunkett, "A History of the Liberty Party with Emphasis upon Its Activities in the Northeastern States," Ph.D. dissertation, Cornell University, 1930, pp. 58–60.

4 *Ibid.*, p. 62: "That Birney [in 1839] was trying to oust the nonvoting abolitionists from the American Society in order to clear the way for the future organization of a party is only too evident."

5 *The Liberator*, June 8, 1838. See also resolutions passed at New Hampshire Anti-Slavery Society annual meeting, *ibid.*, June 15, 1838.

6 *Ibid.*, June 29, 1838.

7 *Ibid.*, August 10, 1838.

8 Goodell (1792–1878) was for a time editor of *The Emancipator*, organ of the New York abolitionists, founded in 1833, which became the official weekly of the AASS. He was editor of *The Friend of Man* from 1836 to 1842, and a prolific pamphleteer, an enthusiastic supporter of the Liberty party, and later a founder of the Liberty League.

9 *The Liberator*, August 3, September 7, 14, 21, 1838. Obviously, Garrison would disagree with the last three sentences. See "Circular" from the Executive Committee of the New-York State Anti-Slavery Society to the Members of its Auxiliary Societies, *ibid.*, March 22, 1839.

10 *Ibid.*, July 20, 1838.

11 The incident is mentioned in Maria Weston Chapman, *Right and Wrong in Massachusetts*, pp. 101–5; Merrill, *Against Wind and Tide*, p. 149; Thomas, *The Liberator: William Lloyd Garrison*, p. 267; Louis Filler, "Parker Pillsbury: An Anti-Slavery Apostle," *New England Quarterly*, XIX (September 1946), 328.

12 See Joshua Leavitt's comments on a reprint of a *Herald of Freedom* article by Nathaniel P. Rogers, *The Emancipator*, April 18, 1839,

and on a resolution recently passed at a Connecticut antislavery meeting, *ibid.*, November 7, 1839; Birney, "View of the Constitution of the American A. S. Society as Connected with the 'No-Government' Question," *ibid.*, May 2, 1839; George Bradburn's remarks at the Albany convention, as reported *ibid.*, August 15, 1839.

13 *The Liberator*, February 1, 1839.

14 Henry B. Stanton to Elizur Wright, Jr., January 26, 1839, Wright Papers, LC: "A bold effort was made at the annual meeting to make the Mass. Anti S. Society subservient to the non-resistance Society, & *it succeeded.* The Annual Report was non-committal on the *duty* of abolitionists to go to the polls & there remember the slave. This was voted down with clamor. A resolution was brought in declaring that it was *the duty* of such abolitionists as could *conscientiously vote*, to go to the polls & vote for the slave. Garrison warmly opposed this, & brought in a substitute, declaring that those abolitionists who believed in political action & went to the polls & there voted against the slave, *were inconsistent with their* professions!—A genuine nonresistant resolution. This substitute was clamorously adopted. Thus it is—the Mass. A. S. Society at its annual meeting in 1839, refuses to declare that it is the duty of voting abolitionists to remember the slave at the polls! In a word, it resolved itself into a non-resistance Society." It should be emphasized once again that before the "plot" developed, the nonresistants would have voted for a resolution declaring it the duty of abolitionist voters to vote for the slave, but that now such a resolution would clearly become a weapon in the hands of those who were determined to discredit the nonresistants, who could now support political-action resolutions only if they were formulated in negative terms, as was Garrison's. Stanton's views are also expressed in his letter to Birney, January 26, 1839, *Birney Letters*, I, 481–83.

15 "TO 'H. C. W.,' *alias* HENRY C. WRIGHT," *The Liberator*, April 5, 1839.

16 Cf. Dwight L. Dumond, *Antislavery: The Crusade for Freedom in America* (Ann Arbor, Mich., 1961; paperback ed., 1966), p. 297: "Garrison . . . was an anarchist. . . ."

17 The distinction between a society's taking a position that only part of it approves and branding the minority recreant to duty is a legalistic distinction, but when a group of strong-minded people work together for a common cause, a certain amount of euphemizing is necessary. A legalistic formula in such a situation is a sign that the various groups are willing to remain united, and it represents recognition that they can do so only if they gloss over differences and frame their statements generally or vaguely enough to offend none of the components in the coalition—provided, of course, that the differences glossed over are not matters of principle.

18 The clause is quoted on page 5 above.

19 *Sixth Annual Report of the Executive Committee of the American Anti-Slavery Society*, pp. 76–82. The political section of the report continues to p. 103. In my effort to understand the thinking of Tappan and other anti-Garrisonians, I have learned much from Bertram Wyatt-Brown, "Partners in Piety: Lewis and Arthur Tappan, Evangelical

Abolitionists, 1828–1841," Ph.D. dissertation, Johns Hopkins University, 1963.

20 "That this society still holds, as it has from the beginning, that the employment of the political franchise, as established by the constitution and laws of the country, so as to promote the abolition of slavery, is of high obligation—a duty, which, as abolitionists, we owe to our enslaved fellow-countrymen groaning under legal oppression" (*Sixth Annual Report*, pp. 41, 43).

21 Wendell Phillips, who was not a nonresistant but agreed with Garrison in refusing allegiance to the government, had his own version: one could ask a pirate captain to treat his captives humanely, without thereby admitting his right to hold them (*The Liberator*, July 26, 1844).

22 Various forms of this disclaimer are to be found throughout the sources. See, for example, Lydia Maria Child to Maria Weston Chapman, April 10, 1839, Child Papers, BPL; Samuel J. May to Francis Jackson, July 25, 1839, Anti-Slavery Letters, BPL; editorial by [Oliver Johnson], *The Liberator*, June 21, 1839; "Address to the Abolitionists of Massachusetts," from Francis Jackson and Garrison, for the Massachusetts Society, *ibid.*, July 19, 1839; letter to editor from "Straight Forward" (a Rhode Island "anti-non-resistant," pro-political-action man), *ibid.*, September 6, 1839; "Letter from Mrs. Child, on the Present State of the Anti-Slavery Cause," *ibid.*, September 6, 1839; and Ellis Gray Loring, "To the Editor of the Emancipator," *ibid.*, May 8, 1840. Passages from the last two documents follow. Mrs. Child: It is not true that the Massachusetts Society is pledged to the nonvoting, nonresistance theory. The board of managers consists of twenty-eight men, of whom only four are conscientiously opposed to voting. "I believe it may be said with truth that ninety-nine hundredths of the Mass. Society go to the polls; and many of them are very active in the exertion of political influence." (Her husband was a Whig.) She explained that support for the freedom of each member to choose his own mode of action did not imply support for nonresistance. If the political abolitionists' demand that voting be a test of membership were proper, then those who believed that boycott of slave-grown produce should be a test of membership could vote that those who disagreed ought to resign. The nonresistants, she said, "have never expressed or evinced a desire that their opponents should be advised to withdraw from the Anti-Slavery Society because they *do* go to the polls." Loring: The Massachusetts Society "is not a non-resistance society in disguise, nor are we allowing non-resistance doctrines to be introduced into our meetings. On the contrary, never has our political standard been higher, our political action more free, active and vigorous, our political success so decisive, as within the last year. I claim, for the old Massachusetts Society, the honor of having . . . sent more abolition voters to the polls, and of having achieved a more brilliant triumph in the Legislature, within twelve months, than has ever been done by any society in this country, paralyzed as we are falsely represented to be, by the infection of non-resistance. . . . It is true, a few of our brethren differ from the majority, as to the duty of exercising one particular form of political action;—but is this to implicate the whole Society? More especially, can it do so, when those brethren have

never brought their peculiar views into our meetings;—no, not even for the purpose of self-vindication?"

23 See Stanton's letter cited in footnote 14 above.

24 Plunkett, "A History of the Liberty Party," pp. 62–65. The Garrisonians even claimed their influence helped the Liberty party. For example, Wendell Phillips wrote: "Wherever Abby Kelley lectured last winter, they followed the next week, and would often, notwithstanding all she could do, get more subscribers for their papers than she could for the *Liberator*. You, who know the *Liberator*, know that it requires a pretty *full*-grown *man* to relish its meat." And: "As fast as *we* . . . make abolitionists, the new converts run right into the Liberty Party, and become almost or wholly hostile to us. This results from the strong leaning of our national character to politics." (Phillips to Elizabeth Pease, October and April 1844, as quoted in Garrisons, *Garrison*, III, 233n.) Other Garrisonians made similar statements from time to time. If they were correct, many of the party's new converts joined it not because the old organization had repelled them but because once it had converted them they affiliated with a mode of abolitionist activity more congenial to their tastes. See also James S. Gibbons to Abby Kelley, September 23, 1842, Stephen S. and Abby Kelley Foster Papers, AAS.

25 I will not attempt a history of political abolitionism, of course; my purpose is to analyze the political abolitionists' ideas on strategy and tactics, ends and means, and compare them with the Garrisonians' ideas about political action.

6

POLITICAL ACTION

MYRON HOLLEY of upstate New York was the first to urge abolitionists to organize their own political party. In a series of thinly attended conventions during 1839, he and a few supporters tried to persuade their fellow members of the AASS that they must make independent nominations for President and Vice-President in time for the 1840 election.[1] At first the only reactions were negative: Birney and Francis Julius LeMoyne, who were nominated by a Holley-led convention in Warsaw, New York, in November 1839, declined, and antislavery societies passed resolutions condemning the innovation. But the prospect that Martin Van Buren and William Henry Harrison, both unacceptable, were to be the major-party candidates gradually convinced some abolitionists that Holley was right; without a separate antislavery ticket many abolitionists would feel disfranchised. In April 1840, a convention in Albany, New York, again nominated Birney, this time with Thomas Earle as his running mate, and this time the nominees accepted, and the new party, named Liberty by Gerrit Smith,[2] was launched on its troubled career. The only precedents for such a step had been a few nominations for local offices, and the poor showing of the

Liberty party in the 1840 election was certainly no demonstration that the tactic itself was incorrect. Not only were the party's leaders inexperienced as political managers and the time too short to overcome the traditional opposition of abolitionists to independent nominations, but the nationwide depression had reduced the financial resources of their would-be contributors, and the A & F, the association on which they had counted to furnish an organized base and a nucleus of party workers, was a failure from the start. All that was needed to ensure that Birney's candidacy would prove a fiasco was the Log Cabin campaign; many abolitionists who might have voted for Birney were caught up in the mass excitement and cast their votes for Harrison.[3] The Liberty party leaders hoped that these defectors would soon repent, and upon Tyler's accession their hope turned to optimism. When Birney was nominated again in the spring of 1841, with more than three years to prepare for the next election, probably half the delegates at the nominating convention, according to the principal student of political abolitionism, expected their party to win in 1844, and even the most cautious assumed that by 1848 it would lead the North.[4] In the 1844 election its vote was again extremely low, but high enough in New York, in the opinion of some interpreters, to give the state and with it the presidency to the Democrat James K. Polk. Some observers therefore thought that Birney's candidacy had been a trick to help the Democrats; a Detroit paper called him a "Polkat in the skin of a mink."[5] In its first two ventures into presidential politics the party had failed in its key task—to convince the Northern electorate that slavery was the principal issue and must take precedence over all others—and when by the fall of 1847 it had become clear that slavery was to be a burning political issue, the Liberty party, ironically, was at a standstill.

Three assumptions underlay the organization and program of the Liberty party: first, that an abolitionist must never vote for any candidate unwilling to use all the powers of the office he aspired to in the cause of abolition; second, that the major parties must necessarily be dominated by the slave power so long as slavery existed; and third, that the abolitionist party was a temporary tactic, which would die with the death of the slave power. Abolitionists, true to form, differed widely among themselves on all three assumptions.

It may be suggested that a fourth assumption ought to be added to the list: that the United States Constitution, rightly interpreted, enabled Congress to abolish slavery in the states. The failure to assume this ought logically to have deprived the Liberty party of its reason for being. That there was a problem here was, however, not clear to the organizers at the start. The conflicting opinions expressed on the constitutionality of slavery, when the question did arise among political abolitionists, will be discussed in Chapter 7.

The first assumption was the first to be debated, since the duty to vote only for abolitionists, taken for granted since the birth of the movement, was the immediate inducement to some abolitionists to make independent nominations after experience had shown that the major parties were unwilling to nominate acceptable candidates. In its first few years the AASS repeated the rule as a formulation of a religious duty; it seemed self-evident that a member who voted for a nonabolitionist simply because he agreed with the candidate's program on other issues was in effect sacrificing the slave's interests to his own. He was, as the members said, in Saint Paul's words, "doing evil that good might come." But later, when the movement began to analyze problems of political tactics, the question turned out to be somewhat more complex. Some abolitionists even discovered that the proper political course could not be deduced from religious premises.

An anonymous New York abolitionist, for example, wrote to *The Liberator* in 1838 of his dismay at finding, as he thought, that Garrison wished to make abolitionism a political question. The only political action he looked forward to was that by Southern legislatures, after their conversion, to abolish slavery in their own localities, for how could abolition in the District of Columbia, enacted by Congress, be enforced over the slaveowners' opposition? Even if Congress could constitutionally legislate on slavery in the states, which he denied, how could it do so against the wishes of the owners? Since a slave-

holder could not be coerced into abolition, he must be converted. This line of reasoning led the writer to a startling
conclusion: that voting abolitionists should vote irrespective of
the slavery question. He disagreed with the advice by the
Massachusetts Anti-Slavery Society's board of managers, to
withhold votes from candidates who did not give the right
answers to abolitionist interrogators; such a policy, he pointed
out, would disfranchise antislavery voters. In a situation in
which nothing could be hoped for from either party on the
slavery issue, should not abolitionists nevertheless have a voice
in choosing their rulers?[6]

At the Albany convention the following July, the assemblage passed the customary resolution that an abolitionist must
not vote for nonabolitionists.[7] That this resolution was no
longer an automatic formula is shown by the opposition of a
few members. Four of them, of whom the best known was the
Negro editor Samuel E. Cornish, submitted a protest that read
in part: "The undersigned cannot consent, that the free exercise of the right of suffrage shall be restricted by the action of
any self-constituted assembly, or to place themselves in a position, little or nothing short of absolute disfranchisement."[8]
George Bradburn had not voted on the resolution, but in a
letter printed in *The Liberator* he explained that he agreed
with the reasoning of Cornish and the others. He quoted them
to the effect that the disfranchisement of Negroes in New
York State was the chief cause of the neglect and disrespect
they suffered, and that if two sets of candidates ran for Assembly seats, one favoring and the other opposing Negro
suffrage in New York, but both indifferent to the question of
slavery, they would vote for the former. Bradburn concurred,
adding that his duty to the slave might on occasion require
him to vote for a nonabolitionist. He amplified the argument a
year later in a discussion of the question whether an abolitionist might in good conscience choose the lesser of two evils. He
replied with a question: When a voter prevents the greater by
choosing the lesser, is he doing evil? Is he not choosing the
greater good? Voting for a proslavery candidate is not necessarily voting for slavery, he argued, any more than voting for

a Unitarian is voting for Unitarianism.⁹ The only alternative
was self-disfranchisement.¹⁰

Such dissents, however, were barely noticed by those leaders who were determined to transfer their religion-based abolition principles into the political arena intact, undiluted, impervious to logrolling compromises. Some, to be sure, resisted
the distasteful new departure of a separate party; Lewis Tappan refused for three years to identify himself publicly with
the Liberty party, although he voted for its candidates.¹¹ In
1840 William Jay wrote that a third party, by drawing reformers from the major parties, would deprive them "of the
little salt that keeps them from utter putrefaction."¹² Others
merely hesitated long enough to read the political barometer in
the antislavery societies and then gladly joined Myron Holley,¹³ Alvan Stewart, Henry B. Stanton, and a few others to
organize a third party. Probably their ingrained revulsion from
politics induced them, when they accepted the need for political action, to organize independently of the major parties,
but now that they were founding their own party, one that
was to be pure, Christian, and uncompromising, they tried
hard to distinguish between good politics and bad politics. The
theoretical formulation of that distinction was the second assumption that underlay the organization of the Liberty party:
that the two major parties were and must be servants of the
slave power. This principle was more taken for granted than
discussed; Gerrit Smith was the only one of the leaders who
discoursed on it at length. On what, he asked, does the policy
of independent nominations rest?

> On the duty, the necessity of abolitionists to break off
> from their national parties—parties which are, and
> which, whilst American slavery exists, must be pro-
> slavery—for the South will enter into none but pro-
> slavery parties[;] let but that duty, that necessity be
> conceded—and even a child can see, that no farther
> concession is needed to justify abolitionists, provided
> voting be a right and a duty, in voting in concert. Even a
> child can see, that the scattering system pre-supposes,
> that the existing parties, one or both, are reclaimable; and

that this system is indefensible, if it be admitted, that these parties, being national, are, and from the nature of the case, must be pro-slavery, whilst American slavery exists.[14]

If the major parties were necessarily servants of the slave power, it followed that even antislavery candidates nominated by them must be only half-abolitionists, and an abolitionist who knew he must vote only for committed enemies of slavery must nominate them himself.

The third assumption followed logically enough, for if the existence of slavery determined the need for a Liberty party, the death of slavery would eliminate that need. Joshua Leavitt, for example, wrote, "we should keep ourselves from entanglements with either of the present parties, so that, when our object is gained, those two party elements may *then* be in a condition to renew their struggle for the mastery, unprejudiced and unaided by our organization."[15] The leaders also assumed that the Liberty party, as a temporary one, must not take stands on all the issues of the day. Its sole reason for being was to persuade Northern voters that slavery was the paramount political issue, and that all other problems not only faded into insignificance beside it, but could not be solved so long as slavery endured.[16] The party must therefore go before the voters as a "one-idea" party. The purity of its principles could not be maintained if it had planks on such issues as the Independent Treasury or the tariff, which would attract political adventurers and involve the party in controversies over those issues. Gideon's army had been strengthened by the restriction of its recruits to the pure and vigilant, and Liberty leaders at first saw their movement as the Gideon's army of American politics.

At first. American political parties do not prosper in proportion to their purity, and principles cannot replace ballots. The absurdly low votes Birney received in 1840 and 1844 spotlighted what soon became a vital question among Libertymen: whether the party should not abandon "one-ideaism" and present the voters with a platform containing planks on all issues an administration must deal with. Perhaps the problem

would never have arisen had abolitionists been thoroughly persuaded by their own propaganda that every other issue was
insignificant compared to slavery. Not only that majority of
antislavery voters who always cast Whig or Democratic ballots, but even Libertymen, could never quite forget their desire for a low or high tariff, for reform of suffrage laws, for a
national bank or the Independent Treasury, and so on.

Ironically, that diversity of opinion on other issues and the
importance of those issues had been strong arguments against
organizing a third party in the first place. In 1838, when the
idea was first discussed seriously, everyone seemed to assume
that one-ideaism was a necessary corollary of third-partyism;
hence, those who opposed organization of a separate party
usually did so in part because they opposed one-ideaism. For
example, among the reasons listed by the board of managers of
the Massachusetts Anti-Slavery Society against a third party
had been that it would require abolitionists to forsake their
interest in other problems besides slavery; it would mean that
abolition would be not their chief object but their only object,
and that of course was not so.[17] William Goodell, arguing
against a third party, had written that if abolitionists attempted, as abolitionists, to exert influence on any legislative
subject except abolition, they would become divided against
themselves.[18] The anonymous New Yorker quoted earlier had
asked whether abolitionists should refuse to work against all
other evils until slavery was ended. To do so, he wrote, would
be to imitate the starving boy who refused a loaf of bread
because he did not receive a cheese with it. *Therefore*, abolitionists must not organize a third party.[19] At the end of 1839,
Gamaliel Bailey editorialized in his *Philanthropist* that a third
party would be based on one principle, since on all other
principles abolitionists were Whigs or Democrats. But a one-
idea party would be absurd; all abolitionists would be asked to
vote for candidates who had only their abolitionism in common, and thus to forget all other issues. Suppose the party won
power: how would the various officials act together on those
other questions?[20]

The diversity of opinion on other issues, which had seemed

to be an argument against organizing a third party, was a strong motive for retaining the party's one-idea policy as long as possible, for no matter what additional planks were added to the platform, some voters would be alienated. One-ideaism was justified more often, however, on grounds of principle. As Dr. James McCune Smith, eminent Negro physician, wrote:

> . . . there is but one way to attack Slavery through Political action: it is to make it the sole idea of that political action. All recognize the converse of this: all admit that the *one idea* of slavery has spread its shoots and its roots and its suckers into every institution in the land. . . . And if the one idea has wrought this, how can we remove the results except by removing the one idea in its essence and in its mode? Any other method would be as futile as the attempt to stop the slave-trade & let slavery alone.[21]

In a letter to a Liberty party convention, Gerrit Smith defended one-ideaism on the same ground but added the practical argument that additional planks would attract nonabolitionists whose accession would adulterate the party. Moreover, he told the assemblage, the original object of the Liberty party was to combine *all* voting abolitionists. You who argue against one-ideaism do not need the additional planks to reinforce your own commitment; therefore you would be adding them to attract people whose commitment is not very strong. You are asking the party to become abolitionist plus something else. But that is exactly what the Northern wings of the major parties claim to be. Like them you will submerge the abolition part of your creed in the "something else," and you will split the present Liberty party membership. Let us, he urged, be confident that a party true to the essential interests of man may be trusted to take care of his minor interests too, whereas a party unwilling to advocate abolition cannot be trusted on any other issue.[22] By the time Smith expressed these views, one-ideaism was already being widely questioned by Liberty-men. After the election the following year, the party's stand-ard bearer, James G. Birney, joined the trend, and within two years after that, Smith himself helped to organize a universal-reform party with himself as its presidential candidate.

Birney had unwittingly encouraged the change when, unaware that candor is rarely compatible with candidacy, he freely expressed his disapproval of manhood suffrage.[23] He soon received a worried letter from an Ohio abolitionist leader asking: Is it true you believe the suffrage ought to be restricted and that some federal officials should be given longer terms?[24] Birney replied that he must decline to answer the queries, since the candidates' views on other questions should not divert attention from the Liberty party's single aim of abolition. He then expounded at great length on democracy. If he had been a member of the Constitutional Convention of 1787, he wrote, and had foreseen the next fifty years, he would have disfranchised all unworthy persons—not only criminals but also those who violently invade the rights of free speech, press, and inquiry; he would have made the suffrage an honor to be earned. He would have lengthened the terms of senators and raised their minimum age. He would have required their advice and consent to removals from office. He would have made the President only a formal head of state, without power, so that parties would have no motive to control him and such spectacles as the Log Cabin campaign would be impossible. He added, however, that he would not advocate these things now, in 1843; it was too late. The states now had the right to regulate the suffrage, and they were competing with one another to see which could debase it most. But he would advocate limiting the President to one term.[25]

Within the next few months Birney received letters from Pittsburgh abolitionists who thought they could get anti-Masonic votes for the Liberty party, provided they could find out Birney's views on Masonry. Birney furnished the history of his connection and then his break with the Masons. Other Pennsylvania leaders wrote him that since the protectionists in their region could not vote for Polk and were unsure about Clay, they might vote the Liberty ticket if they knew how Birney stood on the tariff. The candidate replied that he was generally for a revenue tariff sufficient to meet all government expenses and would want the present duties lowered gradually so as not to hurt any lawful interests. In later replies to inquiries, he disapproved of distribution to the states of proceeds from the sale of public lands, stated that Congress had the power to establish a national bank, and opposed the chartering of a bank before slavery was abolished.[26]

While Birney was undermining one-ideaism by his sheer inability to remain silent, a few other leaders were accomplishing the same result deliberately.[27] Within the next few years a remarkable catalogue of sometimes mutually exclusive proposals emerged; some were proposed as planks for antislavery-party platforms, while others were opinions expressed in discussions of what an antislavery party should or should not advocate. Among them were proposals

for cheap postage;

for abolition of the government post-office monopoly;

for limiting the amount of land that individuals might own;

for reducing the price of public lands gradually every five years, down to 25¢ an acre, and after twenty-five years ceding them to the states;

for limiting sales of public land to actual settlers;

for regulations tending to equalize land distribution;

for free homesteads to actual settlers;

for public lands to be distributed, at cost of distribution, to landless men in small parcels;

for exempting homesteads from execution for debt;

for making homesteads inalienable;

against exempting particular quantities of land from execution;

against limiting acquisition, ownership, or alienation of land;

against distribution of the proceeds of sales of public lands to the states;

for limiting to ten the hours of labor on public works and in establishments chartered by law;

against internal improvements;

for internal improvements;

for prohibition of liquor;

against prohibition of liquor;

against electing to office any seller of liquor or advocate of license laws;

for the Independent Treasury;

for free trade;

for protective tariffs;

for the gradual elimination of the tariff;

for a revenue tariff;

for the abolition of the Custom House;

for the popular election of the President;

for a single term for the President and reduction of his powers;

for raising the age of senators, increasing their powers, lengthening their term of office, and requiring their consent to the removal as well as the appointment of officers;

against lengthening senators' term of office;

for direct election of senators and cabinet members;

for making more government offices elective, including postmasterships;

for woman suffrage;

for universal manhood suffrage;

for forfeiture of the vote by those who violate others' freedom of speech, press, and inquiry;

for restriction of the suffrage to the wise;

against alien suffrage;

against restriction of the suffrage;

against secret societies;

against any statement opposing secret societies;

for a law encouraging "associations for every species of human occupation or business";

for ending the Indian wars (1841);

for ending the Mexican War (1847);

for reducing congressmen's travel allowances;

against any plank advocating reduction of congressmen's travel allowances unless the issue was to be pressed strongly later;

for retrenchment of government expenses;

for abolition of the army and navy;

for abolition of West Point Academy;

for individual financial liability of members of corpora-
    tions;
against legislative monopolies;
for reduction of government salaries;
for abolition of unnecessary offices;
against establishing a United States Bank until slavery was
    abolished;
for judicial reform; and
against voting for persons known to be immoral, unjust, or
    dishonest.[28]

By the middle 1840s the abolitionists' political diversity,
which had been an argument first against the organization of a
third party and later for one-ideaism, had become a strong
motive for abandoning the latter policy. A Michigan editor,
Theodore Foster, placed the issue before Birney in 1845. We
have, he wrote, four alternatives: first, we can refrain from
discussing any other issues; second, each member and paper
can discuss them freely, but the party itself must take no action; third, we can postpone such discussions until the party is
close to winning power and then, in convention, take stands on
the other issues; and fourth, our conventions can freely act on
the other issues, making it clear that they are subordinate to
abolition and that abolitionism is the only test of membership.
The first, continued Foster, is contrary to human nature. The
second policy has been successfully tried, but it is doubtful
that Libertymen will always be willing to ignore issues important to them. They will probably return to their former parties unless state and national issues are recognized in the Liberty platform.[29] The third alternative, he wrote, leaves the
other questions in the hands of politicians. The fourth course
ought to be adopted.[30]

By now Birney was convinced. His discussions of other
issues became proposals for planks rather than mere expressions of personal opinion. At the beginning of 1846 he argued
publicly that the Liberty party could not expect to gain the
support of most Northerners on the slavery issue alone. We
are, he proclaimed, a *reform party* and must take a stand on all
subjects with which the voters are deeply concerned. And he

listed the planks he would propose; in their emphasis on free trade and minimal government they added up to a remarkably Democratic-type program.[31] William Goodell, who had earlier argued so eloquently against independent nominations, had also been converted, and in April 1847 he drafted a call to a convention at which abolitionists were to endorse a long list of proposed reforms and nominate a candidate for President. This list too was of the sort that would appeal to Democratic abolitionists only.

Goodell drew an inevitable but significant conclusion from the abandonment of one-ideaism; he pointed out that the staunchest supporters of that policy were those who were most ready to leave the Liberty party "just this once" to join their old parties on other questions. One-ideaism was the policy of a temporary party, but only a party with a broad platform, containing planks on all questions a government must deal with, could be permanent.[32] Birney agreed. The Liberty party, he wrote in 1847, should be considered not a mere balance-of-power pressure group but a permanent party,[33] and he added his name to the call for the convention.[34] It took place at Macedon Lock, New York, in June 1847, founded the Liberty League, and chose as its candidate Gerrit Smith, who at first had tried to stem the tide toward broadening the platform but had in the past year capitulated. Smith now believed abolitionists would continue to vote for Whigs or Democrats unless they regarded their antislavery party as a permanent party aspiring to power, which a one-idea party could never do.[35] One-ideaists remained in the Liberty party, which in 1848 split again, this time over joining the Free Soil coalition.

The logic that impelled the expansion of the Liberty platform was explained years later by one of the League's organizers, William Goodell: to overcome the weaknesses, discussed above, inherent in a one-idea, temporary, party,

> it was proposed to specify some of the particular measures which the principles and professions of Liberty men required them to espouse, such as free trade, gratuitous distribution of public lands, limitation of land

ownership, the inalienable homestead, retrenchment of expenses, free suffrage, and the abolition of all legalized monopolies and castes.

In further support of this policy, it was urged that slavery was only to be overthrown through the destruction of the minor monopolies and aristocracies subsidized by and sustaining it; and that the forces needed at the ballot box to overthrow slavery must consist, to a great extent, of the masses of men who feel that they have wrongs of their own to be redressed, and who could have no confidence in a Liberty party not committed to universal equality and impartial justice to all. They predicted that unless this advice was heeded, the Liberty party would, ere long, be scattered to the winds. They contended that, as civil government is an ordinance of God for the protection of *all* the rights of *all men*, we have no right to administer it, or to seek to administer it, for any lower or partial ends, and that if any *Anti-Slavery Society* may confine *its* attention to one form of oppression and robbery, it does not follow that the functions of CIVIL GOVERNMENT may be thus circumscribed.[36]

Goodell had incorporated these views in an address he presented at a convention in Port Byron, New York, in June 1845, but it was not adopted. The minority who favored the address, however, were those who organized the Macedon Lock convention two years later and adopted a platform consisting of twenty planks.[37] To a Whig abolitionist, many of these planks undoubtedly appeared more like spikes, calculated to test to the utmost his willingness to undergo martyrdom for the sake of the slave.[38] They included calls for "repeal of all tariffs, whether for protection or revenue," as well as retrenchment of government expenses, abolition of the army and navy, restriction of landholding, and abolition of the government post-office monopoly.[39]

What is remarkable here is the unrecognized assumption that a commitment to "universal liberty and impartial justice" implied assent to Democratic-type planks, that these planks were necessary demands of a "universal reform" party. That assumption was not shared by all political abolitionists. George Bradburn, for one, favored the League's demands individually but urged retention of one-ideaism. He wrote that he was willing to be plundered by tariffs, monopolies in land, and other legislated evils, if by submitting to them he could hasten the end of slavery; hence he believed it would be wrong to refuse to vote for a candidate who could help abolish slavery, because the candidate disagreed with him about lesser iniquities.[40] William Jay did not see all the League's other reforms as integrally connected with abolition of slavery; if my house is afire, he wrote, my neighbors who gather to put out the fire should not stop from time to time to discuss their own problems which do not concern me.[41] *The Liberator*, predictably, ridiculed the Liberty League. Garrison wondered why it limited its creed to twenty articles, for many others might just as properly have been added. He reported that a writer in a Liberty party paper in Utica had proposed nineteen more, "so as to make the exact number thirty-nine; identical with the number embraced in the creed of the English Church."[42]

The point that Garrison made facetiously touches on a problem that had arisen years before within the AASS: the relation of abolitionism to other issues. When some members decided that the abolition of slavery was to be part of a sweeping reformation of society which would include women's rights and nonresistance, they were accused of dragging in extraneous questions. *The Liberator* did not miss the opportunity to call attention to the parallel.[43] The anti-Garrisonians too had connected abolitionism with true Christianity, temperance, and other good things, showing that the issue to them was not between abolition standing alone and abolition plus other reforms; the question was *which* other reforms ought to be endorsed. Now the problem arose in a different form. The Liberty Leaguers formed a "universal reform" party, yet many dedicated reformers opposed some of their proposals, while others would add additional planks. There was, then, a choice not only between one-ideaism and universal reform, but also between different definitions of "universal," and the selection of planks was dictated by the framers' conception of what changes were needed to make justice prevail in American society. The Libertymen had kept their platform narrow in part to avoid alienating potential supporters; the Leaguers defended the broadening of the platform in part to secure additional supporters. The unconscious rationale is at least equally significant, for the question then became, *Which* additional supporters? A plural program could be either very broad or very narrow, depending on the nature of its planks and the size and influence of the groups attracted or repelled by them. Garrison had been accused of narrowing the anti-slavery platform when he preached women's rights and non-resistance, since many potential abolitionists opposed these innovations. Since he restricted his proselytizing to his own paper and the Non-Resistance Society, it may be suggested that the Liberty Leaguers were more guilty of what they had accused him of, for they added to antislavery a long list of reforms some of which must repel that vast majority of abolitionists who were Whigs, while Democrats who were not abolitionists would certainly not join the League in any event.

Yet the political abolitionists had little choice; the abandonment of one-ideaism seems to have been inevitable. A principal thesis of the original Libertymen had been that the slave power had taken over the federal government. The evidence on which they based this assertion included certain government policies in regard to banking and currency problems, foreign trade, immigration, and other subjects, as well as in regard to issues directly related to slavery.[44] The political abolitionists here showed unconsciously how they stood on all those issues. By contending that the government's handling of them proved the dominance of the slave power, they were in effect saying that their handling of them would have been different. In documents written early in the history of the Liberty party, the writers were not fully aware that they were taking sides on many of the important political issues of the day; they assumed that the right position on them was self-evident to every moral person. The broad platform was, then, present in embryo even in the Liberty party's earliest one-idea policy. The party's 1844 platform, for example, professed opposition to the government's policy of doing all it could to secure the markets of the world for the products of slave labor, while those of free labor were mostly confined to the non-paying market of the slave states, and it declared that the government must, in its foreign relations, do all in its power to extend the markets for the products of free labor. The result of that policy, predicted the platform, would be general and permanent prosperity. Another resolution in the 1844 platform declared:

> That we believe intelligence, religion, and morality, to be the indispensable supports of good government, and are therefore in favor of general education; we believe, also, that good government itself is necessary to the welfare of society, and are therefore in favor of rigid public economy, and strict adherence to the principles of justice in every department of the administration.[45]

The development of broad-platformism was thus hastened, not created, by the party's failure to attract the votes of most abolitionists in 1840 and 1844. If one reason for its low votes was most abolitionists' desire to have a say in the disposition of other issues besides slavery, the abandonment of one-ideaism could not solve the party's problem. First, most abolitionists apparently believed that a vote for a splinter party was wasted; Whig abolitionists considered it a vote for the Democrats. Second, the Democratic-type platform which the League adopted could hardly be a vote-getter so long as most abolitionists leaned toward the Whigs.[46]

The abolitionists' inability to agree on "extraneous issues" turns out to have been an argument against organizing the Liberty party, for keeping the Liberty party's one-idea policy, and for abandoning the one-idea policy. It seems, then, that there was a second proposition they agreed on: that they had nothing in common except the basic principles in the AASS constitution. And since that fact was cited in support of mutually exclusive policies, a century's perspective may permit the further observation that it doomed in advance *any* effort to organize politically.

The failure to distinguish between Garrison's opinions as a nonresistant and the tactics he thought the abolitionist movement (as a coalition of adherents of many philosophies) ought to pursue has led to an understandable confusion among historians who discuss his views on political tactics. Noting his repudiation of all forceful government and, after 1842, his denunciation of the United States Constitution, they have dismissed his advocacy of certain types of political action as evidence of muddy thinking and have paid too little attention to the theory underlying that advocacy.[47]

The starting point for his discussion of political action was his conception of the abolitionist movement as a broad coalition. Just as he would not exclude from the AASS any abolitionist whose philosophy differed from his, so he could, without prescribing modes of action, theorize about the sort of political tactics proper for an abolitionist who shared little with him but the principles of the society's constitution—the sinfulness of slavery and the duty of immediate emancipation. Given the average abolitionist's acceptance of the United States government and the propriety of voting, what types of political action, Garrison might ask, were consistent with that abolitionist's principles? Second, which among those tactics was the most effective way of fighting slavery in the political field?

Garrison's answers to the first question coincided with those of the majority of political abolitionists. That is, the abolitionist could with propriety adopt the "scattering" policy, meaning he could cast a write-in vote for an individual not on the ballot, to demonstrate his dissatisfaction with all the regular nominees; in a thoroughly abolitionized district, these scattering votes could, he thought, represent enough strength to force concessions from the regular parties at the next election. The same effect could be produced by temporary nominations by abolitionists. Or, the abolitionist could work actively as part of a pressure group to force a major party to take acceptable positions and nominate antislavery candidates on the local level, while he would of course refuse to vote for its presidential candidates as long as they were acceptable to the party's Southern wing. Eventually, many abolitionized local parties might force a change in the party's national character. The scattering policy could be combined with this second mode of action.[48] Still another possibility was for the abolitionist to join with others to organize a third party. Garrison and most of his group never condemned the Liberty party as wrong in principle. They condemned it when they answered the second question, that concerning the effectiveness of each of the tactics that were in principle acceptable.

> We admit [wrote Garrison] that the *mode* of political action, to be pursued by abolitionists, is not strictly a question of principle, but rather one of sound expediency. We have never opposed the formation of a third party as a measure inherently wrong, but have always contended that the abolitionists have as clear and indisputable right to band themselves together politically for the attainment of their great object, as those of their fellow-citizens who call themselves whigs or democrats. . . . But every reflecting mind may easily perceive, that to disregard the dictates of sound expediency may often prove as injurious to an enterprise as to violate principle. It is solely on this ground that we oppose what is called the "liberty party." We believe it is highly inexpedient, and therefore not the best mode to advance the anti-slavery cause.[49]

Since Garrison the nonresistant opposed all parties on principle so long as the government was based on force, he could not prefer one party to another or condemn one more than another on any but expedient grounds. It would also follow that to the abolitionist who was not a nonresistant there could, he believed, be no principled objection to a third party.

The disagreements on political tactics between the radicals and Libertymen, then, hinged, in Garrison's opinion, on the question of expediency, not principle. They agreed that the two parties were corrupt and the servants of the slave power, but they proposed different ways of reforming them. According to the radicals, the parties were corrupt because the people

were. Only a reformed public opinion could reform the parties
in any meaningful, lasting way. Who, they asked, would join
the third party? Committed abolitionists. Would they be more
useful there or in their old parties? If their task was to convert
the masses of voters, they would be more effective if they
remained where those masses were.[50] In an abolitionized district both parties would have to make concessions to keep
their own abolitionist members from defecting, and a third
party, by withdrawing those members from both major parties, would permit them to continue to ignore the interests of
the slave. But if abolitionists adopted the scattering policy and
demonstrated their refusal to vote for unacceptable candidates
and their willingness to cross party lines to vote for abolitionists despite differences on other issues that separated the
parties, they could constitute a real balance of power between
them.[51] A third party would be a less effective instrument for
influencing public opinion than agitation by the AASS and by
abolitionists voting as individuals. And once public opinion
had been converted, the major parties would, for the sake of
votes, reflect the change in their platforms and nominations,
and a third party would be unnecessary.[52] This argument was
urged whether the third party was of the one-idea or broad-
platform type.

The fullest exposition of the Garrisonian theory is in an
imaginary dialogue, by Lydia Maria Child, between "A" and
"B." In response to "A's" inquiry about the position of the
AASS on political action, "B" explains:

> [It] stands on precisely the same principles that it did the
> first year of its formation. Its object was to change public
> opinion on the subject of slavery, by the persevering
> utterance of truth. This change they expected would
> show itself in a thousand different forms:—such as con-
> flict and separation in churches; new arrangements in
> colleges and schools; new customs in stages and cars; and
> new modifications of policy in the political parties of the
> day. The business of anti-slavery was, and is, to purify
> the *fountain*, whence all these streams flow; if it turns
> aside to take charge of any *one* of the streams, however

important, it is obvious enough that the whole work must retrograde; for, if the fountain be not kept pure, no one of the streams will flow with clear water. But just so sure as the fountain is taken proper care of, the character of all the streams *must* be influenced thereby. We might form ourselves into a railroad society, to furnish cars with the same conveniences for all complexions; but we feel that we are doing a far more effectual work, so as to change popular opinion, that there will be no *need* of a separate train of cars. We might expend all our funds and energies in establishing abolition colleges; but we feel sure that we have the power in our hands to abolitionize *all* colleges.

In answer to a later question, "B" contends that before the Liberty party was organized, both parties in Massachusetts were afraid of abolitionists and hence willing to grant their requests; this is no longer so. "A": But those legislators were not genuine abolitionists, or they would not have refused concessions once the pressure was removed.

B: Those men, let me tell you, did the work of sound anti-slavery; and in doing it, got imbued more or less with anti-slavery sentiment, in spite of themselves. The machinery of a third political party may send into Congress, or the halls of State legislation, a few individuals, who are anti-slavery to the back-bone. But could one Alvan Stewart do as much for our cause in Congress, as twenty of Joshua R. Giddings? Fifty men, who have a strong motive for obliging the abolitionists, could surely do more for our cause, in such a position, than merely two or three radical abolitionists. I too want to see all our legislators anti-slavery; but when that time comes, there will most obviously be no need of a distinct abolition party; and in order to bring about that time, we must diligently exert moral influence to sway *all* parties. . . .

And why, continues "B," assume that the Liberty party will be comprised of more disinterested men? Many are joining it who never were abolitionists. In one county, Democrats join temporarily, to defeat a Whig; in another county, Whigs join to defeat a Democrat. Are these recruits more reliable than major-party legislators who are willing to give abolitionists what they ask? Many Libertymen are sincere abolitionists, but "by the natural laws of attraction, their party will draw around them the selfish and the ambitious." If party machinery is so mischievous, asks "A," how can you work with Whigs and Democrats? "B: By adhering closely to moral influence, we work *through* both parties, but not *with* them. They do our work; we do not *theirs*. We are simply the atmosphere that makes the quicksilver rise or fall."

Later "A" remarks that the South dreads antislavery at the ballot box more than anywhere else, and "B" replies:

> I never doubted that political action would be a powerful engine for the overthrow of slavery.—The only question between you and the American Society seems to be, whether the speediest and most extensive political effect would be produced by the *old* scheme of holding the balance between the two parties; or the *new* scheme of forming a distinct party. I apprehend what the slave-holders would like least of all things, would be to see *both* the great political parties consider it for their interest to nominate abolitionists; and this *would* be the case if anti-slavery voters would only be consistent and firm.

"A": But they will not be consistent and firm; under the old plan they always turned aside to vote for a Harrison or a Van Buren. "B": If that is so, will the Liberty party keep them from doing so? Will a two-thirds abolitionized Democrat, who has joined to defeat a Whig, vote Liberty when his ballot is needed by his own party? An antislavery member of an old party will be more reliable if his party interests coincide with his abolitionism and if his work as an abolitionist will mean an increase in the number of antislavery votes for his own party. But you remove that stimulus when you organize a separate party: you force him to give up his party position on all issues besides slavery. And the success of such a third party would be its undoing, for if it gains enough power to influence legislation in a state, one Libertyman will be protariff and another antitariff, and they will be swallowed by their former parties again. "A" suggests that perhaps these lawmakers will be willing to sacrifice those other considerations for the sake of anti-slavery. In that case, "B" replies, their constituents will complain that their other interests are neglected and will vote the legislators out of office. And so we have come back to moral influence as the legitimate work of an abolitionist. But, asks "A," can we not exert moral influence and work for the Liberty party at the same time? "B": In practice, things have not worked out that way; Libertymen now talk scornfully of moral influence. "A": But now that the Liberty party exists, should we not vote for its candidates? "B": "That is the bait that has hooked half their numbers. . . . *Moral* influence dies under *party* action."[53]

The radicals decried what they believed was the tendency of some to exaggerate the significance of legal enactments; when William Goodell, for example, argued that slavery was the creature of law and that its abolition was "nothing more nor less than the repeal of these slave laws," they replied that slavery was "the creature of avarice and love of domination" and was "only *sanctified* and regulated" by law.[54] Wrote Rogers of New Hampshire:

> The best and utmost that political movements—the constitutions, enactments, and decisions could effect for the slave, is to translate him into that anomaly in a *christian republic*, called a "free nigger." New Hampshire has thus transmuted him by the magic force of its politics. What is the liberty of a New Hampshire emancipated colored man? It barely qualifies him to pass muster as a candidate for the mercy of the Colonization Society. . . . New York has abolished slavery by *law;* yet it is as much as a colored man's life is worth to live in her cities. . . . Slavery has been *legally* abolished in half the states of the Union, and the best they can do for the fugitive slave is to give him race ground to Canada before the Southern bloodhounds and for the freed man of color is to let in upon him the gray hounds of colonization.[55]

Garrison and those who thought like him insisted that to abolish the law would be useless without transformation of the spirit that the law reflected.[56]

The advocates of a third party, wrote Oliver Johnson, have betrayed a degree of impatience with the progress of the cause. They should note that in England the abolitionists continued to hold the balance of power without organizing their own party, until they won. It may be replied, he continued, that the parties in the United States are more subservient to the slave power than they were in England. True, he conceded, but that merely proves that the people here are more corrupted by slavery than were the English; and will a third party counteract that corruption and purify their hearts?

All attempts to abolish slavery by legislation before the people of the country are converted to anti-slavery principles must of necessity be unsuccessful. A political party is not needed as a means of converting the people, and when they *are* converted, such a party will of course be unnecessary. When we say that efforts to abolish slavery by legislation must for the present be necessarily unsuccessful, we do not mean to intimate that such efforts should not constantly and vigorously be made; but only that the want of success should be attributed to the right cause, and not lead to the adoption of a measure which is at best of doubtful utility.[57]

The Libertymen mistook "the right cause" when they contended that the major parties were incorrigibly proslavery and from that contention deduced the need for a third party. The fundamental principles of both parties, said the Garrisonians, were laudable. The Democratic creed preached liberty, reform, and equal rights; the Whig creed, stability, supremacy of law, and security of property; between them the rights of the people and the interests of property were championed. If not for the slave power, temporarily dominating and perverting both, abolitionists who accepted the legitimacy of the government could adhere to one or the other without violating their antislavery principles. Abolitionist agitation, then, must aim to bring both parties back to their own principles, to make the leaders of both act consistently with their own professions.[58] Expecting less from organized political action than did the Libertymen, Garrison could not see a political party, regardless of what it called itself, as the insurance of an office-holder's fidelity to the cause. That role he assigned to unorganized (but infinitely more coercive) public opinion.

Running through all the tactical thinking of Garrison and his followers is an emphasis on what today would be called "building a constituency." Their political theory may be seen as a part of their general theory of agitation, a corollary of which was their conception of the AASS itself as no more than a propaganda center, from which abolitionists with a wide variety of philosophies and affiliations would go, armed with agitational weapons to use in whatever parties, churches, or other organizations they chose to belong to. Without public opinion on its side, the movement could accomplish nothing; with public opinion, it could transform all organizations dependent on public opinion into tactical weapons for the cause.

Garrison did not see political action as a way of achieving his goals by parliamentary means. Those goals were far too radical—far too subversive of the fundamental arrangements of American society—to be realized by the vote of a few hundred men, including slaveholders and their allies, in the Capitol in Washington, even if a majority of them had been willing to so vote, which was inconceivable. It would, therefore, be an oversimplification to say that he refused to engage in political action because such action would represent participation in a government whose legitimacy he, as a nonresistant, denied, although this purely abstract formulation was sufficient for the "ultraists" whose spokesman he was. But what of the principles that should, in Garrison's opinion, guide the tactics of those abolitionists who did not repudiate the coercive United States government? One gets the impression from his writings on the subject that he at least sensed the practical danger that other radicals throughout American history have sometimes encountered: that *ad hoc* alliances for partial ends may under certain circumstances strengthen the hegemony of the enemy by legitimizing the institutions, and the ideological justifications of those institutions, by means of which the enemy exercises his hegemony. The radical who recognizes this danger (or who at least senses it, as I think Garrison did) may form such alliances, but on his own terms, with explicit safeguards against his participation being used to foster illusions that political action is more than a temporary tactic for very limited purposes; he will, that is, make it clear that he is using the political machinery and that it is not using him. It is in the light of Garrison's partial insight into this principle that we should interpret his insistence, as against the Libertymen, that the major parties were redeemable; they were redeemable not as parties but as the politically organized constituencies among which nonradical abolitionists could agitate for abolition.

In view of the radicals' opposition to the third party and their belief that the major parties were redeemable, it is understandable that abolitionists who refused to leave their old parties found more common ground with them than with the Libertymen. And since most abolitionists were Whigs, the Libertymen discovered a convenient weapon against both adversaries: the accusation that Whigs and nonresistants had formed an alliance against the Liberty party.[59] The Libertymen themselves recognized that Garrison never, as an abolitionist, condemned voting per se; they asserted that he was inconsistent when he, a nonresistant, advised voters to vote for abolitionists regardless of party label. That assertion constitutes an implicit admission that his policy was not proscriptive, that he did not consider abolitionists who accepted the legitimacy of political action spurious abolitionists. Libertymen knew they had no reason to fear he would persuade many abolitionists to stay away from the polls. Their real grievance against him was therefore not his antipolitical philosophy as a nonresistant but his anti-third-party position as an abolitionist.[60] That his nonresistance was used as a red herring is suggested by the argument, heavily relied on during the factional struggles, that nonresistance must be officially repudiated because its absurdity and radicalism would alienate most potential supporters. It would follow that after the society had split, the radical remnant, isolated from the more conservative body of abolitionists, would exert negligible influence. Yet while the Liberty party was struggling to attract the support of anti-slavery Whigs and Democrats, it directed its principal polemics against the nonresistants, ostensibly to prevent them from exerting influence against political action of any sort. And the AASS and the Massachusetts Anti-Slavery Society retained the allegiance of thousands of Whig voters in New England who, if the Liberty party's public fears had had substance, would have fought the Garrisonian influence as vehemently as did the Libertymen.[61] Clearly, the real issue was not political action versus nonresistance but third-party political action versus independent political action. Equally clearly, the real threat was not Garrison's influence for nonresistance, which was small, but his influence for independent (non-Liberty-party) political action, which was considerable.

In fact, it is difficult to draw a line between the nonresistants and some major-party abolitionists before the mid-1840s, so far as political tactics are concerned. The independent Whig David Lee Child adhered to the Garrisonian faction in that period; the same is true of George Bradburn, who broke with that faction when he left the Whig for the Liberty party in 1844.[62] Gamaliel Bailey, Birney's successor as editor of *The Philanthropist* (Cincinnati), was certainly no disciple of Garrison, but as long as he opposed the Liberty party his articles were freely reprinted and praised in *The Liberator*.[63] One such article was an editorial in which Bailey observed that abolitionists were a small minority in the free states. If they constituted a majority there would be no need for a third party, because they could force the major parties to nominate suitable candidates. No minority could bring about any legislated action against slavery; hence the advocates of a new party must act on the assumption that this measure was the best way to obtain a majority. Now, a new party could not hold out to its adherents the hope of office or political advancement; nor could it threaten to defeat any lawmaker. Unable to succeed by appealing to motives of self-interest, it must operate by moral means—argument, persuasion. Was the third-party scheme the best way to carry on propaganda? No, declared Bailey, quite the opposite. As long as a major party saw that abolitionists did not threaten it as a party, that they said nothing about its doctrines, that they insisted that their

cause could be supported by all people without interfering
with either party's essential interests, that they asked only that
it be true to its own stated principles, it would not war upon
them. Let the parties have the offices and prestige, he advised.
Our present policy removes as far as possible "every obstacle
between those parties and the force of our arguments."

> If the larger portion of our fellow countrymen are so
> corrupted and unprincipled, that they cannot, by any
> *moral* means we have been accustomed to use, be induced
> to act on our principles, surely, beyond all doubt, it is
> visionary to expect to reform them by a political orga-
> nization, too feeble to bestow political rewards, or inflict
> political punishment.[64]

Garrison could agree with every one of these statements. "The
politics of a people," he wrote, "will always be shaped by its
morals, as the vane on the steeple is ever indicating in what
direction the wind blows."[65]

NOTES

[1] The story of these conventions is well told in Joseph Rayback,
"The Liberty Party Leaders of Ohio: Exponents of Antislavery Coalition," *The Ohio State Archaeological and Historical Quarterly*, XVIII
(April 1948), 165–67; Fladeland, *Birney*, Ch. 9; Theodore C. Smith,
Liberty and Free Soil Parties in the Northwest (New York, 1897), Chs.
4–5; and Dumond, ed., "Introduction," *Birney Letters*, I, ix. Smith's book
is the best discussion of antislavery parties in general; the reader should
consult it for many aspects of the subject not covered here, including
differences between Eastern and Western abolitionists' views.

[2] Smith (1797–1874) was a wealthy landowner, businessman, and
philanthropist in upstate New York, converted from colonizationism to
abolitionism in 1835 by Weld. He was related by marriage to Stanton
and Birney. Although an advocate of sex equality, he exchanged public
polemics with Garrison on several other important issues. Unlike Stanton
and Birney, he never let the disagreements weaken his regard and respect for Garrison, and their personal friendship continued. Smith was
very changeable in his opinions; his innumerable printed open letters
constitute a good weather vane showing the direction of the ideological
wind in the abolitionist movement.

[3] In the 1840 campaign both major parties emphasized personalities
over issues. A Democratic newspaper ridiculed the Whig candidate,
saying if Harrison were offered a pension and a barrel of cider he

would no doubt abandon his bid for the presidency and spend the rest of his life contentedly in a log cabin. The Whigs capitalized on this remark and portrayed their candidate as a man of the people; they organized parades and picnics, distributed large quantities of cider, made the log cabin their emblem, and pictured the Democrat Van Buren as an effete aristocrat. The tactic succeeded, and Harrison won a majority of the votes, including a majority of abolitionists' votes. Harrison died in April 1841, a month after his inauguration, and Vice-President John Tyler, a Virginia slaveholder, became President.

4 Smith, *Liberty and Free Soil Parties,* pp. 53–54.

5 *Ibid.,* p. 81.

6 *The Liberator,* September 14, 1838.

7 Garrison and Ellis Gray Loring, along with their "new-organized" enemies, all voted for it.

8 *The Liberator,* August 16, 1839.

9 Garrison replied that it would be, if the Unitarian was running for the post of religious teacher (*ibid.,* November 6, 1840).

10 *Ibid.,* October 30, 1840.

11 See Tappan to Seth M. Gates, October 21, 1843, and to Gerrit Smith, December 9, 1843, Tappan Papers, LC. *The Emancipator,* November 14, 1839, printed a letter from Tappan to the editor listing eighteen reasons for opposing a third party (reprinted in *The Liberator,* November 14, 1839). In 1840, before the split, Tappan had opposed Joshua Leavitt's use of the AASS's official organ, *The Emancipator,* to propagandize for the Liberty party (see Tappan to Birney, January 23, 1840, Tappan Papers, LC). After the split, when *The Emancipator* became the organ of the A & F, the struggle continued, with Tappan resigning from the executive board in protest (see Tappan to William Jay, June 11, 1841, Tappan Papers, LC). *The Liberator,* December 27, 1839, reprinted from the Cincinnati *Philanthropist* a survey of the attitudes toward a third party expressed by prominent abolitionists and several state antislavery societies and newspapers.

12 Quoted in Plunkett, "A History of the Liberty Party," p. 57.

13 Holley introduced a remarkable resolution (which was not voted on) in a convention in upstate New York in 1840: "Resolved that if there are any members of the American Anti-Slavery Society sincerely desirous of abolishing slavery, in the United States, but opposed to all civil govt. as a *moral wrong,* and therefore not willing to countenance it, by holding any of its offices, or voting for any of its functionaries, though we cannot perceive with what consistency, they can remain members of that society, we cheerfully invite them to cooperate with us, in the exercise of their best powers of moral suasion in favor of abolishing slavery—reminding them however, that *our duty to God,* as asserted in the constitution of that society, will require us to oppose any efforts they may make to dissuade any of its members from voting for abolition legislators." See Holley to Gerrit Smith, March 20, 1840, Gerrit Smith Miller Collection, SU.

14 Smith to William Goodell, reprinted from *The Friend of Man* in *The Liberator,* February 19, 1841. See also Smith to Luther Myrick, January 17, 1841, to William Seward, February 19, 1842, and to Abby

Kelley, July 24, 1843, all in Gerrit Smith Miller Collection, SU. The letter to Seward is incidental evidence of the abolitionists' astounding political naïveté. It was a request to that hardheaded Whig politician to be the Liberty candidate for President. Smith quoted a letter he had received from Birney two weeks earlier suggesting Seward as nominee. Smith based his request on Seward's opposition to slavery, but, he added, he realized that like many Whigs, Seward was still probably hoping the Whig party would abolish slavery and that he would hence decline the nomination, knowing the Liberty party had originated in the conviction that both major parties must be proslavery so long as slavery existed. "You are, perhaps, surprised, seeing that the abolitionists have already nominated Mr. Birney for that office, at my asking whether you will consent to be named by them for President. There is no man, whom the abolitionists would take more pleasure in electing to this office than Mr. Birney. . . . Nevertheless, inasmuch as they believe that your nomination would greatly hasten the triumph of their cause, they would prefer to have you the candidate in his stead. With him or with any other candidate, who has little or no influence with the Whig or Democratic party, they would not expect to get the vote of a single State. With yourself, they would have hopes of carrying several states; and would even not despair of carrying the nation." Seward declined the honor (see Smith to Seward, March 5, 1842, same collection). See Dumond, ed., *Birney Letters*, I, ix–x, where the editor explains that some Libertymen believed from the start that efforts to reform the major parties must be futile and that by 1844 many more agreed, believing that since the South would not participate in any national party that was not proslavery, the major parties would remain proslavery as long as slavery existed.

[15] Leavitt to Birney, January 18, 1842, *Birney Letters*, II, 660. See also Gerrit Smith to Abby Kelley, July 24, 1843, Gerrit Smith Miller Collection, SU.

[16] This idea was expressed repeatedly. The following formulation of it is significant only because written by Joshua Leavitt, editor of *The Emancipator*, despite protests that the AASS's organ must not take sides. He wrote that the opposers were wrong in saying that as long as the American people were divided by various interests it would be impossible to induce them to organize a party united to act on one great interest. Leavitt replied that slavery was the overriding interest and no other problem could be solved before abolition. He closed thus: "Is there not ground for the presumption, that brothers Tappan, Gates, Garrison, Bailey, and the others, would not reason as they do, were not their minds unconsciously influenced by other interests, personal, social, political or commercial, more than by the ONE IDEA of abolishing slavery[?]" ("Independent Anti-Slavery Nominations," *The Emancipator*, December 12, 1839).

[17] "To the Abolitionists of Massachusetts," *The Liberator*, August 10, 1838.

[18] Goodell, "Political Action against Slavery. No. 3," reprinted from *The Friend of Man* in *The Liberator*, September 7, 1838.

[19] *Ibid.*, September 14, 1838.

[20] Reprinted *ibid.*, December 6, 1839.

21 James McCune Smith to Gerrit Smith, May 12, 1841, Gerrit Smith Miller Collection, SU. The theory that slavery lay at the root of all other national problems was one that abolitionists accepted a priori; it did not generally follow from an examination of those other problems. Hence a Whig abolitionist could link abolition to Whig solutions and a Democratic abolitionist could link it to Democratic solutions.

22 Gerrit Smith "to the President of the National Convention of the Liberty Party, which is to be held in the City of Buffalo August 30th & 31st, 1843," August 10, 1843, Gerrit Smith Miller Collection, SU.

23 See Birney to Daniel H. Fitzhugh, March 20, 1843, Birney Papers, UM; and the following documents in *Birney Letters*, Vol. II: Birney to Lewis Tappan, January 14, 1842, p. 659; Theodore D. Weld to Birney, January 22, 1842, p. 662; Joshua Leavitt to Birney, February 14, 1842, p. 674, and February 28, 1843, pp. 719-20; Gamaliel Bailey to Birney, March 31, 1843, p. 727; and especially Birney to Bailey, April 16, 1843, pp. 732-34.

24 Samuel Lewis to Birney, May 28, 1843, *ibid.*, pp. 738-39.

25 Birney to Lewis, July 13, 1843, *ibid.*, pp. 743-47.

26 See *ibid.*: Joseph P. Gazzam to Birney, December 27, 1843, pp. 765-66; Reece C. Fleeson to Birney, January 10, 1844, p. 773; Birney to Fleeson, January 20, 1844, pp. 774-76; Russell Errett to Birney, July 13, 1844, pp. 820-21; William H. Stephenson to Birney, July 23, 1844, pp. 822-23; Birney to Errett, August 5, 1844, pp. 829-30, 832; Birney to Hartford (Ohio) Committee, August 15, 1844, pp. 833-34.

27 As early as October 1840, Joshua Leavitt suggested that voting abolitionists could be brought to support free trade, and hence the Liberty party should endorse it, to secure the support of Democrats. And, he added, support for the anti-Corn Law movement in England would attract a following in the West (Leavitt to Birney, October 1, 1840, *ibid.*, p. 604). See also Garrisons, *Garrison*, II, 435: the authors quote an 1840 Liberty party resolution that although abolition was the most important question in national politics, it was not the only one in which the party was interested; that its principle that all men "are, *as men,* entitled to an equal participation in the benefits of our Government, does decide all these questions in favor of the general good, by deciding them in favor of the widest and largest liberty that can flourish under just laws." The authors comment: "This was the price of a vice-presidential candidate whose hobby was monopoly." The Massachusetts Liberty party, they add, sent to the national party resolutions on the Corn Laws, immigration, manufacturing and the tariff, banks, and other issues. For a similar trend in 1841, see Fladeland, *Birney*, p. 212.

28 *The Finance of Cheap Postage* (New York, 1849), by Joshua Leavitt, Secretary of the Boston Cheap Postage Association, copy in Leavitt Papers, LC; Lewis Tappan to George H. Evans, October 11, 1847, and October 16, 1849, Tappan Papers, LC; *Speech of Gerrit Smith Made in the National Liberty Party Convention at Buffalo, September 17th, 1851,* circular, Box I of Smith Family Papers, NYPL; copy of Gerrit Smith to E. Crosswell, April 9, 1840, Gerrit Smith Letterbooks, Gerrit Smith Miller Collection, SU; Thomas Earle to Gerrit Smith, May 1, 1848, Julius LeMoyne to Smith, May 21, 1850, and LeMoyne to Smith,

June 17, 1850, all *ibid.; To the Editors of the Emancipator, Boston,* circular by Gerrit Smith, Vol. 18, James G. Birney Papers, UM; two printed circulars, one signed by Leavitt as secretary of the Boston Cheap Postage Association, 1849, the other signed by, among others, Lewis Tappan as treasurer of the New-York Cheap Postage Association, 1849, *ibid.;* documents in *Birney Letters,* Vol. II, cited in footnotes 23 to 26 above; Theodore Foster to Birney, July 7, 1845, September 29, 1845, December 7, 1845, and May 4, 1846, *ibid.,* pp. 951, 973-74, 983, 1015; statement by Birney in *The Signal of Liberty* of September 29, 1845, *ibid.,* pp. 971n-72n; Birney to the President of the Michigan State Anti-Slavery Society, January 1, 1846, *ibid.,* pp. 993-96; Guy Beckley to Birney, January 5, 1846, *ibid.,* p. 998; William Goodell to Birney, April 1, 1847, *ibid.,* pp. 1048-51; Beriah Green to Birney, April 23, 1847, *ibid.,* pp. 1066-67; Ephriam H. Sanford to Birney, October 31, 1848, *ibid.,* pp. 1116-18; Fladeland, *Birney,* pp. 212, 220-22, 232-33, 258-59; Harlow, Gerrit Smith, pp. 86-87, 110-12; Plunkett, "History of the Liberty Party," pp. 162-64.

29 Here he listed Michigan issues such as reduction of salaries, legal reform, abolition of militia training, sale of the railroads to private owners, issue of more scrip, and the license question; and national questions such as reduction of navy expenses, abolition of West Point, and cheap postage. Significantly, he seems to have taken it for granted that all good men favored these measures. In later letters Foster lengthened the list of planks he favored.

30 Theodore Foster to Birney, July 7, 1845, *Birney Letters,* II, 950-52. For Foster's diligent work in inducing the Michigan Liberty party to broaden its platform, see his letters to Birney of September 29, 1845, *ibid.,* pp. 973-74; October 16, 1845, pp. 980-81; December 7, 1845, pp. 982-84; February 13, 1846, pp. 1002-4; March 30, 1846, pp. 1007-9; May 5, 1846, pp. 1014-16; and article by Foster and Guy Beckley, March 1847, *ibid.,* pp. 1057n-59n.

31 Birney to the President of the Michigan State Anti-Slavery Society, January 1, 1846, *ibid.,* pp. 990-96.

32 Goodell to Birney, April 1, 1847, *ibid.,* pp. 1047-57. Beriah Green, who favored the broad platform, hoped Birney would not sign Goodell's manifesto because of the second plank, which called for broad suffrage; Green favored restriction of the vote to the wise (Green to Birney, May 5, 1847, *ibid.,* p. 1066).

33 Birney to Guy Beckley, April 6, 1847, *ibid.,* p. 1061.

34 Birney to Goodell, April 26, 1847, *ibid.,* pp. 1071-72. For other correspondence preliminary to the convention, see James C. Jackson to Birney, April 23, 1847, and Birney to Jackson, May 17, 1847, *ibid.,* pp. 1067-70, 1073-74.

35 Smith's change of views is described in Harlow, *Gerrit Smith,* pp. 175-79. For background on the formation of the Liberty League, see also Thomas, *The Liberator: William Lloyd Garrison,* pp. 344-45; Fladeland, *Birney,* p. 262; Plunkett, "History of the Liberty Party," Ch. 6; T. C. Smith, *Liberty and Free Soil Parties,* pp. 100-102. See also "A Fourth Party," editorial in *The Liberator,* July 2, 1847; Henry C. Wright, "Mass Meeting of the Liberty Party at Buffalo," *ibid.,* November 19, 1847;

Letter of Gerrit Smith to the Liberty Party of New-Hampshire, March 18, 1848, leaflet in Lysander Spooner Papers, NYHS; Goodell, *Slavery and Anti-Slavery,* pp. 473–78.

36 *Ibid.,* pp. 474–75.

37 See *ibid.,* and Plunkett, "History of the Liberty Party," p. 162. Some sources state there were nineteen planks.

38 "The 'Liberty Party,'" wrote Mrs. Child some years earlier, "not only compels men to renounce *all* their political predilections, except opposition to slavery; but it is in grain loco-foco. Leavitt, Wright, Goodell, Jackson, Smith[,] Stewart, are democrats, in the technical sense; and the papers of that party throughout the country betray a decided lurch toward that side; Therefore, as a *general* thing abolition whigs" steer clear of it (Lydia Maria Child to Ellis Gray Loring, March 9, 1842, Child Papers, NYPL).

39 Plunkett, "History of the Liberty Party," pp. 163–64.

40 Bradburn to Gerrit Smith, October 8, 1847, Gerrit Smith Miller Collection, SU. Another late defense of one-ideaism is Lewis Tappan to F. J. LeMoyne, December 26, 1849, "Letters of Dr. F. J. LeMoyne, an Abolitionist of Western Pennsylvania," *Journal of Negro History,* XVIII (October 1933), 455–56.

41 Jay to Gerrit Smith, September 25, 1846, Gerrit Smith Miller Collection, SU.

42 "A Fourth Party," *The Liberator,* July 2, 1847. Another editorial in the same issue ridiculed the group that had withdrawn from the Liberty party because its platform of liberating the suffering millions on Southern plantations was too narrow and who held a "national" convention (of about seventy persons), the first of the four parties to do so. "The race, however, is not always to the swift; and it is possible that, though late in the field, either the Whigs or the Democrats may gain the victory."

43 See "Extraneous Points," *ibid.,* July 2, 1847.

44 See Julian P. Bretz, "The Economic Background of the Liberty Party," *American Historical Review,* XXXIV (January 1929), 257–60.

45 Kirk H. Porter and Donald B. Johnson, compilers, *National Party Platforms, 1840–1960* (Urbana, Ill., 1961), pp. 6, 7 (twenty-first and twenty-fourth resolutions).

46 Some abolitionists, however, were Whigs only because they believed the Whig party sounder than the Democratic party on the slavery issue. This was true of George Bradburn, who favored the Liberty League's planks (see page 155 above) but up to a few years before had belonged to the Whig party.

47 See Thomas, *The Liberator: William Lloyd Garrison,* pp. 275–76, 285–88, 325–26. Merrill, *Against Wind and Tide,* has an extremely brief summary, without comment. One would not learn from Barnes, *The Anti-Slavery Impulse,* or Filler, *The Crusade against Slavery,* that Garrison even had a theory of political action. See also Dumond, ed., "Introduction," *Birney Letters,* I, ix.

48 One or more of these points may be found in each of the following (as well as in many more documents in the same period): "To the Abolitionists of Massachusetts," by Francis Jackson and Amos A. Phelps,

for the board of managers of the Massachusetts Anti-Slavery Society, *The Liberator*, August 10, 1838; Oliver Johnson, "Hear Both Sides," *ibid.*, September 14, 1838; [Oliver Johnson?], "Anti-Slavery Political Party," *ibid.*, June 26, 1840; E[dmund] Q[uincy], "Liberty Party," *ibid.*, September 22, 1843; resolutions presented by Garrison for the business committee, reported in "The Twelfth Annual Meeting of the Massachusetts Anti-Slavery Society," *ibid.*, February 2, 1844; "Extracts from the Twelfth Annual Report of the Managers of the Massachusetts Anti-Slavery Society for 1844," *ibid.*, March 22, 1844.

49 " 'Dying Away'—Another Richmond in the Field—Political Action," *ibid.*, October 1, 1841. (Thomas, *The Liberator: William Lloyd Garrison*, pp. 325-26, cites this statement to prove that Garrison did oppose the Liberty party on principle, but he quotes it in an 1843-1844 context, showing Garrison's alleged reaction to the increasing strength of the Liberty party, and he comments, "Such statements fooled no one. . . ." Yet by October 1841, such successes as the party was to enjoy were in the future. According to Fladeland, *Birney*, p. 188, about one tenth of eligible voters in antislavery societies voted for Birney in 1840.) See also resolution passed at the AASS convention in 1842, reported in *The Liberator*, May 27, 1842. Such statements appeared from time to time in that paper throughout the active life of the Liberty party. Those written by Edmund Quincy in the mid-1840s, when he was editor pro tem. in Garrison's absence, stressed the alleged recreancy of Birney and other Liberty leaders as reason for opposing the party, whereas Garrison most often emphasized arguments against third-partyism per se. In emphasizing their theoretical differences I do not mean to deny that animus influenced their thinking. Historians have dealt at more than adequate length on that motive, and since in my opinion the animus does not fully account for the views expressed, the theories deserve attention on their merits. The conviction that party politics was corrupting caused Mrs. Child to assert that abstention from it was a question of principle. Third-partyism was more corrupting than agitation within the two major parties, she wrote, since it required closer contact with party machinery (see "The Third Party," *ibid.*, July 9, 1841). The difference between her position and Garrison's was, however, largely one of terminology. Abby Kelley shared Mrs. Child's view. See James S. Gibbons to Elizabeth Pease, January 31, 1842, Anti-Slavery Letters, BPL.

50 This may seem inconsistent with the come-outer principle defended by Garrisonians (especially Maria Weston Chapman), who stressed the educational value of bearing witness to an ideal by ostentatiously withdrawing from institutions that trampled on it. Again it should be pointed out that these tactical suggestions were intended to apply only to those abolitionists who did not subscribe to nonresistance, come-outerism, and other aspects of Garrison's radical creed, those who believed in working within the framework of the United States government.

51 See two editorials by Garrison, "Gerrit Smith on Political Action" and "The Licence Law—Political Action," *The Liberator*, January 31 and February 21, 1840.

52 See "To the Abolitionists of Massachusetts," *ibid.*, August 10, 1838;

[Oliver Johnson?], "Anti-Slavery Political Party," *ibid.*, June 26, 1840; L[ydia] M. C[hild], "Talk about Political Party," reprinted from *The National Anti-Slavery Standard* in *The Liberator*, August 5, 1842; E[dmund] Q[uincy], "Liberty Party," *ibid.*, September 22, 1843.

53 "Talk about Political Party," *ibid.*, August 5, 1842. In the issue of September 2, Garrison endorsed "B's" position and defended Mrs. Child's article from the ridicule by Beriah Green in a letter from Green printed in an upstate New York paper.

54 Goodell, "Political Action against Slavery," No. 2, *ibid.*, August 31, 1838; resolution passed at New-England Anti-Slavery Convention, *ibid.*, June 7, 1839.

55 Quoted in Robert Adams, "Nathaniel Peabody Rogers: 1794–1846," *New England Quarterly*, XX (September 1947), 372. See also an 1847 speech by Frederick Douglass, in Philip S. Foner, ed., *The Life and Writings of Frederick Douglass*, I (New York, 1950), 278.

56 Senator Thomas Morris, wrote Garrison, "assumes that 'political action is necessary to produce moral reformation in a nation.' This is to reverse the order of events. Moral reformation is necessary to produce an enlightened, conscientious, impartial political action. A man must first be abolitionized before he will be able or willing to burst the shackles of party, and give his vote for the slave. . . ." *The Liberator*, August 16, 1839.

57 [Oliver Johnson?], "Anti-Slavery Political Party," *ibid.*, June 26, 1840. An earlier part of that editorial warrants quotation: "We are confident that our opinion upon this point is not the result of our peculiar views of the inherent character of government, but of a careful estimate of all the considerations which should have weight with a person who regards it not only right in itself, but a duty, to exercise the elective franchise. That slavery in our country will eventually be abolished by law, (so far as it can be done by such means,) unless the views of the people in relation to government shall undergo a speedy and almost miraculous change, and that every consideration of expediency and duty must naturally operate to induce abolitionists, who vote, to carry out their principles by consistent and persevering political action, is what we fully believe. We urge no arguments, on the anti-slavery platform, to dissuade men from voting. The question is not, whether the ballot-box is not an important instrumentality, which should be wielded by every voter for the promotion of the cause of humanity and freedom; nor whether anti-slavery voters are not under the most sacred obligations to bestow their suffrages upon men who have given unequivocal evidence of their fidelity to the principles of impartial justice; but it is, whether the desired object can be most speedily and effectually accomplished by an organized and independent political party, or by the modes of action hitherto pursued, modified somewhat, perhaps, in the light of past experience. It does not follow, that he who opposes the plan of independent nominations must therefore stay away from the polls, or vote for the pro-slavery candidates of the present parties." And he went on to argue for the scattering policy.

58 "To the Abolitionists of Massachusetts," *ibid.*, August 10, 1838. See also Johnson's article cited in note 57 above; Garrison, " 'Dying Away'—

Another Richmond in the Field—Political Action," *ibid.*, October 1, 1841; E[dmund] Q[uincy], "Liberty Party," *ibid.*, September 22, 1843; Garrison, "The Liberty Party . . . ," *ibid.*, March 12, 1847.

59 See especially [William Goodell], "Circular. *To the Abolitionists of New-York who believe it wrong and absurd to retain a connexion with the* PROSLAVERY PARTIES, *commonly called* WHIG *and* DEMOCRATIC," reprinted from the Cazenovia (New York) *Abolitionist* in *The Liberator*, November 4, 1842.

60 See Goodell, *Slavery and Anti-Slavery*, pp. 518–19. Nonresistants, he wrote, comprised less than one percent of the Massachusetts Society's membership and numbered no more than 100 or 200 in all New England in 1841–1842 and even fewer elsewhere. In the same passage Goodell argued that there was a practical alliance between the Democratic and Whig abolitionists and the nonresistants against the Liberty party.

61 Their vehemence sometimes bordered on the vitriolic, exceeding anything written by Garrison, although his screeds have been emphasized by historians. See, for example, *The True History of the Late Division in the Anti-Slavery Societies*, Being Part of the Second Annual Report of the Executive Committee of the Massachusetts Abolition Society [led by Libertymen] (Boston, 1841) (the part on political action is pp. 22–26); Goodell's Circular, cited in note 59 above; "The American Anti-Slavery Society," by the Rev. C. T. Torrey, reprinted from *The Tocsin of Liberty* in *The Liberator*, November 4, 1842; "A Hundred Conventions," reprinted from *The Herkimer Journal* in *The Liberator*, August 4, 1843.

62 See his letter *ibid.*, August 16, 1844. It should be added that Samuel E. Sewall, a Libertyman, was a Garrisonian also and that loyalty to that group does not by itself indicate concurrence with the views of Garrison. In the cases of Child and Bradburn, however, I believe that two motives were present: first, belief in the "broad platform" policy of AASS organization and opposition to proscriptionism, and second, agreement with Garrison on political tactics (and, incidentally, women's rights). See *ibid.*, March 5, 1841, for Garrison's comment on Bradburn, then a member of the Massachusetts House of Representatives from Nantucket. Reprinting a letter to the editor of *The Boston Atlas* praising Bradburn, Garrison wrote that it should be read by "the editor of the Friend of Man [Goodell], and all others who insist that no man can be a true abolitionist who is elected to office by the whig or democratic party."

63 For his low opinion of Garrison, see Bailey to Birney, October 14, 1837, and April 18, 1840, *Birney Letters*, I, 428, 556–57. In an editorial reprinted in *The Liberator*, December 6, 1839, Bailey wrote that many of his views on third party coincided with those expressed in a recent address by the Massachusetts Anti-Slavery Society's board of managers. Bailey supported Harrison in 1840, but his views on issues other than slavery coincided with those of the Democrats. See Bailey to Birney, February 21, 1840, and March 3, 1840, *Birney Letters*, I, 531–32, 535–38.

64 "A Separate Political Organization," reprinted in *The Liberator*, December 6, 1839. In an article reprinted *ibid.*, July 17, 1840, Bailey argued that a vote for Birney would help elect Van Buren, and that

although the Whigs, if elected, would be no more friendly to abolitionists than would the Democrats, abolitionists could exert more influence
on the Whigs. Within a year, however, Bailey went over to the Liberty
party. His conversion is noted in Bretz, "The Economic Background of
the Liberty Party," *American Historical Review*, XXXIV (January
1929), 256.

65 "The Liberty Party . . .," *The Liberator*, March 12, 1847. Expressing the same thought in negative terms, he wrote, "Political action is not
moral action, any more than a box on the ear is an argument." "James G.
Birney—The Liberty Party," *ibid.*, March 13, 1846.

7

PRINCIPLE
AND EXPEDIENCY

A CHRONIC PROBLEM of all movements for change is the relation of principle to expediency. The various schools of abolitionist thought approached the problem in different ways, and their approaches may be compared by analyzing their solutions to several key tactical questions, among them the appropriate response to the development of the Free Soil movement of 1848 and the correct interpretation of the United States Constitution.

The various theories of political action discussed in Chapter 6 suggest how each group would react to the Free Soil movement. Most radicals and two-party abolitionists, for different reasons, welcomed it. The Libertymen divided; some went along with the experiment, while others feared and deplored it, for reasons similar to those of the radicals for welcoming it. The Liberty Leaguers took part in the Free Soil convention, but most refused to accept its candidate and platform.[1]

Julian P. Bretz has shown how the Liberty party's argument in the early 1840s that the slave power controlled the government and caused the depression tended to secularize the party, for that thesis encouraged it to appeal principally to the interests of Northern whites. "With secularization," he adds, "went, almost as a matter of course, the development of more moderate anti-slavery doctrines." Among the causes of this change was the fact that parties must compromise with principle.

> The Liberty party might continue to insist that its paramount object was human freedom, but the fact remained that its activities were chiefly directed against the slave power as a political and economic force, and not against the existence of slavery in the states. The separation of the national government from slavery was, politically, an attainable end, while emancipation was not.[2]

The party's platform in 1844 bears out Bretz's judgment; it does not call for federal interference with slavery in the states, but merely demands "the absolute and unqualified divorce of the General Government from Slavery."[3]

A straw in the wind was the 1846 coalition of the New Hampshire Liberty party with Whigs and independent Democrats to elect a Whig governor and send John P. Hale to Congress. Another indication of the direction in which the political wind was blowing was the Liberty party's own nomination of Hale for President in 1848. To some Libertymen this straw was the last: Hale was considered a nonextensionist, not an abolitionist. What had happened to the party's fundamental principle that an abolitionist must never vote for a nonabolitionist? If such a departure from principle could be justified by the need for votes, the next step, though distasteful, was certainly logical: to replace Hale by a candidate who was even more "available"—Martin Van Buren. Some Libertymen could not conceive of supporting the man who in 1836 had pledged to veto any bill to abolish slavery in the District of Columbia. His nominator at the Free Soil convention, however, announced that Van Buren would now be willing to sign such a bill, and the former President received a majority on the first ballot. Hale withdrew, and his supporters made the vote unanimous. Those Libertymen who could not stomach Van Buren joined the Leaguers in nominating Gerrit Smith.[4]

The efforts by some Liberty party leaders to broaden their party's public appeal had begun years before. As early as 1842,

Salmon P. Chase, future Secretary of the Treasury under Lincoln, and other Libertymen in Ohio had worked to replace Birney by a more moderate candidate and to modify the party's platform.[5] After 1845, according to Joseph P. Rayback, their movement was aided by a number of developments: the start of the attempt by Birney and others to transform the Liberty party into a universal-reform party, which alienated many moderates; the founding in Washington, D.C., of *The National Era*, the Liberty party organ edited by Gamaliel Bailey, which enabled the Ohio group to publicize its program; Birney's ill health, which freed many Libertymen to support another candidate; the party's poor showing in the 1845 and 1846 elections; and "the introduction of the Wilmot Proviso, with its accompanying upsurge of antislavery feeling among the rank and file of the older political organizations and the fusion of all these elements in many local elections, which made it apparent that Chase's schemes were not without merit."[6] The logical next step of the coalitionists was to join antislavery Whigs and Barnburner Democrats (reform Democrats in New York State) in the Free Soil convention in 1848. Those political abolitionists who had recoiled at the nomination of Hale had already been alienated by what they interpreted as the sacrifice of principle to expediency, and many others who considered it a high but justified price for a broad popular base found it possible to pay a somewhat higher price for an even broader popular base. Part of that higher price was the nomination of Van Buren, leader of the Barnburner element in the Free Soil coalition.

Some Libertymen who had accepted Hale's candidacy drew back, not only from the nomination of the former President but from the much more significant part of the purchase price: a weaker platform. Moreover, according to Eric Foner, "the Free Soilers were the first major antislavery group to avoid the question of Negro rights in their national platform," owing to the Barnburners' opposition.[7] On the slavery question, the major difference between the Liberty platform of 1844 and the Free Soil platform of 1848 was that the latter contained an explicit disclaimer of any intention to interfere with slavery in the states. In addition, the Free Soilers omitted the Libertymen's denunciation of the three-fifths and fugitive-slave clauses in the Constitution.[8] The A & F, which had endorsed Hale (whereupon Birney, in disgust, had resigned as one of its vice-presidents[9]), addressed an impassioned plea to Libertymen not to let themselves be swallowed up in a new coalition with large segments of the old parties, a coalition that demanded not abolition but nonextension.

> Do not, we beseech you, retreat—under the pretence that you can thus urge on more effectually those who have just commenced the march of liberty. This is not the way to influence men nor to preserve your own integrity. Sound philosophy and political experience show that those worthy to conquer must lead, and that they who are feeling the first aspirations of freedom will follow those who bear the loftiest standard.
>
> Is it said, this is a "crisis"—a "special case"—"unite this once," and the Liberty party hereafter can act as efficiently as before? This is the stereotyped declaration on the eve of every Presidential election. . . . At every election temptations will be presented to postpone action on the great objects of your association, to carry some collateral issue, and thus friends or foes essay to make you instrumental in achieving inferior good at the expense of fundamental principles. . . . Never risk the success of the cause by making an issue on a minor point.[10]

The Liberty Leaguers, who made an issue on nineteen minor points, agreed fully with the Libertymen who refused to board the Van Buren bandwagon. Their common ground was the Free Soil party's failure to make an issue on the major point: abolition. In his history of the antislavery movement, William Goodell observed that the Free Soil program endorsed cheap postage, internal improvements, retrenchment of government expenses, free homesteads, a revenue tariff, and other reforms; it had as many collateral planks as the Liberty League's platform, "but omitting '*the one idea*' of a direct abolition of slavery. Yet it was eagerly embraced by many

who had scarcely ceased from protesting against the introduction of other topics by the Liberty League, in connection with
the highest standard of anti-slavery action."[11]

From the Libertymen's point of view, the Free Soil party
combined the worst features of the major parties and the
Liberty League—respectively, the absence of an abolition
plank and a multitude of distracting demands that appealed
only to the selfish interests of Northern whites. From the Liberty Leaguers' point of view, the Free Soil party combined the
worst features of the major parties and the Liberty party—
respectively, the absence of an abolition plank and a consequent refusal to relate slavery to all the other evils that beset
American society. While the substitution of nonextension for
abolition caused some abolitionists to denounce the Free Soil
movement, it caused other political abolitionists to embrace it,
for it provided them with the opportunity to satisfy their own
desire to work within the political main stream.

Like those who nominated Gerrit Smith, the radical abolitionists pointed out that the Free Soil party had lowered the
abolition standard, but like the coalitionists they welcomed
free-soilism. With the exception of a few individuals, the
radicals hailed it not for what it was but for what it represented: the growth of antislavery sentiment to the point where
large segments of the old parties were willing to break with
their parties and take a more advanced position.

The differences between the majority and the minority of
radicals had been forecast in a debate at the annual meeting of
the AASS in May 1846. Sidney Howard Gay offered a resolution praising Senator Joshua R. Giddings for being "as faithful
as his position will permit him to be to his duty." Stephen S.
and Abby Kelley Foster objected to praising a man who was
not an abolitionist, but Gay and Garrison argued that Giddings had done what he considered his duty and deserved
commendation as a friend of the slave. Mrs. Foster proposed
that the resolution be amended to insert the word *false* before
position, and the modified resolution passed.[12] An even clearer
forecast of the radicals' attitude toward the Free Soil movement
was a resolution passed early in 1848 by the Massachusetts

Anti-Slavery Society. The society rejoiced at the widespread support for the Wilmot Proviso, as evidence of awakening opposition to slavery, and it felt certain that many people thought the Proviso would prevent extension of slavery; yet it disagreed with such people, for "the attempt to restrain slavery by laws and constitutions is precisely equivalent to damming up the Mississippi with bulrushes."[13]

The organization of the Independent Democratic, or Free Soil, party evoked a number of detailed statements of the radical position by Edmund Quincy, one of the editors pro tem. of *The Liberator* in the summer of 1848, when Garrison was ill.[14] The first major editorial on the subject opened with the observation that for almost thirty years there had been but one party in the United States—the slavery party—which had been governing the country "through the factions springing from local or economical interests, into which the population of the country has, from time to time, divided itself." Most people did not realize that their parties were mere instruments of the slave power, but, largely owing to the unremitting agitation by abolitionists, they were now beginning to see that their parties were powerless for good. The disintegration of these parties, continued Quincy, was cause for rejoicing. Yet the new movement was far behind the abolitionists, whose task now was to remain in the van in order to lead the new movement to yet loftier heights. Abolitionists must recognize that free-soilism proposed merely to prevent the enemy from occupying new regions. Useful as this service would be, it must be regarded as subordinate to the abolitionists' demand for the destruction of the enemy. "But while the Abolitionists who accept the morality and the method of the American Anti-Slavery Society, cannot act with the Free Soil party in its organization and at the polls, they must watch its progress with lively interest, and cannot help giving it incidental assistance." Here Quincy distinguished between the Free Soil and Liberty parties. Although he acknowledged that the latter included "in its ranks, and even among its prominent candidates, sincere abolitionists and well-meaning men," he declared that it was an antagonist, not an ally, of the antislavery movement, having been formed to fight abolition rather than slavery. The Free Soil party, on the contrary, sprang "from an honest hatred of Slavery, or genuine jealousy of its encroachments, and it is led by men whose purity of purpose and personal honor are above suspicion. Its direction is the same as ours. Our relations are not incompatible with mutual respect, sympathy, and, to a degree, co-operation." The steadfast and uncompromising adherence to abolition principles that had educated the public mind up to free-soilism must be maintained to carry that mind to an ever more advanced position.

> The greatest possible expediency is a rigid adherence to the highest absolute right. Even for the multiplying of Free Soil votes this would be the best policy. Wherever the Abolitionists . . . have thus aroused the moral sense and made the conscience uncomfortable and desirous of relief, in nine cases out of ten the persons thus acted upon would seek it, in the first instance, in a Free Soil vote. . . . [I]t was our agitation alone that kept the Third [Liberty] party alive, until it was merged in the Independent Democratic party. . . .[15]

In the next issue, Quincy continued his analysis. He asserted that even if the Free Soil party should succeed in its object, slavery would continue to exist and flourish. Hence, the new party was "a hopeful movement rather with regard to the hopeless character of the parties from which its constituent elements have separated themselves than to the broad views and high objects of the party itself." Abolitionists should welcome it only as a sign of discontent with the existing political situation and as a reaching out for something better. "If it stop where it is, and make no forward movement hereafter, it would be better for it and its members if it had never been born." The abolitionist movement was revolutionary, he added, in that it struck "at an essential element—at the government—of our Institutions. . . . The Free Soil party, however, is not in its nature and purposes a Revolutionary party. For it does not aim at the life, but only at the growth of Slavery. . . ."[16]

The fundamental difference between the attitudes toward the Free Soil party adopted by the radicals and by the coalitionists is suggested by the latter's approach to the race issue. A recent study explains that although it was the Barnburners' opposition that caused the 1848 platform to omit a call for equal rights for Negroes, the Free Soil platform continued to avoid that issue after the Barnburners had returned to the Democratic party. The Whigs and Libertymen who in 1852 controlled the Free Soil party "realized that in a society characterized by an all but universal belief in white supremacy, no political party could function effectively which included a call for equal rights in its national platform."[17] Here is suggested the difference between the concept of an antislavery party as the abolitionist vanguard, the chief instrument for abolishing slavery, and the Garrisonian concept of the party as only the most advanced portion to date of the broad constituency among which the AASS as the abolitionist vanguard agitated. When the Libertymen in the Free Soil party played down the equal-rights issue, to gain wide support among a racist constituency, they were separating what had always been linked in the antislavery society constitutions and abolitionist propaganda: abolition of slavery and conversion of the white man to the acceptance of the Negro as his brother. In fact, the abolitionists' denial that their agitation would lead to bloodshed had always been based on the insistence that abolition would result from that conversion. A large segment of the political abolitionist movement was now tacitly giving up this traditional assumption and substituting for it the thesis that abolition could be effected by political means alone. This thesis rested, consciously or not, on a theory of what an antislavery party in the North could do to end slavery in the South, and that theory, in turn, must include an idea of what the Constitution of the United States permitted or required the federal government to do about slavery.

BY THAT TIME three abolitionist theories of the connection between antislavery political action and the nature of the Constitution had emerged. First, the coalitionists, with minor differences among them, generally believed that the Constitution was antislavery in over-all spirit but contained several clauses that for the time being legitimized slavery in the states. The task of antislavery political action was to divorce the federal government from slavery, that is, to abolish slavery in places where Congress exercised sole jurisdiction (the District of Columbia and the territories); to abolish the interstate slave trade, a business which in this theory came within the purview of the commerce clause; and to admit no new states with proslavery constitutions. Such actions would place the institution of slavery under official odium, prevent it from expanding, block the redistribution of human chattels from the upper to the lower South, and doom slavery to extinction. Second, the Liberty Leaguers, and most of those Liberty party men who refused to join the Free Soil coalition, interpreted the Constitution as a thoroughly antislavery document and insisted it gave Congress technically the right, and morally the duty, to abolish slavery in the states. Hence a party that called for nonextension rather than abolition relinquished the fundamental principle that gave the abolitionist movement its reason for being. A party that acknowledged the constitutionality of slavery in the states, asserted this contingent of the movement, was to that extent a proslavery party and gave up the Constitution to the slave power. Third, the Garrisonians believed the Constitution a proslavery document, conceived in compromise and dedicated to the perpetuity of slavery. One reason they welcomed the Free Soil party was that in their view it opposed slavery as far as a party could within the framework of the American constitutional system. Of the three theories, the Garrisonian was the only one that saw a legitimate distinction between the vanguard abolitionist movement and an antislavery political movement, two groups that perforce operated on different principles but were nevertheless not hostile to one another.[18]

Until the early 1840s, abolitionists' statements about the Constitution were random, superficial, and contradictory; citations from them would have little significance for an analysis of the leaders' opinions about the government and the problem of relating expediency to principle in political action. The many early statements that the Constitution did not guarantee slavery or that it outlawed slavery did not reflect systematic analysis of that document. They represent a more or less automatic use of a ready-made weapon wielded by people who wanted to convert the public and who intuitively knew that it was to their advantage to have as many revered institutions on their side as possible. And the many statements disclaiming any unconstitutional purpose and assuring Southerners that abolitionists relied on them rather than on the federal government to abolish slavery represent equally automatic uses of a tactical device by people who intuitively understood that they should not unnecessarily antagonize potential converts. Carefully worked-out theories began to take form in response to a number of later developments: the earlier signs of what was to become Garrison's disunionist position, the publication in 1840 of Madison's notes on the Convention of 1787,[19] the government's steps toward annexation of Texas, the Supreme Court's decision in *Prigg v. Pennsylvania,* and the Liberty party's need to justify its existence within the nation's political framework, yet distinct from the two major parties.

Lysander Spooner posed the problem with remarkable bluntness: "If abolitionists think that the constitution supports slavery, they ought not to ask for power under it, nor to vote for any one who will support it. Revolution should be their principle." The majority of Northerners, he wrote, opposed slavery; all they needed was to be shown that abolition was consistent with "their constitutional faith." On the other hand:

> To say, as many abolitionists do, that they will do all they constitutionally can towards abolishing slavery, is virtually saying that they will do nothing, if they grant at the same time, that the constitution supports slavery. To suppress the slave trade between the States, as some propose, is certainly violating the spirit, and probably the law, of the constitution, if slavery be constitutional.[20]

It would perhaps be uncharitable to assume that the logical relation of theory to practice, here so clearly expressed, provided some political abolitionists with their motive for finding slavery unconstitutional. At the very least, the reader must

admire the clarity with which Spooner, a Massachusetts lawyer, saw how a painstaking analysis of the points at which
slavery conflicted with the Constitution coincided with the
desire of many abolitionists to adopt arguments and tactics not
only within a revered tradition but professedly rescuing that
tradition from those who would pervert it. By the late 1840s,
the anticoalition political abolitionists and the Garrisonians had
made the choice: those who nominated Gerrit Smith in 1848
were sure the Constitution was thoroughly antislavery, and
the Garrisonians had earlier discovered it was thoroughly proslavery. Hence both groups stood apart from the Free Soil
party.

The position of those Western Libertymen who were to
enter the Free Soil coalition was spelled out by one of their
leaders in a letter to Gerrit Smith in 1842. "[W]hile we maintain a steadfast adherence to our principles," wrote Salmon P.
Chase,

> we think it not advisable to incur any unnecessary
> odium. . . . [T]he allegation against us of an intention
> to interfere with slavery in the States by the exercise of
> physical or political power prejudices against us many
> worthy and sensible people, who think that the Constitu-
> tion authorizes no such interference. We are ourselves
> almost unanimous in this opinion. We think, therefore,
> that it is unwise by any part of our political action, to
> afford occasion for such a charge against us. We prefer
> to let the burden of devising the best mode and of reduc-
> ing to practice the best mode of negro emancipation in
> the Slave states, rest upon those States. We believe that if
> the General Government can be made to act right and to
> set an example in favor of liberty, there are several slave
> states which would hasten to follow it, and that the
> example of them would speedily be followed by the rest.
> We prefer, therefore, to direct all the energies of our
> political action against the unconstitutional encroach-
> ments of the Slave Power and against Slavery itself
> wherever it may exist without constitutional sanction.
> Standing on this ground and directing our exertions to
> those objects we obtain the cooperation of many who are

not prepared to go beyond, and who, nevertheless, will go for amendments to the Constitution, in case it shall be found impossible to deliver the country from the manifold evils which result from slavery without such amendments.

When I say that we are against slavery wherever it exists without constitutional warrant I mean that we are against Slavery in the District of Columbia, in Florida & on the seas; in short we hold that no man can be constitutionally held as property in this country except *in a state* where the local constitution maintains slavery. . . . Slavery is against common law & na[tural rig]ht and can exist only in virtue of municipal law of the State.[21]

When the Free Soil convention met in Buffalo in August 1848, the disparate elements worked out an arrangement whereby the Libertymen secured the platform they wanted and the Barnburners furnished the candidate. The platform can thus be considered to represent at least the public views of Chase, Joshua Leavitt, Henry B. Stanton, William Lewis, and other abolitionists in the coalition. Among its planks were several dealing with the constitutionality of slavery. They stated that slavery depended on state law alone, Congress having no power over slavery in the states; that the early policy of the Union was to discourage slavery; that the federal government had no power to deprive anyone of life, liberty, or property without due process of law (but that presumably the Fifth Amendment did not prohibit the states from doing so); that Congress had no power to institute slavery anywhere; that it was the federal government's duty to abolish slavery where it possessed power and to prohibit its extension; and that Congress must not admit any more slave states or permit slavery in any territory.[22]

The theory that the Constitution outlawed slavery in the states took shape slowly. The Liberty party did not take an official position until the mid-forties,[23] although it is hard to see how, without one, a group advocating abolition of slavery throughout the nation could justify its existence for several years as a party within the American political framework. As late as May 1844, its standard bearer was expressing conventional views on the question. "Slavery," wrote Birney,

> so far from promoting any of the objects of the Constitution, is hostile to every one of them—to Union, to justice, to domestic tranquil[l]ity, to the common defense, to the permanent welfare and the security of Liberty. . . . The National legislation ought, to the very verge of Constitutional law, to favor and exalt our free institutions. . . . Do the Free States deplore the existence of slavery and wish for its extinction without violence to the Constitutional rights of the Slave States? . . . [Let them] demand of the appointing power that no slaveholders be appointed to offices under the gov't. If this was done Slavery would die out in five years without violation of the letter or the spirit of the Constitution.[24]

Shortly thereafter, Birney advocated the same policy of appointing only nonslaveholders to office, but this time he added, "My mind strongly inclines to the opinion, that, if Congress can rightfully abolish slavery in time of *war*, it may also abolish it in time of *peace*." In support of this inclination he argued that the principles of liberty asserted in the Declaration of Independence had been substantially incorporated into the Constitution, and that the Fifth Amendment, declaring that no person should be deprived of liberty without due process of law, furnished the federal government with the necessary authorization.[25] In subsequent letters on the constitutional question, Birney stressed one theme: that since Congress had no constitutional power to establish slavery, it had exceeded its delegated powers every time it admitted a slave state.[26] It would seem, then, that he would still consider slavery in the original thirteen states to be constitutional. By 1850 he had finally relinquished that belief and pronounced the theory that under the Constitution all slaves in the United States could be liberated "the only one that can be well defended."[27]

Birney's caution was not emulated by William Goodell, Lysander Spooner, and Gerrit Smith.[28] Their doctrine—that the Constitution was an antislavery document—was, according to Theodore C. Smith, "a questionable theory at best." Nevertheless, he writes, it was "very welcome to the souls of impatient abolitionists," and three conventions in the Midwest and one in Boston endorsed it.[29] It was embodied most fully in Goodell's *Views of American Constitutional Law* and Spooner's *The Unconstitutionality of Slavery*, published in 1844 and 1845 respectively, and became one of the issues on which the Liberty Leaguers split from the more cautious leaders of the Liberty party in 1847.[30]

Spooner, a lawyer, opens by expounding a number of general principles in the light of which he later examines the Constitution of the United States. First, all law is grounded in the natural rights of individuals; law is that rule or principle of justice which protects those rights. No statute that conflicts with this higher law can be binding. Second, the legitimate object of government is to authorize the adoption of means, consistent with natural justice, to protect men's natural rights. Laws consistent with this object are binding, for government is created by a voluntary contract among men. Since the object of the contract is to protect natural rights, a contract between men to commit murder or between two nations to plunder a third is void and of no obligation. The third principle follows from the first two: since a constitution sets forth the terms of the contract, "*constitutional law, under any form of government, consists only of those principles, of the written constitution, that are consistent with natural law, and man's natural rights.*" Slavery obviously is unconstitutional according to this doctrine.[31]

Spooner then analyzes the American colonial charters and statutes, the Declaration of Independence, the state constitutions of 1789, the Articles of Confederation, the Constitution, the intentions of the Convention of 1787, and subsequent practice. He first deprives the slaveholders of colonial precedent by arguing that toleration of slavery in the colonies is no evidence of its legality. On the contrary, slavery was illegal according to English common law, which the settlers brought with them to America.[32] Slavery can be legalized, if at all, only by positive legislation that precisely describes the persons to be enslaved, and no colonial statutes did so.[33] But even if

slavery had been lawful before 1776, the Declaration of Independence, which was "the constitutional law of this country
for certain purposes," abolished it. Hence, even if there had
been slaves in the colonies, the Declaration freed them, "and
the burden would then be upon the slaveholder to show that
slavery had *since* been *constitutionally* established."[34] Every
passage in state constitutions that recognizes slavery was inserted after the adoption of the Constitution of the United
States, Spooner continues. The use of the word "freemen" in
some of them, he insists, does not weaken his argument, for
"freemen" is not necessarily the opposite of "slaves." It is an
old English term used to distinguish citizens having certain
privileges from aliens who did not have them. But even if the
word is used to distinguish between free men and slaves, the
term is insufficient to legitimize slavery, according to the
principle that

> Slavery is so entirely contrary to natural right; so en-
> tirely destitute of authority from natural law; so palpably
> inconsistent with all the legitimate objects of govern-
> ment, that nothing but express and explicit provision can
> be recognized, in law, as giving it any authority. . . . It
> is a rule of law, in the construction of all statutes, con-
> tracts and legal instruments whatsoever—*that is, those
> which courts design, not to invalidate, but to enforce*—
> that where words are susceptible of two meanings, one
> consistent, and the other inconsistent, with liberty, jus-
> tice and right, that sense is always to be adopted, which is
> consistent with right, unless there be something in other
> parts of the instrument sufficient to prove that the other
> is the true meaning.[35]

Up to this point, Spooner contends, he has proved that
slavery did not legally exist in the United States before 1787.
Did the Constitution establish it? Even defenders of slavery do
not assert, he writes, that the Constitution created the institution; "the most they claim is, that it recognized it as an institution already legally existing, under the authority of the State
governments; and that it virtually guaranteed to the States the

right of continuing it in existence during their pleasure." But since he has already proved that it did not legally exist in the states, he can, he says, rest his case here. And since the Constitution made all the people of the United States citizens, no state could thereafter reduce any of its people to slavery, for the Constitution of the United States was made the supreme law of the land.[36]

Yet Spooner chooses to examine the Constitution itself, to refute the arguments of those who say it sanctions slavery. Those arguments, he writes, are not and cannot be based on the actual words of the document, for everyone admits that the words are ambiguous. Some therefore say that certain words in the Constitution are capable of being interpreted in a proslavery way and that that interpretation is buttressed by historical and circumstantial evidence. But, replies Spooner, this is substituting

> the supposed intentions of those who drafted the constitution, for the intentions of the constitution itself; and, secondly, it personifies the constitution as a crafty individual; capable of both open and secret intentions; capable of legally participating in, and giving effect to all the subtleties and double dealings of knavish men. . . .

On the contrary, he insists: "Its intentions are no guide to its legal meaning . . . ; but its legal meaning is the sole guide to its intentions." How is its legal meaning to be discerned? Anything consistent with natural right may be legalized and sanctioned by implication and inference, but anything contrary to natural right can be sanctioned, if at all, only by distinct, unequivocal, and unambiguous terms "to which no other meaning can be given." Judges have always known that nothing contrary to natural justice can be made law even by explicit enactment. But in England and the United States judges have depended on executives and legislatures for appointment and have in practice compromised with this vital principle. In so doing, however, they have avoided direct collision by insisting that the terms of a statute in conflict with natural law

be so explicit that they cannot deny its authority without
"flatly denying the authority of those who enacted it."[37]

In the light of these principles of construction, Spooner
examines the words of the Constitution. The so-called fugitive-
slave clause does not, he points out, contain the words *slave* or
slavery. Since of two alternative constructions the one consistent with freedom is to be preferred, he declares that some
other kind of service or labor must be found for the clause to
apply to. Using historical evidence (which he earlier declared
irrelevant), he finds that at the time of the 1787 Convention,
indentured servants constituted a distinct class, referred to by
many laws. "Persons held to service or labor" thus were indentured servants and apprentices. Furthermore, the phrase is
not a legal description of slaves, for "slavery is property in
man. It is not necessarily attended with either 'service or
labor,'" since very young and very old slaves do not work.[38]

A similar analysis is made of the three-fifths clause, the
proslavery interpretation of which depends on a distinction
between "free" persons and "all others." According to his
principle that of two possible constructions the "innocent"
one is to be used, Spooner argues that "free" is not the opposite of "slave." In old English usage it described persons pos-
sessing certain privileges denied to aliens.[39] Spooner applies
similar reasoning to demonstrate that the other clauses so often
cited to show the constitutionality of slavery are susceptible to
interpretations consistent with freedom.[40]

Spooner disposes of legal precedent with the argument that
the legal meaning of a written constitution cannot be changed
by practice, or it ceases to be a standard for practice. Hence it
does not matter what meaning the government has placed on
the Constitution; what does matter is the meaning the government was bound to place on it from the beginning.[41] Did the
people really understand the Constitution to sanction slavery?
The answer, writes Spooner, is of no legal import, yet it is
pertinent. The slaveholders were a minority, but they were
united and influential, dominated the poor whites, and controlled the state governments. But he had earlier proved that
all thirteen original states had had "free" constitutions in 1787;

hence, it is absurd to say that the people intended to establish a Constitution over all that legalized slavery.[42] Similar reasoning fills the remaining nine chapters of this fascinating tract.

In grappling with the obvious question—why slaveholders would have consented to the compact he has described— Spooner declares that in law it is considered reasonable for a man to do justice contrary to his apparent pecuniary interests. In fact, "when communities establish governments for the purpose of maintaining justice and right, the assent of all the thieves, robbers, pirates, and slaveholders, is as much presumed as is the assent of the most honest portion of [the] community."[43]

Repeatedly Spooner insists that the Constitution was in reality very different from what everyone thought it was. The same extreme emphasis on theoretical principles is apparent in the author's assumption of the tactical value of his efforts. He took it for granted that the same natural reason, unaffected by interest, custom, or prejudice, that determined the real nature of the Constitution, would convert his readers to the Truth. He remarked to a correspondent that John C. Calhoun had correctly characterized Northern public opinion: five percent of Northerners were for slavery, five percent abolitionist, twenty percent opportunists who would side with the strongest party, and the remaining seventy percent people who disliked slavery but were unwilling to defy the Constitution. Spooner concluded that if abolitionists showed slavery to be unconstitutional, they would have the support of ninety-five percent of the North. Does this not prove, he asked, that our most important task is to spread the truth about the Constitution?[44] Just as the Constitution must be interpreted in accordance with the principles of natural justice, so, assumed Spooner, it would be read by the light of disinterested natural reason, if abolitionists shed that light by distributing his treatise.

SPOONER'S REASONING, wrote Garrison, was "ingenious— perhaps, as an effort of logic, unanswerable." But Garrison thought it likely that the American people, when they adopted the Constitution, knew what they were doing. "Fact is to be preferred to logic; intention is mightier than legal interpretation," and the important thing is not "the words of the bargain," but "the bargain itself."[45]

The distinction, discussed in earlier chapters, between Garrison's beliefs as a nonresistant and his position as an abolitionist is especially necessary to an understanding of his well-known but little analyzed theory that the Constitution was a proslavery document. When in 1837 he repudiated allegiance to forceful government, he did so as a nonresistant, to whom the relation of the United States Constitution to slavery was irrelevant; proslavery or antislavery, the Constitution was the fundamental law of a coercive regime. Not until a few years later did Garrison the abolitionist fully work out a theory that the Constitution was a proslavery document, a theory that won the concurrence of the non-nonresistant Wendell Phillips and coincided with the interpretation of the non-nonresistant John C. Calhoun, and that did not appear to all nonresistants to be a necessary corollary of their pacifist philosophy.[46]

The first signs of the direction in which his constitutional thinking was heading were a few minor articles pointing out proslavery clauses in the Constitution and the slaveholders' dependence on the Union to protect them against their human chattels.[47] By the beginning of 1842 Garrison was ready to urge his new theory from the antislavery platform, and he did so at a meeting of a society controlled by his followers.[48] On that occasion he presented and defended the following resolutions:

> Whereas, the existence of slavery is incompatible with the enjoyment of liberty in any country;
> And whereas, it is morally and politically impossible for a just or equal union to be formed between Liberty and Slavery;
> And whereas, in the adoption of the American Constitution, and in the formation of the Federal Government, a guilty and fatal compromise was made by the people of the North with southern oppressors, by which slavery has been nourished, protected and enlarged up to the

present hour, to the impoverishment and disgrace of the nation, the sacrifice of civil and religious freedom, and the crucifixion of humanity;

And whereas, the slaveholding States make even moral opposition to their slave system a capital offence, and avow their determination to perpetuate that system at all hazards, and under all circumstances;

And whereas, the right of petition has been repeatedly cloven down on the floor of Congress, and is no longer enjoyed by the people of the free States—the liberty of speech and the press is not tolerated in one half of the Union—and they are regarded and treated as outlaws by the South, who advocate the cause of universal emancipation; therefore,

1. Resolved, That the American Union is, and ever has been since the adoption of the Constitution, a rope of sand—a fanciful nonentity—a mere piece of parchment —'a rhetorical flourish and splendid absurdity'—and a concentration of the physical force of the nation to destroy liberty, and to uphold slavery.

2. Resolved, That the safety, prosperity and perpetuity of the non-slaveholding States require that their connexion be immediately dissolved with the slave States in form, as it is now in fact.

3. Resolved, That the southern slave system is wholly dependant [*sic*] upon the physical force of the North for its existence; and therefore that a dissolution of the Union would certainly abolish that system, and thus remove from the South the heaviest curse that was ever inflicted upon any portion of the globe, and bestow upon her the richest blessings of heaven. . . .

6. Resolved, That the petition presented to the United States House of Representatives, by John Quincy Adams, from sundry inhabitants of Haverhill, in this county, praying Congress to take measures for a peaceful dissolution of the Union, meets our deliberate and cordial approval. . . .

These sentiments were a bit strong even for the Essex County society, and the resolutions were tabled.[49] By the middle of April several Garrisonian societies had passed disunion resolutions and the time seemed ripe to have the national society itself face the question boldly. Garrison accordingly wrote an editorial that called for a large attendance at the May convention of the AASS, and in it he ventured the opinion that "Many important topics will be presented for consideration. . . . The milk that has hitherto been used must now give place to meat." Until now the abolitionist movement has, he explained, discussed first principles, but these have been settled; it is no longer necessary to argue the right of men to liberty. Most abolitionists now agree also that the church, at first counted on as their strongest ally, is utterly destitute of the spirit of Christ. But, Garrison continued,

> there are other questions which are not so definitely settled, and to these should special attention be drawn during the anniversary week.
> The first of these, in importance, is the duty of making the REPEAL OF THE UNION between the North and the South, the grand rallying point until it be accomplished, or slavery cease to pollute our soil.[50]

Other newspapers, predictably, publicized these treasonable thoughts. Garrison reprinted an editorial from a New York paper and in his reply repeated the alternatives he had presented in his April 22 piece, but this time the words *or slavery cease to pollute our soil* were italicized. "You can be free," he announced,

> without the shedding of blood. Demand the repeal of the Union, or the abolition of slavery—not as a THREAT, but as a MORAL OBLIGATION—as the performance of an imperative duty to clear your garments from pollution, and your souls from blood-guiltiness. This you have a right to do, by the very theory of your government.

Whereupon he appealed to the Declaration of Independence, Chief Justice Marshall, Thomas Jefferson, and other authorities for the doctrine that the majority had the right to change the government. He ended by asking Northerners in general: If the South depends on you to protect slavery, then who but you are the real slaveholders?[51]

Although Garrison assured his readers that the views expressed in his April 22 editorial were his own, the meat was too strong even for some members of the AASS who had been able to digest his earlier courses. Others among them could swallow disunionism but not the public's insistence on identifying Garrison's views with the official policy of the organization. The executive committee of the AASS therefore published a statement regretting

> that certain publications in the Boston Liberator have been so construed as to commit the Society in the public view in favor of an object which appears to them entirely foreign to the purpose for which it was organized, viz. *Dissolution of the Union*. . . .
>
> This Committee deem it a duty to the Society which they represent, no less than to their fellow citizens, and to themselves personally, to declare that they have not, at any time, either directly or impliedly, authorized such publication; and that it is no part of the object of the American Anti-Slavery Society to promote the dissolution of the Union. The specific objects for which it was organized, are, the abolition of slavery, and the improvement of the colored people; to gain which, it proposes to employ no means but such as are strictly consistent with morality and the rights of citizenship.

It closed by stating that the society was not committed to discuss any particular topic at its coming convention, but that it would not be deterred by threats of violence from doing what it deemed its duty.

Garrison commented that the executive committee had a right to disclaim responsibility for what he had written but not to convey the impression that the course he proposed would be foreign to the purposes of the society or that it would be immoral for the society to discuss the expediency of withdrawing from the Union.[52] To ensure that the approaching convention would be free to discuss the question without the possibly inhibiting effect of his presence, Garrison announced that he would not attend.[53] His views were defended there by Wendell Phillips and Abby Kelley, but, according to

Garrison's account, no vote was taken on the disunion question, the members deciding that the discussion ought to continue uninfluenced by an official declaration of the society.[54]

The furor died down, and little was written in *The Liberator* about disunionism for the rest of the year. In January 1843 the annual meeting of the Massachusetts Anti-Slavery Society was torn by bitter debate over disunionist resolutions,[55] and in March Garrison began heading his editorial column with one resolution adopted at that meeting: "*Resolved*, THAT THE COMPACT WHICH EXISTS BETWEEN THE NORTH AND THE SOUTH IS A 'COVENANT WITH DEATH, AND AN AGREEMENT WITH HELL,'—INVOLVING BOTH PARTIES IN ATROCIOUS CRIMINALITY,—AND SHOULD BE IMMEDIATELY ANNULLED."[56] But political and religious controversies continued to monopolize the paper's attention. In January 1844 Garrison again presented disunion resolutions at the annual meeting of the Massachusetts Society, and again they were tabled,[57] but if the moderate David Lee Child may be believed, "the doctrine of 'Repeal,' as it is called, is gaining, and must gain ground. With me it is a question of time. I am in favor of dissolution, if we cannot have abolition; but I could wish to see all reasonable means used of reforming, before we destroy the Constitution."[58]

Disunionism became the official creed of the AASS by a 59–21 vote at its annual convention in May 1844. The minority included David Lee Child, Thomas Earle, Ellis Gray Loring, and William A. White, who protested the vote, and Child resigned as editor of the society's organ, *The National Anti-Slavery Standard*. Child's letter quoted above and Earle's position at the convention make it clear that their differences with the majority were primarily tactical.[59] The main contribution to the debate was a long address by Garrison "To the Friends of Freedom in the U. States." He contended that "the existing national compact . . . is 'a convenant with death, and an agreement with hell'; inasmuch as it was effected by a bloody compromise . . . ; that it enjoins obligations and duties, which are incompatible with allegiance to God, and with the enjoyment of freedom and equal rights"; that its natural results have been the growth of slavery, imprisonment of northern Negro seamen in Southern ports, theft of the North's wealth, denial of the right of petition, and other outrages; and that friends of liberty have the duty to withdraw their allegiance to it "and by a moral and peaceful revolution to effect its overthrow; in accordance with the doctrines laid down in the American Declaration of Independence." To bring about this peaceful revolution, Garrison proposed eight tactics for the society to pursue. First, the disunion slogan must be given wide publicity. Second, the people of the North must be shown that Union involves them in guilt. Third, disunionism must be discussed prominently in the society's official organ. Fourth, agents must travel and spread the truth to the extent made possible by the society's means. Fifth, the society must discountenance any political party that favors continuing the alliance with the slaveholding states or allowing slaveholders in Congress. Sixth, the society must "persuade northern voters, that the strongest political influence which they can wield for the overthrow of slavery, is, to cease sustaining the existing compact, by withdrawing from the polls, and calmly waiting for the time when a righteous government shall supersede the institutions of tyranny." Seventh, the society must circulate a pledge for men, women, and children to sign, embodying disunion principles. And eighth, the society must try to change public sentiment in the North so as to convince the South that only abolition could make Americans a united people.

The protests presented to the convention demonstrate that there was little love for the Constitution among the members. The chief objections to the new policy were tactical, except for one argument that seems to have caused some bitterness and that appeared in both Loring's and Earle's statements. They contended that the adoption of disunionism was a departure from the society's tradition of leaving modes of action up to individual members, and that the society had constituted itself a tribunal to settle matters of conscience and was in effect as proscriptive as the schismatics of 1840 had tried to make it.

Garrison replied to this damaging argument in a long editorial in the issue of May 24. He opened with a comment that the protests came from tried abolitionists and deserved careful consideration. But they were mistaken; the society had adopted no new test of membership and had not narrowed its platform. Must it adopt only policies that won unanimous assent? There must be unanimity on principles, but if unanimity were required in the application of principles, the society could not function. This year's minority might become next year's majority. Further, the endorsement of disunionism was not the adoption of a creed. The majority had simply announced its convictions, with no thought of proscribing the minority, asking them to resign, or casting doubt on their fidelity to the cause. The comparison with the schismatics was unfair, he argued, for Birney and his cohorts had declared voting a religious duty and had insisted that only those who accepted that theory could be abolitionists in good standing. Not only did the society at the present time not proscribe those who disagreed with the disunionist position, but that position itself was not a creed in the sense in which Birney's "religious duty of voting" had been. That is, the society now said that it was the duty of abolitionists to abstain from *"voting to sustain a blood-cemented Union and a pro-slavery Constitution,"* not to abstain from voting per se or under a form of government in "harmony with the will of God and the freedom of the human mind." This explanation evidently failed to satisfy the doubters, for the accusation of proscriptionism reappeared on subsequent occasions.[60]

Earle's protest also contended that the disunion resolution had been "adopted almost exclusively by the votes of the non-resistant opponents of all human governments, . . . and is, in effect, exclusion of all but that class, from the Society, or a requisition upon them to sustain, by their contributions and countenance, the doctrine of opposition to human government." Garrison replied that he did not know whether most votes for the resolution had been cast by nonresistants. But suppose they had been; if those individuals cast their votes in good faith as abolitionists, should they be reproached because they were also nonresistants? Earle's accusation was echoed by Amos A. Phelps in *The Anti-Slavery Reporter*, which he

edited, and by Gerrit Smith.[61] Garrison replied to Smith in
the September 20 issue and commented that Francis Jackson,
Wendell Phillips, and other non-nonresistants considered the
Constitution proslavery, and he angrily pointed out once more
the

> difference between seceding from a particular govern-
> ment, because of its pro-slavery character, and opposing
> every form of government which is upheld by military
> power—between refusing to support the present Consti-
> tution of the United States, on the ground that it sanc-
> tions the slave system, and opposing every Constitution
> which is enforced at the point of a bayonet—between
> objecting to voting for men who, if elected, must swear
> to sustain oppression, and denouncing voting at the polls
> *per se.* . . .[62]

Garrison ended the editorial with "Let Christ fulfill his mission, for the government is laid on his shoulders; and he (in the
person of his followers, of course,) shall put down all rule, and
all authority and power." These undoubtedly "anti-institutional" sentiments were, it must be reiterated, expressed by
Garrison the individual; they were not part of the doctrine
endorsed by any antislavery society. Earle's final objection was
that the resolution proposed to dissolve the Union before the
society had petitioned for a change in the objectionable features of the Constitution. What! cried Garrison; after the
right of petition has been trampled in the dust and abolitionists
treated as outlaws?

All the arguments on both sides were aired once again at the
New-England Anti-Slavery Convention in May 1844, but on
that occasion disunionism was endorsed by a vote of 250 to
24.[63]

Throughout his career, whenever Garrison took a position
far in advance of others, he always defended his action in part
on the ground that it forced people to think. He must therefore have been gratified by the change in views announced by
two of the best-known protesters at these conventions, J. Miller McKim and David Lee Child. McKim's switch was explained in an article in *The Pennsylvania Freeman,* which he

edited.[64] Child took longer to come around; it was the final consummation of the plot to annex the foreign state of Texas that impelled him to write a letter, which Garrison read to the AASS convention in May 1846. Child wrote that he had hoped that "the audacious encroachments" of the slave power on the Constitution and its "undisguised prostitution of all the powers of the government" would arouse the North to resist. But Northerners dashed his hopes by acquiescing in the unconstitutional joint resolution annexing Texas, a clear evasion of the requirement that two thirds of the Senate concur with the President in any arrangement with a foreign state. As though that were not enough, Congress ignored the Constitution when it admitted the senators and representatives from Texas, despite the constitutional provision that congressmen should be citizens for seven years and senators for nine years; Texas's representatives had not been citizens of the United States for six months. Furthermore, wrote Child, in neither political party could he perceive any remedy for this unsupportable state of things, to which his own state of Massachusetts had tamely submitted. To him the Union was now "loathsome," and he thoroughly approved of the policy of the AASS. "I find in it, and in no other organized or associate action, consolation and hope for American slaves, and for Americans who do not mean to be slaves."[65]

The joint resolution whereby Congress offered annexation to Texas forced a curious ally into the Garrison camp. Judge William Jay, conservative son of the Founding Father John Jay and, unlike Child, never in any way sympathetic to Garrisonian radicalism, announced his conversion to disunionism in a letter to Henry I. Bowditch. Although he retained, on technical grounds, his conviction that an abolitionist could swear to support the Constitution,[66] he declared that he was now abandoning his previous opposition to disunionism. The Constitution's toleration of slavery, Jay explained, did not warrant dissolution, for slavery was confined within limits and as long as it remained so, its extinction was inevitable. Nor did every violation of the Constitution justify dissolution. But the joint resolution, violating the Senate's right to vote by a two-thirds majority on transactions with a foreign state, destroyed the compact itself; it enabled slavery to burst the bounds within which it had been confined and ensured a permanent proslavery majority in the Senate and consequent slaveholding control of the federal government. Its consequences would be the indefinite extension of the southern boundary of the United States, seizure of foreign territory, and spread of slavery into the new acquisitions.

> A mutual compact cannot be binding on one party alone. The compromise of the Constitution, respecting slavery, of which we have heard so much, was nothing more than the absence of any grant of power to the Federal Government, either to abolish, or to nurse, cherish, or protect it, as a national institution. This compromise is now terminated by the late usurpation, and we are left at liberty . . . to war upon slavery by every possible means not forbidden by the law of God. The Constitution is converted into an instrument of cruelty, oppression, and wickedness. It has ceased to be the Constitution, which I have, on various occasions, sworn to support. . . .
>
> Dissolution must take place, and the sooner the better.

Jay contended that duty to the slaves did not, as some abolitionists believed, require maintenance of the Union. The morals and happiness of the children of Northerners ought, he said, to have more weight than the vain hope of freeing the slaves who would populate Texas and the territories to its south. On the other hand, a continuance of the Union would more likely enslave the North than free the South, and "A separation will more easily be effected *now* than when the relative strength of the South shall have been greatly augmented."

Jay then enumerated certain "Present duties of the North." The constitutional right of slaveowners to hunt fugitives in the North must be regarded as abolished. Any individual in the free states who helps to capture a fugitive or who owns a slave must be punished. Whenever a Negro citizen of a Northern state is imprisoned in the South on account of his color, "an adequate number of the citizens of the State committing the outrage, who may be found on our soil," must be seized and held as hostages. Congress and the state legislatures must be petitioned "to take measures for an amicable dissolution of the Union." Jay closed with the remark that he was surprised at how many people, in private conversation, agreed with him.[67]

While Jay's call for disunion was a demand for a simple geographical separation of the free from the slave states, primarily in self-defense, Garrison's call for disunion was strictly an agitational weapon. As always, his arguments were refined in response to others' attacks. In the summer of 1844 Gerrit Smith wrote that Northern disunionism was a case of the pot calling the kettle black: "The slaveholding North, so far from being less guilty than the slaveholding South, is as much guiltier, as greater light and weaker temptation can make it." Agitation for disunion, he contended, would foster the delusion that the North was guiltless and had no other duty than to get out of the bad company into which it had been drawn. Shall we, he asked, blame the Constitution because it does not prohibit slavery? It does not prohibit many other evils; but may we then infer that it is responsible for gambling and drunkenness? Smith repeated that the blame belonged not on the Constitution but on Northerners who could, whenever they chose, elect an antislavery administration in Washington, abolish slavery in areas under congressional jurisdiction, and thus doom the institution. Disunionism operated to relieve Northern consciences, by blaming the Constitution and the Union for the sin of the North.[68]

Garrison denied that he was calling for a simple separation of the North from the South:

The appeal of the Society was not a geographical one, but is addressed to every individual who professes to abhor slavery, wherever he resides on American soil. . . . It has nothing sectional in its spirit or design, any further than one portion of the country may be more disposed to give heed to it than another, owing to a difference in the moral and intellectual condition of the inhabitants.

But suppose the AASS did call upon the North to separate from the South: why should it not ask the people of the North to repudiate their alliance with slaveholders? And suppose Smith were correct in regarding the North as the guiltier section; why, asked Garrison, should not the guiltier section be the first called to repentance? Why should not those who forge the chains be called upon to desist? To tell the North to repudiate its alliance with the South is not to salve Northern consciences, he argued; on the contrary, it is to charge the North with being an accessory to the crime of slavery. But, he repeated, the call for disunion was not addressed to Northern-ers in particular; it was addressed to all the people, "SLAVE-HOLDERS included—to the whole country. It is a simple declara-tion, that liberty and slavery cannot coalesce or exist under the same government; that tyrants, and the enemies of tyranny, can never walk together on amicable and equal terms. . . ." In reply to Smith's statement that in the event of a separation he would go with the South as the less guilty section, Garrison demanded:

> Who proposes a separation between Northern and Southern SLAVEHOLDERS? Who advocates a geo-graphical secession, unless it be preceded by a geographi-cal reformation—and how is that secession possible, so long as both parts of the country remain pro-slavery in spirit? . . . This revolution is to be commenced by *free-men*, carried on by FREEMEN, consummated by FREE-MEN.[69]

The call for disunion was precisely analogous to the call for immediate emancipation and the call for Christlike perfection; it was the statement of a moral imperative, a reveille to the conscience; and it was made by an agitator who knew that those who heard the call were in no condition immediately to translate it into practice.

If abolitionists who wished to operate within the nation's governmental framework needed to discover that the Consti-tution was antislavery or at worst neutral, the radicals were ideologically free to construe the Constitution as the evidence seemed to them to dictate. By temperament standing outside the American value system, they felt no urge to blink at what appeared to have been the immoral connivance of Northerners with Southerners in the Constitutional Convention of 1787, and it is at this point that the alliance of the radicals with the two-party abolitionists obviously had to break down. This is not to say that the interpretation of the Constitution as proslavery was a corollary of nonresistance, for, as noted before, Garrison's constitutional theory coincided with that of the Southerners and of certain abolitionists who were not nonresistants. These abolitionists were, however, radicals too, though not of the nonresistant variety; they too looked at American institutions from the outside and were ideologically free to approve or condemn them, although perhaps their alienation from the received values of their society inclined them toward the latter course.

Not Garrison but Wendell Phillips and Dr. William Ingersoll Bowditch worked out the detailed theory of the Constitution as a proslavery document. As might be expected, Bowditch's analysis occupies far fewer pages than Spooner's.[70] He begins by agreeing with Spooner that ideally human law codifies absolute justice and ought to be relatively constant. Legislators have never yet, however, succeeded in making laws coincide with a people's highest ideas of justice; yet the laws enacted are nevertheless laws. English precedents are irrelevant to the present issue, for the first colonists brought with them only that part of English law that was applicable to their new situation.[71] English courts could not limit the colonists' discretion on the subject of slavery, for those courts had no appellate jurisdiction over colonial courts, and Parliament and the King in council never tried to discourage slavery in America. Furthermore, contends Bowditch, it would be incorrect to argue that the rights to the writ of habeas corpus and to trial by jury outlawed slavery in the colonies, for they had existed side by side with slavery in England for centuries; habeas corpus is intended to prevent unlawful restraint, and if the law recognizes slavery the writ cannot free a slave. Colonial legislatures were competent to legislate on slavery as on other matters of internal policy, and they did so.[72]

Bowditch then rebuts the argument that the Declaration of Independence was part of constitutional law for the purpose of establishing as law the natural right of individuals to liberty. There is, he says, no historical evidence that the people expressly or impliedly gave Congress the power to abolish slavery. It is, then, necessary to examine the first state constitutions and the United States Constitution, and he begins this examination by stating two rules of construction, on the authority of Justice Story, Chief Justice Marshall, and other jurists. First, the words of the Constitution are to be understood in their plain, common sense in the time they were written, unless their context demands a different construction. If acceptance of the common meaning would result in absurdity or injustice, it would be monstrous to construe the words literally, but slavery was not at that time considered absurd or unjust by most people. Second, to discover the true meaning of the words of the Constitution one may examine any evidence that reveals what the social, political, or religious institutions were at the time the document was written.[73]

Spooner had argued that if a word is susceptible to two meanings, one consistent and the other incompatible with justice, the former is to be chosen unless the context requires the latter. Bowditch replies that he knows of only one court decision to support this rule, but that even if it were correct it could apply only to a law and not to a constitution. The people declared the United States Constitution the supreme law of the land. Hence the Constitution must be constant and uniform over a long period. If the meaning of a clause depends on justice, there must be some standard that will always proclaim the same criteria of justice. But there is no such standard; our notions of justice change. Hence, according to Spooner's rule of construction, the Constitution is *not* the supreme law of the land.[74]

So far, says Bowditch, he has proved that slavery existed legally in the colonies. The state constitutions could have abolished it, but they did not. Nor did the Articles of Confederation, which denied to Congress any power not expressly delegated to it. Clearly, the expression *free inhabitants* in the

Articles means those who are not slaves; "free inhabitants" in article 4 include paupers, vagabonds, and fugitives from justice, but the clause excepts them from the guarantee of the privileges and immunities of "free citizens." An examination of the Constitution yields the same results. In the three-fifths clause the "other persons" are obviously slaves, because those bound to service for a term of years are included in the whole number of "free persons." With respect to the slave importation clause, Bowditch refutes Spooner's contention that it could refer to voluntary immigration; Bowditch argues that if *migration* and *importation* had meant the same thing, both words would not have been used. With respect to the fugitive slave clause, Bowditch states that the phrase *persons held to service or labor* was a customary description of slaves at the time of the Convention. He adds that ordinarily the laws of one state do not apply in another, that a slave escaping to a free state would by this rule of law be free, and that the fugitive slave clause was therefore an explicit exception in favor of slavery.[75] The results of all these constitutional compromises, writes Bowditch, have been further compromises and the steady advance of slavery.[76]

Those compromises are discussed in detail in Wendell Phillips's pamphlet *The Constitution a Pro-Slavery Compact*,[77] which contains quotations from and discussions of Madison's notes on the Constitutional Convention, debates in the Confederation Congress and in the state ratification conventions, the Federalist Papers, and other documents. According to Phillips:

> If the unanimous, concurrent, unbroken practice of every department of the Government, judicial, legislative, and executive, and the acquiescence of the whole people for fifty years, do not prove which is the true construction, then how and where can such a question ever be settled? If the people and the courts of the land do not know what they themselves mean, who has authority to settle their meaning for them? . . . What the Constitution may become a century hence, we know not; we speak of it *as it is*, and repudiate it *as it is*.[78]

Some people insist that the revolutionary spirit of the late eighteenth century could not have permitted such an infamous bargain. But, says Phillips, the Constitution was written by "forty of the shrewdest men and lawyers in the land," who spent months in "anxious deliberation." Fifty years have gone by, and at least twenty million of their children have died, courts have passed judgment, political parties have competed, and everyone has agreed on what the Constitution has meant. "[M]ust not he be a desperate man, who, after all this, sets out to prove that the fathers were bunglers and the sons fools, and that slavery is not referred to at all?"

> But if, on the contrary, our fathers failed in their pur-
> pose, and the Constitution is all pure and untouched by
> slavery,—then, Union itself is impossible, without guilt.
> For it is undeniable that the fifty years passed under this
> (anti-slavery) Constitution show us the slaves trebling in
> numbers;—slaveholders, monopolizing the offices and dic-
> tating the policy of the Government;—prostituting the
> strength and influence of the nation to the support of
> slavery here and elsewhere;—trampling on the rights of
> the free States, and making the citizens of the country
> their tools. To continue this disastrous alliance longer is
> madness. The trial of fifty years with the best of men and
> the best of Constitutions, on this supposition, only proves
> that it is impossible for free and slave States to unite on
> any terms, without all becoming partners in the guilt,
> and responsible for the sin of slavery.[79]

Despite the flood of articles and speeches, some readers of *The Liberator* who agreed that the Constitution was proslav-ery balked at disunionism. Wendell Phillips undertook to answer them at the beginning of 1848, in a three-part editorial. First, he explained, we ask for dissolution of the Union be-cause it is our duty to cease to do evil. To the objection that that duty can be done by securing amendments, he replied that three quarters of the states must concur and that in the mean-time those who attempt that course

> must remain in the Union, voting, acting, paying, arm-
> ing, swearing, hunting slaves, putting down insurrections,

etc. etc. till the required number are converted to their side. . . . Dissolution of the Union is a course, by which a man or State may immediately disconnect themselves from the sin of sustaining slavery.—The distant hope of Constitutional amendment not only allows, but makes it *necessary*, that we should remain in the Union, performing its sinful requirements while they continue the law of the land, in order to effect our object.

Dissolution, he declared, can be the work of a minority, but before we can amend the Constitution, we must become a majority. Second, no amendment that can be secured would reach the root of the problem. Amendment can change the *terms* of the contract, but guilt lies in Union itself between slave and free states; consequently only an abolition amendment can be of any use, and such an amendment would of course be unacceptable to the South, which would sooner accept disunion. Third:

To propose a dissolution of the Union is the best way of holding up such a mirror to the national mind, as makes it to see its own deformity. It gives men an opportunity of measuring themselves by a rule of absolute right. . . . Disunion startles a man to thought. It takes a lazy abolitionist by the throat, and thunders in his ear, "*Thou* art the slaveholder."

Aside from our desire to free ourselves from guilt, he remarked in closing, our only object in preaching disunionism is the abolition of slavery, which would quickly follow dissolution of the Union.[80]

Returning to the question of political tactics, we may now note that the disunionists' approach to that question coincided with their constitutional theory. They made two principal points. First, a disunionist did not deprive himself of political influence by refusing to vote under a proslavery Constitution. Second, the Free Soil party took the most antislavery position possible under the Constitution, and it was the Liberty-party–Liberty-League position that threatened actual dissolution of the Union.

On the first point, they repeatedly explained that they were not averse to practical alliances with those who disagreed with them, provided such alliances did not entail sacrifice of principle. But, they maintained, the power to do good and to wield influence would be destroyed by opportunistic and unprincipled behavior. How much moral and political power for good will we possess, asked Garrison, after we have acquiesced to a moral and political union with slaveholders? Can we swear to execute the compromises of the Constitution and in the next breath pledge that we will exert all our moral and political power to destroy them? Or, as Phillips put it, how much influence can he have "who looks one way and rows another"? Adherence to principle is, in any case, the most expedient course, for, as Phillips wrote, "God, . . . when he established the right, saw to it that it should always be the safest and best. He never laid upon a poor finite worm the staggering load of following out into infinity the complex results of his actions. If we do justice, God will ensure that happiness results."[81] On another occasion, he recalled that Granville Sharp had resigned his place as an underclerk in the War Office to avoid having to authorize shipment of arms to put down the revolted colonies. The Libertymen, wrote Phillips, would have cried out " '[Y]ou are losing your influence!' " "And," he added, "indeed it is melancholy to reflect how, from that moment, the mighty clerk of the War Office dwindled into the mere Granville Sharp of history!"[82]

On the second point, Garrison noted that if, as some Libertymen maintained, the Constitution was antislavery, then every slaveholder was legally as well as morally a manstealer, and the first thing their party must do, if elected, would be to declare slavery illegal and the slaves free. The sequel, he added, is predictable: "civil and servile war, blood flowing like water, the Union dashed to fragments." Of course, consequences are not to be regarded where duty is plain. If the Liberty party is clear as to the unconstitutionality of slavery, let it at once inscribe that principle on its banners, "that the country may no longer be kept in suspense; and then we will see whether it will not be regarded as a Disunion party."[83] But in fact the

Liberty party is two-faced, he announced; it professes to be warmly attached to the Union, yet it places a construction upon the Constitution which, if any party attempted to put it into practice, would "blow the Union 'sky high.' "[84]

The Free Soil party, on the other hand, is perfectly candid, observed Edmund Quincy. Van Buren, its standard bearer, states its grievance against the South: the North entered the constitutional compact and agreed to protect slaveholders with the guarantees of the Constitution, with the expectation of receiving in return political supremacy within the Union. In that expectation it has been disappointed, "and it is not the atrocity of the bargain that shocks Mr. Van Buren so much, but the being overreached in the consideration." But Van Buren wants to prevent the extension of slavery. This, wrote Quincy, is a step in the right direction, although it may as well not be taken unless it leads to further steps. But "there is no other step to be taken within the Constitution. This touches its extremest bounds." Hence it is absurd for anyone willing to act under the Constitution to demand more.[85] A few months later, *The Liberator* reprinted the "Address of Southern Delegates in Congress to Their Constituents," written by Calhoun, in which he complained that it was no longer easy to recover fugitive slaves in most Northern states. Garrison rejoiced that Northern public opinion had changed and would continue to change in this respect, but, he added, "if the people of the North feel that they can no longer execute the pro-slavery guaranties of the Constitution, they owe it to justice, honor, probity no longer to swear to support that instrument. . . . It is wrong and treacherous for them to swear to do that which they do not mean to perform." The Massachusetts Anti-Slavery Society, meeting at about the same time, resolved that if the Southerners feared the Free Soil party, it was because they feared that if elected its candidates would be false to their oaths of office and would covertly exploit the antislavery sentiment in their communities to go beyond the pledges in its platform.[86]

A frank agitation of the disunionist slogan was justified as the only way to prevent the otherwise inevitable breakup of the Union, for only abolition could prevent the Union from being dissolved "in form, as it is in fact," and the disunion agitation was now, contended the Garrisonians, the most effective way of working for abolition. Or, as the motto at the head of *The Liberator*'s editorial column proclaimed during part of 1842, "A repeal of the Union between Northern liberty and Southern slavery is essential to the abolition of the one and the preservation of the other."[87]

Each faction of abolitionists saw a necessary and logical relation between its constitutional theory and its political-action policy. The Liberty Leaguers and those Liberty party men who remained aloof from the Free Soil movement believed that under the Constitution no one could legally be a slave. They further believed that if Northerners could be persuaded to accept this as the correct reading of the Constitution, ninety-five percent of the North would join the antislavery movement and the slaveholders, overwhelmed by numbers, would consent to abolition. Some of the coalitionists believed that the Constitution was neutral on the question of slavery, others that it contained clauses permitting slavery in the states but was in spirit antislavery. They were willing, some of them eager, to assure Southerners that they would not attempt to outlaw slavery in the states under the Constitution as it was but would, if elected, work for an amendment and would outlaw slavery in places under congressional jurisdiction. They were convinced that such a program would produce abolition in the border states, then in the middle tier of Southern states (which would then be the "border" states), and finally in the deep South. The Garrisonians insisted that the Constitution was a proslavery compact between North and South at the Negro's expense, that if a party advocating a reneging on that agreement grew in power in the North and captured the government, the South would be justly aggrieved and would have no other recourse than to leave the Union thus perverted from its original purpose. They therefore wanted to persuade Northerners of the real nature of the Constitution so that the North would present the South with two alternatives: to end slavery or to end the Union that the slaveholders needed for their own protection. They believed that if this policy had been adopted and not undercut by the majority of abolitionists, the provocation would never have been given to the South to secede. As Garrison's sons wrote in the 1880s in their comment on political-action speeches at the 1839 convention of the AASS, "in the declaration that the *only* force which can reach the citadel is the ballot-box, and that the ballot-box is the *only peaceful* mode of securing abolition, we recognize a new departure, which led directly up to the election of Abraham Lincoln—and to civil war."[88]

The abolitionists who declared the Constitution an antislavery document and those who believed it neutral or amendable were both, in the Garrisonian view, pursuing dangerous courses. The former, realizing the impossibility of amendment, declared amendment unnecessary. The latter would accomplish abolition in the South by political means alone. Ultimately, both courses would enforce abolition in the face of the slaveholders' united opposition. The only alternative to force was moral suasion. Whether the Garrisonians were realistic in hoping a sufficient number of slaveholders could be converted is debatable; equally debatable is the realism of the other factions in believing the South would accept their interpretations of the Constitution and the political policies implied in them. Insofar as political action remained a mode of agitation and did not require a compromise of principle, the Garrisonians had no objection to it, for their practical policies always concentrated on awakening consciences, disseminating the truth, building a constituency. What they opposed and feared was an attempt to embody antislavery sentiment in political (and hence coercive) measures before the constituency, North and South, had been built.

Garrison's interpretation of the Constitution is now regarded as the correct one; it is his political-action policy, justified by the constitutional theory, that historians find unrealistic. The "sensible" and "realistic" abolitionists who went into politics devised a legalistic, incorrect reading of the Constitution as their theoretical justification. Each faction saw a logical connection between its theory and its practice, and if they were right, the historians are wrong. A recent survey of changing interpretations of Garrison suggests that historians have felt more kinship with the middle-of-the-road liberal abolitionists, those who worked within the constitutional framework, than with radicals of the Garrison stripe.[89] It may also be suggested that many scholars find it difficult to empathize with the activist inspired by a canon of values and committed to realize them by consistent behavior regardless of the consequences to personal popularity that flow from defiance of orthodoxy. If that is so, they can easily, or perhaps unwittingly, sever the activist's theory from his practice—on the one hand, accept Garrison's reading of the Constitution but consider absurd the practical policy deducible from it, and on the other hand regard the political abolitionists' exegesis of the Constitution to be historically false, yet consider realistic the policy that translated that exegesis into practice. But perhaps in this instance the logician is nearer the truth. The policy of the "realistic" political abolitionists did not, after all, produce peaceful abolition, and the alternatives that Garrison presented —reconstruction of the Constitution and the Union *or* disunion—were presented by life itself a score of years later.[90]

DURING THE LIFE of their movement, abolitionists were presented with other choices from time to time that required them to weigh principle against expediency—or rather (since they assumed as a matter of faith that adherence to principle was always the most expedient course), to discover where the principle lay in alternative tactics. Two controversies reflect the difficulty, for reformers, of tracing the connection between the religious duty to be free of the sin they were trying to extirpate and the practical results of doing that duty. These two controversies were over the suggested tactic of boycotting slave-grown produce and over the purchase of Frederick Douglass's freedom.

The free-produce movement, as is well known, was chiefly a Quaker tactic. Quaker, and some non-Quaker, abolitionists proposed resolutions at antislavery meetings[91] and wrote articles advocating abstention from slave-grown produce, taking it for granted that that policy was both a requirement of Christian principle and a means of weakening the slaveholders' grasp on their bondsmen.[92] Many other abolitionists supported the policy without, apparently, questioning its rightness or efficacy.[93] Still others, upon reflection, found neither of the two justifications self-evident. For example, it was argued that a Northerner could not admonish slaveholders if he himself participated in the sin of enslaving his fellow men. But did a purchaser of a cotton garment participate in the sin? Certainly, replied the boycotter; if you buy a horse from a horse thief, knowing he stole it, you are using stolen property and encouraging the thief to steal again. The cases are not analogous, argued the doubter, for by buying the cotton garment you are buying not the stolen article—the slave, who has been robbed of himself—but a commodity one step removed from the theft. That is, if the stolen horse has pulled a farmer's plow, the purchaser of the farmer's crop is not implicated in the theft.[94]

Another way of attacking the doctrine that abolitionists had the religious duty to boycott slave-grown produce was to point out that Christ himself ate with publicans and sinners; no one would argue that he thereby became implicated in their sins. A third line of attack mixed the question of principle with the question of practical consequences of the policy; this was done in two ways. First, not only the cotton garment, but every commodity on the market buttressed somehow, to some extent, the slaveowner's hold on his slaves, and the abolitionist could not refrain from buying them without withdrawing from the world.[95] Garrison explained in 1847 that he had earlier advocated the boycott but now believed he had erred. Slave-labor products, he argued,

> are so mixed up with the commerce, manufactures and agriculture of the world—so modified or augmented in value by the industry of other nations,—so indissolubly

connected with the credit and currency of the country,
—that, to attempt to seek the subversion of slavery by
refusing to use them, or to attach moral guilt to the
consumer of them, is, in our opinion, preposterous and
unjust. . . .[96]

Second, many large contributors to the abolitionist cause were
involved in commerce that to some degree was linked with the
Southern market. That was so even if, like James Mott, they
shifted their line of business away from cotton (they would
not deal in tobacco in any case), or, like David Lee Child, tried
to grow sugar beets in order to do without cane sugar. If all
such links were broken, the capacity of many to contribute to
the cause would be diminished sufficiently to cripple abolitionist activity.[97] Surely God did not require such a policy.

Such considerations led some abolitionists to question
whether a religious principle was involved at all. To Garrison
the criterion became almost solely a practical one: would the
boycott by abolitionists weaken the slave power and the slave
system? He concluded that it would not. Samuel May, Jr.,
likened their abstention to bailing out the ocean with a spoon.
Wendell Phillips, Garrison, and Abby Kelley noted the inconsistency of boycotting American cotton in favor of British
textiles; if the criterion was that slave labor was unpaid, the
boycott should extend to English and Irish cloth, for the
workers who produced it were for all practical purposes
unpaid.[98] Garrison hinted at another way of attacking the
policy. The free-produce movement implicitly assumed that
slavery was profitable for most cotton growers. Garrison
denied that it was, except for a few planters. The system of
slavery, he wrote,

smites the most fertile soil with barrenness, and ends in
widespread bankruptcy. That is its righteous retribution,
the testimony of God against it, and his method of dis-
suading from its prosecution—not abstinence from its
productions. . . . This is our reply to the argument, that
slaveholders are stimulated by a thirst for gold. Be it
so—they have mistaken the road to wealth, and their
disappointment is inevitable. . . . But the master-passion

in the bosom of the slaveholder is not the love of gain,
but the possession of absolute power, unlimited sov-
ereignty.

Garrison then added what by then were familiar arguments: first, that if abolitionists must never use products
tainted with oppression, "we must needs go out of the world
to escape contamination," and second, that the argument
proved too much, for it would require abstention also from
commodities produced by "English factory workers or Rus-
sian serfs."[99]

The free-produce question remained mooted in the anti-
slavery societies, but it led to no serious antagonisms or splits;
abolitionists on both sides were content to work with those
who differed with them on that issue. This debate was one of a
number of ways in which they grappled with the question of
how an abolitionized North could have an impact on the interests and consciences of the slaveholders.

A second controversy occupied abolitionists for a brief
period in 1847. During Frederick Douglass's tour of Britain in
1846, English friends collected his purchase price so that he
could return to his native land a free man. The abolitionist
movement in the United States promptly divided into two
schools of thought. The dividing line did not, incidentally,
coincide with that between Garrisonians and others. Elizur
Wright's Boston *Chronotype* found itself agreeing with the
Philadelphia Female Anti-Slavery Society, *The Anti-Slavery
Bugle* of Salem, Ohio, and *The National Anti-Slavery Standard*, staunch supporters of Garrison, in protesting the purchase
as a betrayal of the abolitionist principle that a slaveholder
must not be paid for releasing his captives; while Garrison
insisted that no principle was involved.

The Philadelphia Female Anti-Slavery Society dealt separately with the questions of principle and expediency, devot-
ing one resolution to each. On the former, it resolved that the
transaction represented an acknowledgment of the owner's
right to Douglass as a chattel; on the latter, it argued that the
ransom took from Douglass "one of the strongest claims to the
sympathy of the community." *The Pennsylvania Freeman*

added that the English friends were giving the master the money to buy another slave. And the *Freeman* concurred with the Philadelphia ladies that now Douglass could no longer lecture as a slave, in which capacity he had exerted immense moral power.[100] These evidently were the sentiments of a large portion of the movement. Samuel May, Jr., wrote to a British friend that the ransom was "exceedingly 'unpopular' among the Abolitionists here. Not one paper (I believe) save the 'Liberator,' has defended it."[101]

Henry C. Wright argued that every man has a natural and inalienable right to himself; hence there can be no property in man; hence Thomas Auld could not own Douglass or sell him; hence no one had the right to buy him. Douglass replied that the transaction at issue would have violated this principle if the buyers had purchased him to enslave him or to compensate Auld for the loss of property rightfully his. But they had neither of these objects. Douglass's freedom and the happiness of his family were worth, to his English friends, the £150 Auld demanded, and which they paid not to compensate him but to induce him to release Douglass from his legal power. Douglass admonished Wright not to confuse "the purchase of legal freedom with abstract right and natural freedom."[102]

A white man was of course in a better position to reply to the argument that Douglass would be a less effective lecturer than when he was a fugitive slave. Garrison pointed out that in Boston Douglass could have been seized and returned South. Some abolitionists suggested that such an occurrence would have brought valuable publicity to the cause. But who, asked Garrison, would like to be kidnapped, tortured, perhaps killed to create an excitement?

It is very easy to give up another to such a doom, by philosophically speculating upon the excellent consequences attending it—but it is not quite so easy to put ourselves in the place of the victim. That alters the case amazingly! No doubt, if Abby Kelley Foster should be kidnapped, and carried to the South, her abduction would do more for the overthrow of slavery than all her powerful labors—but who can complacently speculate

upon the results of such a seizure? If she were in as great
danger as Douglass would have been, or under the same
legal liability to be dragged off at any moment, who
would feel like raising an objection to extricate her from
that danger, to remove that liability, by the payment of a
paltry sum of money?

Who would himself risk such a fate if he could help it? "Not
one of those, we believe, who, oddly enough as abolitionists,
lament that Douglass is no longer able to say he is a slave!"
Some abolitionists had drawn a parallel between ransoming
Douglass and compensating all slaveholders. Garrison denied
its validity,

> not as to principle, we admit, but as to sound policy. It
> might be highly expedient to redeem one slave by pur-
> chase, but quite as inexpedient to negotiate for the pur-
> chase of three millions. Still, we would rather—if this
> must be the alternative—that the most exorbitant pe-
> cuniary exactions of the slave tyrants should be complied
> with, than that their victims should never be set free. We
> do not think this alternative is presented, in regard to the
> slaves as a body; we are certain it sometimes is, as affect-
> ing the release of the slave as an individual. . . . He who
> submits to be robbed, while he denounces the robbery, is
> not to be charged with sanctioning the conduct of the
> robber. To save a fellow-being, it is no crime sometimes
> to comply with even unjust demands.[103]

John L. Thomas, in his biography of Garrison, believes that
"It was on occasions like these that his humanitarian feelings
broke the restraints of dogma and sent his principles fly-
ing."[104] I would argue that Garrison was enunciating a consistently held tactical theory that reconciled humanitarian feelings with principle. Where the result of a policy could not be
predicted, he and Phillips often said that one must do one's
duty and leave the consequences to God. But where the proposed action would clearly defeat the principle it was to serve,
he would re-examine both and if necessary revise one or the
other to satisfy his compelling urge for consistency. On other
occasions as well, Garrison distinguished between principles,

which must never be compromised, and policy, which to serve principle must be flexible.

Ten years earlier he had expressed concern about the danger that Weld would face if he remained in Troy, New York, where he had been mobbed. Garrison thought Weld ought to leave Troy and go to Newport, Rhode Island, to testify before a legislative committee. As he wrote to a Providence abolitionist:

> Weld is as brave as he is good; and while the mob are gnashing their teeth upon him, and brickbats are flying, I do not blame him that he is resolved to maintain his ground at Troy. Still, he has a sufficient excuse for leaving that city, to shield him from the charge of cowardice or desertion—and it is, in my opinion, vastly more important that he should be at Newport, than that he should put down all opposition at Troy—for what is Troy compared to the nation?, and it is a *national* effect at which we must aim before your legislative committee.

During Weld's absence from Troy, "the leaven of sympathy, of humanity, of truth," would be working, to greet him upon his return. Even if the Newport hearings had not been so important, Garrison was unsure if Weld should remain in Troy, since the authorities were unable to maintain the public peace. Weld had already displayed unexampled courage there and could properly leave to go to places where the people would hear him gladly.

> Such an act would be sound policy, and not in any degree allied to fear or apostacy. It would be merely shifting ground, without abandoning an iota of principle. It is not as if he were actually in the keeping of a mob, or confined in a prison, and then under these circumstances required to abjure his abolition sentiments, and be dumb. No: in such a case, it would be his duty to go to the gibbet or the stake, rather than to comply with such an impious requisition.

But such is not the case; hence why try to shout down the mob, perhaps at the cost of life, when one might preach elsewhere to willing ears, especially when it is so important that abolitionists testify at Newport? "I hope he will go before your committee; for Newport is a strong citadel of the enemy, and abolitionists, the strongest and boldest of them, are even *invited within the walls*, and may peradventure carry the place by a single assault."[105]

Three years after the Douglass purchase episode, another question arose, of a less momentous nature, concerning the practical working out of the rule that principles must never be compromised but that policy must be, wherever expedient. The 1850 convention of the AASS in New York was broken up by a band of rowdies who had, among their antics, ridiculed Charles C. Burleigh's long hair and beard. Garrison wrote that if the crowd had only listened to Burleigh for ten minutes they would have changed their opinion of this fine man. But, he added, along with most of Burleigh's friends he regretted the style in which Burleigh chose to wear his hair and beard,

> because it is so wide a departure from customary usage as to excite general remark and provoke popular raillery, thus subtracting from his usefulness as a public lecturer. . . . We are not given to hair-splitting in matters pertaining either to the head or chin, and despise a slavish conformity to fashion; but all things that are lawful are not always expedient. Where there is no moral principle involved, it is sometimes wise to sacrifice what is convenient or agreeable to us, that no unnecessary obstacle may be thrown in the way of a great or good cause in which we may be engaged, and which has arrayed against it all that is formidable in universal apostasy, and inveterate in long cherished prejudice.[106]

All the problems discussed so far are aspects of a larger problem under which questions of reconciling expediency and principle may be subsumed. The "principle" was that to which the abolitionists were dedicated to convert their countrymen. The "expediency" was the effectiveness of their agitation in producing the conversions. We may, then, turn to an examination of certain larger problems of conversion and agitation.

NOTES

[1] For the complicated maneuverings within the Liberty party and the attitudes of various Libertymen and Leaguers before and during the Free Soil convention in 1848, see Theodore C. Smith, *Liberty and Free Soil Parties*, Chs. 8–10; and Richard H. Sewell, "John P. Hale and the Liberty Party, 1847–1848," *New England Quarterly*, XXXVII (June 1964), 200–223 (alternatively, Sewell, *John P. Hale and the Politics of Abolition* [Cambridge, Mass., 1965], Ch. 6). I shall not attempt to duplicate these excellent accounts but shall merely survey those incidents and opinions that throw light on how the various groups saw the relation between abolition principles and political tactics.

[2] "The Economic Background of the Liberty Party," *American Historical Review*, XXXIV (January 1929), 263–64.

[3] Kirk H. Porter and Donald B. Johnson, comps., *National Party Platforms*, p. 4 (second resolution).

[4] T. C. Smith, *Liberty and Free Soil Parties*, pp. 120, 132, 138–39, 141–42; Harlow, *Gerrit Smith*, pp. 183–85; Sewell, "Hale," *passim*. For non-Garrisonian abolitionists' comments on these events, see Theodore Foster to James G. Birney, August 1, 1846, *Birney Letters*, II, 1025–26; Birney to Lewis Tappan, July 10, 1848, *ibid.*, pp. 1108–9; Birney's diary entry of February 15, 1850, *ibid.*, p. 1133n (the manuscript diary in Birney Papers, LC, dates this entry February 17, and there are other minor deviations from the printed version); George Bradburn to Gerrit Smith, October 23, 1847, Samuel R. Ward to Smith, August 14, 1848, and F. Julius LeMoyne to Smith, September 3, 1848, and May 21, 1850, all in Gerrit Smith Miller Collection, SU; Lewis Tappan to Joseph Sturge, November 8, 1848, Tappan Papers, LC; *Letter of Gerrit Smith to the Liberty Party of New-Hampshire*, March 18, 1848, Lysander Spooner Papers, NYHS; Lewis Tappan to LeMoyne, November 18, 1848, and December 18, 1848, in "Letters of Dr. F. J. LeMoyne," *Journal of Negro History*, XVIII (October 1933), 451, 452.

[5] See Joseph Rayback, "The Liberty Party Leaders of Ohio: Exponents of Antislavery Coalition," *The Ohio State Archaeological and Historical Quarterly*, LVII (April 1948), 170–71; Fladeland, *Birney*, pp. 216–20.

[6] Rayback, pp. 173–74. The Wilmot Proviso was introduced in the U.S. House of Representatives in the summer of 1846 in response to the realization that the United States would acquire territory by the treaty that would end the Mexican War. The measure, which never became law, would have prohibited slavery in the Mexican Cession.

[7] Eric Foner, "Politics and Prejudice: The Free Soil Party and the Negro, 1849–1852," *Journal of Negro History*, L (October 1965), 239.

[8] See Porter and Johnson, comps., *National Party Platforms*, pp. 4–7, 13.

[9] See Birney to Lewis Tappan, July 10, 1848, *Birney Letters*, II, 1108–9.

[10] "Address to the Friends of Liberty, by the Executive Committee

of the American and Foreign Anti-Slavery Society," July 4, 1848, in
Ruchames, ed., *The Abolitionists*, pp. 209–18. The quotation is on p.
214.

11 Goodell, *Slavery and Anti-Slavery*, pp. 479–81. On p. 484 he discusses the inexpediency of departures from principle, using language
very similar to the one-ideaist A & F's as quoted above.

12 "Twelfth Annual Meeting of the American Anti-Slavery Society,"
The Liberator, May 22, 1846. The same position was taken in a resolution two years later: "Resolved, That while we appreciate the presence
of Mr. Hale in the United States Senate, delight in the frankness and self-
devotion of Palfrey, and in the gallantry, courage and boldness of Giddings, on the subject of slavery, when brought to the consideration of
Congress, we deplore the melancholy necessity of their position, which
obliges them to stop so far short of what the hour and the duty of every
American citizen require. . . ." "Annual Meeting of the American Anti-
Slavery Society," *ibid.*, May 19, 1848. Garrison's attitude toward Hale is
interestingly analyzed in Samuel May, Jr., to J. B. Estlin, July 16, 1848,
May Papers, BPL.

13 "Sixteenth Annual Meeting of the Mass. Anti Slavery Society,"
The Liberator, February 4, 1848.

14 Quincy (1808–1877) was the scion of an eminent Boston family
and son of Josiah Quincy, president of Harvard. He joined the abolitionist movement in 1837 and became a frequent contributor to *The Liberator*, sometimes acting as editor during Garrison's absence, in which
capacity he faithfully reflected Garrison's views in his editorials.

15 "The Abolitionists and the Free Soil Party," *ibid.*, August 11,
1848.

16 "The New Party," *ibid.*, August 18, 1848. The slogan of revolution
was used by other Garrisonians as well. See, for example, Wendell
Phillips, *The Constitution a Proslavery Compact* (New York, 1856; first
published in 1844 or 1845), p. 169: "Up, then, with the banner of
revolution." He added that he meant peaceful revolution, achieved by
moral suasion. Quincy's position on the relation of abolitionism to free-
soilism became the standard radical position: see, for example, resolution
passed at "Seventeenth Annual Meeting of the Massachusetts A. Slavery
Society," *The Liberator*, February 2, 1849; Garrison to Samuel May, Jr.,
December 2, 1848, Garrison Papers, BPL (after an analysis identical to
Quincy's, Garrison adds that abolitionists should for the time being shoot
their heaviest ammunition at the Whigs); and Garrison to his wife, July
26, 1848, Garrisons, *Garrison*, III, 231.

17 Eric Foner, "Politics and Prejudice," pp. 239–40.

18 The various constitutional theories worked out by abolitionists
have been analyzed elsewhere (although Garrison's has been inade-
quately treated) and will be discussed here only insofar as they relate to
the purposes of this chapter. See Russel B. Nye, *Fettered Freedom*, Ch.
6; Margaret L. Plunkett, "A History of the Liberty Party with Emphasis
upon Its Activities in the Northeastern States," Ph.D. dissertation,
Cornell University, 1930, Ch. 5 (this is the fullest analysis); Theodore C.
Smith, *Liberty and Free Soil Parties*, pp. 89, 98–99, 119, 140; Betty Flade-

land, *Birney*, pp. 149, 178–80, 236, 263–64; Philip S. Foner, *Frederick Douglass* (New York, 1964), pp. 140–42, 159, 163–64; Ralph V. Harlow, *Gerrit Smith, Philanthropist and Reformer*, pp. 280–83; Walter M. Merrill, *Against Wind and Tide*, pp. 203–9; John L. Thomas, *The Liberator: William Lloyd Garrison*, pp. 161, 216–18, 328–32. See also Staughton Lynd, "The Abolitionist Critique of the United States Constitution," in Martin Duberman, ed., *The Antislavery Vanguard*, pp. 209–39. The article is chiefly an analysis of the 1787 Convention, showing that Garrison's interpretation of the writers' intentions was correct.

[19] Garrison's disunionism is discussed in the section beginning on page 195 below. The proceedings of the convention that wrote the U.S. Constitution had been secret; when they were published they provided documentation for the contention of some abolitionists that the Founding Fathers deliberately wrote safeguards for slavery into the Constitution.

[20] Lysander Spooner, *The Unconstitutionality of Slavery*, pp. 290n, 291, 290.

[21] Chase to Smith, May 14, 1842, Gerrit Smith Miller Collection, SU. Cf. Chase to James G. Birney, April 2, 1844, *Birney Letters*, II, 806, in which he contends that since the adoption of the Fifth Amendment slavery has not constitutionally existed in any state. But a year later he was a member of the committee that called the Southern and Western Convention of the Friends of Constitutional Liberty, and the call, as quoted *ibid.*, pp. 934n–35n, pledged the convention to "use all Constitutional and honorable means, to effect the extinction of Slavery in their respective States, and its reduction to its Constitutional limits in the United States." Perhaps the fact that of these three documents only the letter to Birney dealt with Chase's private views explains the inconsistency. The position taken in the letter to Smith is identical to that in an editorial, "Defining Its Position," reprinted in *The Liberator*, January 22, 1847, from *The National Era*, Liberty Party organ in Washington, D.C.

[22] T. C. Smith, *Liberty and Free Soil Parties*, pp. 139–40; Porter and Johnson, comps., *National Party Platforms*, p. 13.

[23] Plunkett, "History of the Liberty Party," p. 156, gives the year as 1843. T. C. Smith, *Liberty and Free Soil Parties*, p. 89, states that the doctrine appeared in 1845. The Liberty party apparently continued to contain members with widely differing views on the question (see George Bradburn to Gerrit Smith, October 8, 1847, Gerrit Smith Miller Collection, SU).

[24] Birney to Benjamin F. Hoffman, May 2, 1844, *Birney Letters*, II, 814–15. Birney to Russell Errett, August 5, 1844, *ibid.*, p. 831: "[H]ow could the Liberty party extinguish Slavery seeing as it is admitted on all hands that the General Government,—except as a war measure to save *itself*—has no constitutional power over that institution in the *States?*" His answer was the same as in the letter to Hoffman.

[25] Birney to Hartford Committee, August 15, 1844, *ibid.*, pp. 834–35.

[26] Birney to Linnaeus P. Noble, September 13, 1847, *ibid.*, p. 1081; to William C. Bryant, October 18, 1847, *ibid.*, pp. 1083–84.

[27] Birney to George Porter, December 30, 1850, Birney Papers, UM.

28 Plunkett, "History of the Liberty Party," notes that most of the abolitionists who said the Constitution was antislavery were not lawyers (note 45, p. 8 of endnotes to Ch. 5).

29 *Liberty and Free Soil Parties*, p. 89. Cf. Dwight L. Dumond, *Antislavery*, who calls this theory an "advanced position" (p. 294) and "the more advanced position" (p. 303), and writes that in 1848 not all abolitionists were "so far advanced" (p. 304).

30 The Spooner pamphlet is excerpted in John L. Thomas, ed., *Slavery Attacked: The Abolitionist Crusade* (Englewood Cliffs, N.J., 1965), pp. 115–17; and the Goodell pamphlet is excerpted in William H. and Jane H. Pease, eds., *The Antislavery Argument* (Indianapolis, 1965), pp. 360–70.

31 Spooner, *The Unconstitutionality of Slavery*, pp. 6–15.

32 *Ibid.*, p. 23.

33 *Ibid.*, pp. 32–36.

34 *Ibid.*, pp. 36–37.

35 *Ibid.*, pp. 39, 43–44.

36 *Ibid.*, pp. 54–56.

37 *Ibid.*, pp. 54–63.

38 *Ibid.*, pp. 67–69.

39 *Ibid.*, pp. 73–74.

40 The importation clause is analyzed *ibid.*, pp. 81–86; the clause obligating the government to protect the states from domestic violence, on pp. 87–88. Spooner discusses the positive provisions of the Constitution that favor freedom on pp. 90–114. His explanation of why the word *persons* in the clause describing eligibility for the presidency really means *male persons* (pp. 99n–100n) evoked a gleeful retort from Wendell Phillips, who accused Spooner of contradicting his principle that words should be construed consistently with the widest freedom. Spooner's announcement that the Constitution's use of the masculine pronoun was to be construed literally, in defiance of the customary use of *man* and *he* for *human race* and *he and she*, would, said Phillips, lead to absurd inferences: the Bible says, "He that believeth shall be saved—he that believeth not shall be damned." So, declared Phillips, "women are neither to be saved nor damned!! And the Constitution itself, in the 5th Amendment, has, 'no person shall be compelled to be witness against HIMSELF. . . .'" Phillips to Garrison, *The Liberator*, August 29, 1845.

41 Spooner, Ch. 10.

42 *Ibid.*, Ch. 11. After having admitted possible majority approval for slavery within certain states and shown that the constitutions were technically "free" despite public opinion, Spooner here deduces the public's intentions (previously ruled out as proper evidence) from the fact that the state constitutions were "free"!

43 *Ibid.*, p. 186.

44 Spooner to S. P. Andrews, March 31, 1847, Spooner Papers, NYHS. This document is a covering letter accompanying Spooner's correspondence with Gerrit Smith, which he was sending to Andrews. The Calhoun speech is in all editions of Spooner's book after the first. See also Gerrit Smith to Spooner, March 20, 1847, and *Letter of Gerrit Smith to S. P. Chase, on the Unconstitutionality of Every Part of*

American Slavery (Albany, N.Y., 1847), Gerrit Smith Miller Collection, SU; and Lysander Spooner to Gerrit Smith, September 8, 1844, Spooner Papers, BPL. Wendell Phillips's article, cited in note 40 above, was a reply to an editorial, "Slavery Unconstitutional," by Garrison, in *The Liberator*, August 22, 1845, which had favorably contrasted Spooner's forthright position with the hedging position taken by many abolitionists including Birney; had paid tribute to Spooner's "unquestionably lofty and humane motives" in trying to give abolitionists a powerful weapon; but had disagreed with Spooner's theory. Phillips thought Garrison too generous.

45 *Ibid.*

46 John Demos, in "The Antislavery Movement and the Problem of Violent 'Means,'" *New England Quarterly*, XXXVII (December 1964), 501–26, points out the distinction between Garrison's earlier repudiation of force and his later repudiation of the Constitution, but he implies that the latter was a rationalization of the former.

47 For example, see "U.S. Circuit Court," *The Liberator*, October 19, 1838, and "Progress of the Anti-Slavery Movement," *ibid.*, January 28, 1842.

48 "Meeting of the Essex County [Massachusetts] A. S. Society," *ibid.*, February 25, 1842. But see Edmund Quincy to J. Miller McKim, August 4, 1844, Anti-Slavery Letters, BPL: "Garrison has been ready for the question these three years & so has Phillips & the rest of what Elizur Wright calls the Boston Clique; but we have never urged it to a decision until the way had been fully prepared for it by full discussion."

49 Disunion resolutions were presented at other meetings from this time on; see news items in issues of March 11, April 22, and April 29, on proceedings at meetings of the Worcester County North Division Anti-Slavery Society, Women's Anti-Slavery Conference of Essex County, Boston Female Anti-Slavery Society, and Middlesex County Anti-Slavery Society. Issues in this period also contain reprints of articles in other papers discussing the question, as well as disunion petitions to Congress.

50 "The Annual Meeting at New-York," *The Liberator*, April 22, 1842.

51 "Repeal of the Union," *ibid.*, May 6, 1842.

52 "Extraordinary Disclaimer," *ibid.*, May 6, 1842. The disclaimer was signed by James S. Gibbons, chairman of the committee, and Lydia Maria Child, recording secretary. Mrs. Child had earlier editorialized in *The National Anti-Slavery Standard* that "it is more than two years since we came to the conclusion, that there was no other way for the free States to clear themselves of being accomplices in tremendous guilt," than disunion. She recounted various political events that showed "plainly enough that the very existence of our civil liberty is endangered by the continuance of slavery," and concluded, "If the South is determined, at all hazards, to sustain her guilty system, and to implicate the free States therein, what can the North do to satisfy her own conscience, and secure her own freedom, unless it be to take measures for a peaceable separation?" Her endorsement of the disclaimer must therefore not be construed as opposition to disunionism per se. See "The Union," *The Liberator*, March 4, 1842. As for Gibbons, he had as little

reverence as Garrison for "sounding brass" (the Union), but insisted that the disunionist doctrine was foreign to the purposes of the society and in any case would be inexpedient. See his "Dissolution of the Union," reprinted from the *Standard* in *The Liberator*, May 13, 1842.

53 "Ninth Annual Meeting of the American A. S. Society," *ibid.*, May 13, 1842.

54 "Cheering Meetings in New York," *ibid.*, May 20, 1842. See *ibid.*, June 3, 1842, for proceedings of "The New-England Anti-Slavery Convention," at which Garrison presented disunionist resolutions and heated debate took place, with the convention taking no action on the question.

55 "Eleventh Annual Meeting of the Massachusetts Anti-Slavery Society," *ibid.*, February 3, 1843.

56 *Ibid.*, March 17, 1843.

57 "The Twelfth Annual Meeting of the Massachusetts Anti-Slavery Society," *ibid.*, February 2, 1844.

58 "Letter from the Editor," reprinted from the *Standard* in *The Liberator*, February 16, 1844.

59 "Annual Meeting in New York," *ibid.*, May 17, 1844; "Business Meetings of the American Anti-Slavery Society for 1844," *ibid.*, May 24, 1844. The individuals who voted are listed in the issue of May 31, which also contains an article correcting some errors in the report in the previous issue. Child (1794–1874) was the husband of Lydia Maria Child and her successor as editor of the *Standard* till his resignation. Among his various activities was an attempt to develop a sugar-beet industry so that Northerners would not have to buy slave-grown cane sugar. Earle (1796–1849), of Philadelphia, had declined the Liberty party nomination for Vice-President in 1840; he was a lawyer, Democrat, and moderate supporter of Garrison. Loring (1803–1858) was a patrician Boston lawyer and early Garrison convert. White was a Boston philanthropist especially interested in the labor-reform movement.

60 See, for example, George Bradburn's protest at the New-England Anti-Slavery Convention in May, reported *ibid.*, June 7, 1844.

61 "The Disunion Pledge," *ibid.*, July 25, 1845; "Gerrit Smith's Constitutional Argument," *ibid.*, August 30, 1844. The failure to distinguish between Garrison's views as a nonresistant and his views as an abolitionist official causes Merrill (*Against Wind and Tide*, p. 209) to accuse Garrison of hypocrisy. According to Merrill, Gerrit Smith resigned from the AASS, contending that disunionism was a nonresistant theory. "Garrison," comments Merrill, "was indignant and insisted rather disingenuously in three long editorials that the constitutional argument was not based on nonresistance and that indeed there was a great variety of religious and political positions represented in the membership of the American society." In view of the facts that there *was* a great variety of such positions in the AASS and that non-nonresistants said precisely the same things about the Constitution as Garrison, the charge of disingenuousness demands substantiation by evidence, which is not provided.

62 *The Liberator*, June 7 and 14, 1844.

63 William Goodell, in *Slavery and Anti-Slavery*, p. 527, writes that the nonresistants' "favorite policy of *not* voting could now be placed on an anti-slavery basis, and openly urged 'on the anti-slavery platform,'

with the aid of anti-slavery funds, instead of depending upon the still moderate number of 'Non-Resistants,' who were consistent enough to abandon the polls." Does he not here admit that before this time non-voting had *not* been urged on the antislavery platform with the aid of antislavery funds?

64 "Change of Opinion," *The Liberator*, June 28, 1844.

65 "Twelfth Annual Meeting of the American Anti-Slavery Society," *ibid.*, May 22, 1846.

66 See Jay to Lewis Tappan, July 3, 1846, Tappan Papers, LC, in which he reaffirms views expressed more fully in earlier letters, for example, to Ellis Gray Loring, September 13, 1843, Anti-Slavery Letters, BPL. He had never endorsed what he believed were the fanciful theories that the Fifth Amendment made slavery unconstitutional (a view publicized by Alvan Stewart) or that Congress during war could abolish slavery. For refutations of both, see Jay to Lewis Tappan, October 5, 1844, Tappan Papers, LC (the Fifth Amendment theory he refers to as Alvan Stewart's "great revelation, a revelation which has no more effect upon my faith than Joe Smith's about the golden Bible"). In a letter to Gerrit Smith, October 21, 1843, Gerrit Smith Miller Collection, SU, Jay wrote that if Texas was annexed he would become a disunionist. Jay's new position is mentioned in Samuel May, Jr., to J. B. Estlin, December 29, 1845, May Papers, BPL.

67 "Annexation of Texas. Duties of the North," reprinted from *The Boston Atlas* in *The Liberator*, April 11, 1845. The article opens with a letter to the editor of the *Atlas* from Henry I. Bowditch in which he states that Jay's letter, enclosed, is in reply to a letter he had written to Jay asking whether the judge retained his earlier views on the Constitution.

68 "Gerrit Smith's Constitutional Argument," *The Liberator*, August 30, 1844.

69 "Gerrit Smith's Constitutional Argument. No. III," *ibid.*, October 4, 1844.

70 [William I. Bowditch], *The Constitutionality of Slavery* (Boston, 1848), is a 48-page pamphlet; the text begins on p. 3. Spooner's book has 294 pages in the 1860 edition, somewhat fewer in the first edition.

71 Bowditch, pp. 7–8. English law and court decisions are, however, discussed on pp. 4–7.

72 *Ibid.*, pp. 8–22.

73 *Ibid.*, pp. 22–26.

74 *Ibid.*, pp. 26–27.

75 *Ibid.*, pp. 28–41. Other clauses in the Constitution are discussed on pp. 42–43. One interesting argument is based on the clause guaranteeing the states a republican form of government. Some abolitionists believed that that clause alone prohibited slavery, since slavery and republicanism are incompatible. On the contrary, says Bowditch, it proves that those who wrote the Constitution believed the two institutions were compatible and that all the states had republican governments in 1787.

76 *Ibid.*, pp. 43–46.

77 New York, 1856. This is the third edition and contains some material not in the first. According to Carlos Martyn, *Wendell Phillips:*

The Agitator (New York, 1890), p. 170, the first edition was published in 1845. Irving Bartlett, *Wendell Phillips: Brahmin Radical* (Boston, 1961), p. 119, dates it 1844. The pamphlet grew out of articles that Phillips wrote for *The Liberator* during 1844.

78 Phillips, *The Constitution a Pro-Slavery Compact*, p. 8.

79 *Ibid.*, pp. 8–9. For additional *Liberator* arguments in support of the Garrisonian position, see especially Phillips, "The No-Voting Theory," July 26, 1844; Phillips, "Non-Voting Theory—Reply to Messrs. White, Earle, and Bowditch," October 25, 1844; Garrison, "Dissolution—Judge Jay's Letter," May 2, 1845. See also Foner, ed., *Life and Writings of Frederick Douglass* (New York, 1950), many speeches and articles before 1851; for example, passages on pp. 187–88, 207–9, 274–75, 328–29 of Vol. I.

80 "Dissolution of the Union," *The Liberator*, January 14, 1848.

81 Phillips, "The No-Voting Theory," *ibid.*, July 26, 1844; Phillips to S. H. Gay, reprinted from the *Standard* in *The Liberator*, October 25, 1844; Garrison, "Speech of Mr. Wilson," *ibid.*, March 6, 1846.

82 Martyn, *Wendell Phillips: The Agitator*, p. 173. Sharp was a British abolitionist and philanthropist. He argued the famous Sommersett case which in 1772 resulted in slaves being declared free in England.

83 "James G. Birney—The Liberty Party," *The Liberator*, March 13, 1846.

84 "Disunion under a Mask," *ibid.*, March 5, 1847.

85 "Mr. Van Buren's Letter," *ibid.*, September 8, 1848.

86 "The Southern Manifesto," and "Seventeenth Annual Meeting of the Massachusetts Anti-Slavery Society," *ibid.*, February 2, 1848.

87 For both quotations, see Garrisons, *Garrison*, II, 50, 56.

88 *Ibid.*, II, 310.

89 David Alan Williams, "William Lloyd Garrison, the Historians, and the Abolitionist Movement," *Essex Institute Historical Collections*, XCVIII (April 1962), 84–99.

90 William H. and Jane H. Pease, in their introduction to *The Antislavery Argument*, p. lxxxiv, write: "It is odd, perhaps, that those who had insisted on disunion in the 1840's and 1850's should, when the war came, have so frequently demanded the preservation of the Union and insisted that the rule of war be made the instrument for ending the slavery that they so deplored but had been unable to abolish." If the purpose of the disunionist agitation is understood, the agitators' unionism during the war is not odd but logical. It was, first, a propaganda device, to pose sharply the issue of the relation of the government to slavery; and it was, second, always presented in terms of alternatives—abolition or disunion—so that Southerners, knowing their system could not survive without federal protection and knowing therefore that slavery must go in either case, would choose abolition. The Garrisonians never rejected the Union per se; they rejected a Union *for slavery*.

91 William Jay objected to such resolutions on the ground that they dragged an "extraneous issue" into society meetings despite the constitution's silence on the question. See his letter entitled "Slave Labor Productions," *The Liberator*, June 18, 1836. He had read that an AASS meeting had passed a resolution by Gerrit Smith "That THIS SOCIETY earnestly and affectionately invites its members, and the members of its

Auxiliaries, diligently and prayerfully to examine the question, whether they can innocently make an *ordinary* use, or be concerned in the traffic of the productions of slave labor?" Jay did not object to the principle, but he argued that the resolution was improper; the society had formed only for purposes enumerated in its constitution. That constitution was an implied contract that restrained the society "from requiring its members to assent to any opinion or to concur in the pursuit of any object not contemplated" in it. That the resolution was itself noncommittal on the question did not justify it; in fact, its insinuation that purchase of slave-made products was sinful was, he argued, dishonest. If abolitionists were to act efficiently they must be united, and hence they must refrain from trying to coerce one another's opinions. Abolitionists favoring the boycott doctrine had the right to promulgate it on their own responsibility and to organize separate societies, but they had no right to set forth a principle, in the name of the antislavery societies, to which only a small minority of members could assent and which was not contemplated by all those who agreed to the principles of the constitution.

⁹² See "Sketches of the Sayings and Doings at the N.E. Anti-Slavery Convention," *ibid.*, June 4, 1847, for an account of one of the debates on this issue in that period. Rev. Henry Grew, Lucretia Mott, and Nathaniel Southard argued for and Stephen S. Foster and Wendell Phillips argued against making the boycott incumbent on abolitionists. "Free Produce Convention," *ibid.*, November 15, 1839, and "Free Produce Association," *ibid.*, November 24, 1843, name prominent abolitionists present at conventions of those who considered the boycott necessary for consistent abolitionism. They included Gerrit Smith, Elizabeth J. Neall, Mary Grew, Sarah Pugh, James and Lucretia Mott, J. Miller McKim, Charles C. Burleigh, William Bassett, and David Lee Child.

⁹³ Other resolutions or arguments defending the obligation to boycott may be found in letter to editor from William Bassett, *ibid.*, December 1, 1837; "Proceedings of an Anti-Slavery Convention of Women, . . . Philadelphia . . . ," *ibid.*, July 27, 1838; many documents in Stephen S. and Abby Kelley Foster Papers, AAS, 1838–1839; Thankful Southwick's resolution, reported in *Proceedings of the Anti-Slavery Convention of American Women* (Philadelphia, 1838), p. 7.

⁹⁴ Elizur Wright, Jr., "On Abstinence from the Products of Slave Labor," *Quarterly Anti-Slavery Magazine*, I (July 1836), 396.

⁹⁵ Abby Kelley wrote that if she must not partake of the fruits of any "system of fraud or oppression," she must not "use any thing from those terrible manufactories where the operatives starve, or suffer, while the manufacturer rolls in luxury—I settle all this matter now, therefore, by knowing it is right for me to use any persons property for *his own benefit*—the slave's property I can use to batter down his prison door and that of the oppressed every where to draw them from under the heels of the tramplers—In one word, it is my duty to use these things, for to abstain would compel me to the life of a recluse" and to be unable to "plead the cause of the poor and needy" (Kelley to Gerrit Smith, August 7, 1843, Gerrit Smith Miller Collection, SU). James G. Birney reported in 1836 that his view of the problem had changed. He still believed abolitionists ought to boycott slave-grown produce, but he

simply could not in practice. See Birney to Lewis Tappan, March 17, 1836, Tappan Papers, LC, and Birney to Gerrit Smith, June 1, 1846, in Dumond, ed., *Birney Letters*, II, 1023.

96 "Products of Slave Labor," *The Liberator*, March 5, 1847.

97 Elizur Wright, Jr., "On Abstinence from Products of Slave Labor," p. 398, argued that it was the abolitionists' duty to abstain as far as they could "without impairing our influence in the cause of human rights." That influence would be impaired if, in substituting linen for cotton, one had less to contribute to the cause. Moreover, Wright was wary "of the exaltation of *physical expedients* into the place of *moral power*, for the removal of slavery. Starving is not convincing."

98 See Abby Kelley's letter quoted in note 95 above; Phillips to Richard Webb, January 13, 1848, Anti-Slavery Letters, BPL; Garrison, "Products of Slave Labor," *The Liberator*, March 5, 1847.

99 "The Free Produce Question," *ibid.*, March 1, 1850. For Garrison's changing opinions on this issue, see Garrisons, *Garrison*, I, 263–64; II, 52–53. In another connection Edmund Quincy amplified Garrison's point that the slaveholders were not motivated by love of riches. They were not such fools, he wrote, that they could not see that the South would be richer and happier without slavery. "Slavery exists, mainly, *because it puts the entire political power of this great nation into the hands of a small oligarchy, the title of which is derived from the ownership of human flesh.*" Single individuals sometimes give up their power, but oligarchies never ("Revolution the Only Remedy," *The Liberator*, October 23, 1846). This is one of the many exceptions to the abolitionist faith in the convertibility of the slaveowners, discussed in Chapter 8 below.

100 *The Liberator*, March 19, 1847; February 12, 1847.

101 Samuel May, Jr., to J. B. Estlin, February 25, 1847, May Papers, BPL.

102 Douglass to Wright, December 22, 1846, in Foner, ed., *Life and Writings of Frederick Douglass*, I, 200–202. The letter is in *The Liberator*, January 29, 1847.

103 "The Ransom of Douglass," *ibid.*, March 5, 1847. See also Garrison to Elizabeth Pease, April 1, 1847, Garrison Papers, BPL. Among other articles in *The Liberator* on the question, see "The Ransom of Douglass," January 15, 1847; "The Ransom: Letter to Frederick Douglass [from Henry C. Wright], with His Reply," January 29, 1847. See Gerrit Smith to Seth M. Gates, February 24, 1839, Gerrit Smith Miller Collection, SU, for a good discussion of the pros and cons long before the Douglass issue arose (Smith's position was the same as Garrison's).

104 *The Liberator: William Lloyd Garrison*, p. 340.

105 Garrison to William M. Chace, June 11, 1836, Garrison Papers, BPL.

106 "Charles C. Burleigh," *The Liberator*, May 24, 1850. In view of the present-day analogies that may be drawn, it should be pointed out that Garrison's stand implied faith that the crowd could be converted; in other circumstances an unorthodox life style may be a *principled* demonstration of alienation from conventional values.

8

CLASSES
AND SECTIONS

THE COMPLAINTS of the modern black-power agitator about the well-meaning white liberal recall the abolitionist's complaint about the average Northerner of his day. The white liberal today favors race equality but "not too fast," and the agitator asks: "How does your passive approval of a theoretical equality diminish actual oppression? Whatever your intentions, is not your abstract support actually an impediment to the sort of action that can bring significant change; is it not a respectable façade to shield the more obviously intransigent?" Most Northerners before the Civil War, and indeed many slaveholders, were "against slavery." But "the Constitution prevented Northerners from doing anything about it," or "the Negroes would not work if free," or "property rights must be respected." Even where opposition to slavery was evidently sincere, there was patently an enormous difference between conviction and commitment, faith and works, theory and practice. The Rev. Orange Scott of Lowell, Massachusetts, speaking at the annual meeting of the Massachusetts Anti-Slavery Society in 1837, addressed a question to those who favored abolition but opposed the abolitionists' measures:

[In] what do you differ from what has always been the sentiment of our whole country? Until very recently, nobody has attempted to defend slavery *in the abstract*. But, what has this sentiment amounted to? Slavery has grown up under it till it is now become a great Oak, which defies the storms of public sentiment—ay, the winds of heaven too! . . . Suppose an individual should say, "I am benevolent, *except the measures*." . . . Every body is willing to say to the poor, "Be ye warmed, be ye filled;" but when we come to the *measures* for feeding and clothing them, the miser starts back! Such benevolence does no good. . . . Mr. Jefferson, and William Wirt, and many other patriots and philanthropists, have been opposed to slavery; but what has their opposition amounted to?[1]

The abolitionists recognized also that they must continually reinforce their own commitment to their cause. The frequent meetings and intragroup journals of any movement for change serve an indispensable function even when they repeatedly pass the same resolutions and proclaim familiar truths to the already committed. These activities help to assure members that they are part of a group with a historic mission, are not fighting alone, and have somewhere to go and others to turn to when public opprobrium weakens their dedication.[2]

The twin tasks of refreshing the commitment of abolitionists and of converting outsiders' passive disapproval of slavery into active opposition differed only in emphasis, especially after the movement had grown from a handful of pioneers into a network of societies with thousands of members. In propaganda aimed at both groups, the abolitionists relied heavily on the same arguments: among others, that slavery denied the humanity of the Negro and prevented the slave from having normal family relations and religious life, that the North shared the slaveowners' guilt, that absolute power of one individual over another encourages atrocities, that slavery was responsible for the degraded condition of Northern free Negroes, and that the talent and manliness of Negroes such as Frederick Douglass and Charles Lenox Remond demonstrated the inherent equality of the races. There was, in addition, a somewhat different tactic employed by abolitionists both among themselves and in their public propaganda. It may be illustrated by William Lloyd Garrison's reaction to an experience he had while on a trip to Britain.

One summer day in 1846 in Liverpool, Garrison was accosted by a prostitute. Later he told of how he had imagined that wretched woman as his sister or daughter. Merrill supposes that this fantasy was Garrison's way of "successfully avoiding temptation."[3] Whether or not that is so, there is abundant evidence that his response manifested an attitude consciously cultivated by abolitionists. On other occasions he deliberately pictured himself in the place of the oppressed. For example, in a speech at the Massachusetts State House, he exclaimed, "Who can contemplate the wife of his bosom—the children of his love—subjected to this fearful suffering and indignity, and for one moment entertain the idea" of gradual abolition?[4] On the first anniversary of his marriage, he wrote to his brother-in-law describing his happiness and extolling the institution of marriage; and he added, how horrible it would be if he and Helen were slaves and were separated by sale. All the more reason, then, to rededicate his life to the abolition of slavery.[5]

This theme, which for convenience will be referred to as "empathy," appears repeatedly in abolitionists' private discourse and public propaganda, in exhortations among themselves to increase their zeal and in efforts to induce complacent whites to imagine themselves in the place of the slaves. Its shorthand expression was the New Testament verse Hebrews 13:3, seldom placed within quotation marks, never identified, and always made an integral part of the writers' own sentences: "Remember them that are in bonds, as bound with them."[6]

If the abolitionist movement had been composed chiefly of its own intended beneficiaries, one of the two uses of the empathy theme would of course have been unnecessary. Negroes in the North—those active in the convention movement, the vigilance associations, and other societies—had no need to remind themselves of their bond with the slaves of the South. But the abolitionist movement comprised mainly white men and women, most of whom had never been South. The empathy theme can thus be seen, perhaps, as a substitute for direct involvement in the suffering that the movement was dedicated to end.

It appeared in other forms as well. When Abby Kelley Foster was asked how she could leave her baby with others, to travel the abolitionist lecture circuit, she replied, "For the sake of the mothers who are robbed of all their children."[7] The abolitionist educator Beriah Green, answering the perennial question asked by Northerners, "What can *we* do?" replied in part:

> You can act as if you felt that you were bound with those who are in bonds; as if their cause was all your own; as if every blow that cuts their flesh, lacerated yours. You can plead their cause with the earnestness, and zeal, and decision, which self-defence demands.[8]

Green's reference to self-defense is significant, for the effort to induce empathy with the slaves in complacent Northerners was more than a heuristic device, although it was that too. Abolitionist propaganda reiterated that Northern whites were in fact indirectly "bound with" the slaves. Paradoxically, the North was not only accessory to the enslavement of Negroes; it was at the same time a secondary victim of the slaveowners. With their strong religious motive for proclaiming the duty of emancipation regardless of consequences, the abolitionists could not in good conscience appeal to the North solely or chiefly on the basis of interest. The empathy theme enabled them in a remarkable way to combine interest with principle, for if a Northern white could be made to feel bound with the slave he would fight the slave power to defend himself, as Beriah Green suggested, as well as to exculpate himself. To free the slave would be to free himself of both guilt and bondage; the two motives would become one.

The abolitionists' theory that the North was both accomplice and victim of the slave power, combined with their theory of conversion (discussed in Chapter 4), suggests a framework for studying certain leading themes in their propaganda approaches to both North and South. We shall examine first their conception of the slave system and how Northerners became its victims and partners in oppressing Negroes in the North as well as in the South; then we shall discuss how the abolitionists' empathy theme and conception of the nature of slavery affected their approach to the Northern working class; then, shifting our attention to the South, we shall investigate the way abolitionists viewed the slaveowners and the possibility of converting them.

GIVEN THE radical abolitionist's special theological premises, and his extravagantly simple view of the relation among belief, motivation, and behavior, the conclusions follow like the consecutive clicks of a row of falling dominoes. The special significance of Stephen S. Foster and a handful of other abolitionists whose unconventional behavior has tempted historians to give them disproportionate attention is that they accepted every corollary, and every corollary of every corollary, of a syllogism constructed from those premises. Their tenets and church-disrupting activities demonstrate where this "domino logic" might lead, whereas the more moderate Garrison shrank from following it to its farthest conclusions.[9] If the sin of slavery existed partly by virtue of the aid that Northerners gave it, and if God commanded every person to wage war upon all sin (and of course God would not command an impossibility), then a Northerner who aided slavery in any way was guilty of heinous sin. Anyone who failed to use an opportunity to fight slavery was at that moment aiding the slave power. Hence a man who was anything but a full-time battler against slavery was as bad as a slaveholder.[10] His guilt was so enormous, and the identification of the average Northern white with the slaveholder so complete, that the Foster mentality could not separate them or mitigate the

Northerner's guilt sufficiently to see him as also a victim. Garrison and most of the radical abolitionists, along with the more conservative abolitionists, recognized degrees of guilt. For propaganda purposes they occasionally would picture the Northerner as the greater sinner[11] (having less excuse than the slaveowner), but almost always they distinguished sufficiently between the aggressive slave power and the Northern white to portray the latter as a victim as well as an accomplice of the former. The North, said the annual report of the Massachusetts Anti-Slavery Society in 1849, "has been willing to purchase the delusive benefits of a deceptive Union at the successive cost of these concessions of its own true interest and the interests of humanity."[12] "These concessions" were the splitting off of Kentucky from Virginia, giving the slaveholders another state, the purchase of the Louisiana Territory and admission of the State of Louisiana, the War of 1812, the tariff (presumably that of 1816), the Missouri Compromise, nullification and the tariff compromise, the Florida war, the annexation of Texas, the Mexican War, and the conquest of the Mexican Cession—all by means of the federal government acting as the instrument of the slave power.[13]

The most conservative abolitionists concurred with the Garrison-dominated Massachusetts Society on this point. James G. Birney asserted in 1840 that "the North, in relation to the South, is as a conquered province," for in the last six years its rights have been invaded one by one, and since the Missouri Compromise the government has been in the hands of the slave power. The North, he added, is beginning to show signs of alarm and is making efforts to redeem herself;

> but she yet requires a great deal more of agitation to rouse her up to a full perception of the danger into which she has been brought, and to the necessity, *if she would save her own liberty*, either of severing her connections with the South, or of acting incessantly on the South for the abolition of slavery.[14]

Arguments purporting to show that the Constitution prevented Northerners from abolishing slavery were clearly beside the point, for the North, according to this well-developed category of abolitionist propaganda, must fight to defend its own share in federal power and its own freedom of speech, petition, and travel. Slavery could not exist alongside liberty to petition Congress, liberty to discuss slavery in the press and in meetings, liberty of Northerners to travel in the South. The slave power was aggressive by nature, and concessions by the North were self-defeating. Since those concessions helped the slave power and hurt the Northerners who made them, abolitionists could point out the expediency of ceasing to commit this sin. Northerners who were "against slavery" but unwilling to act on their conviction might be roused to defend their own freedom and in the process discover that they were in fact "bound with" the slave.

One important difference between abolitionism and the modern Negro freedom movements is that the latter is an attempt to practice freedom, whereas the former was not. It was not primarily a movement of Negroes asserting the rights of free people, but a movement to convert whites to the belief that Negroes ought to have those rights.[15] It was therefore more of a propaganda movement and essentially directed toward changing the minds of whites rather than the circumstances of Negroes. Its very existence thus depended on access to the public ear, and abolitionists were careful to point out that restrictions on their own freedom to speak and publish were restrictions on the North's freedom to hear and read.[16] That is why the linking of abolitionism with the cause of free speech for whites was a legitimate tactic, even though it might seem to start from the racist premise that it was ethical to emphasize their own stake in the free-speech battle, to rouse whites to anger, rather than to concentrate on the denial of the Negroes' very humanity.[17] The legitimacy of this tactic was well expressed by Francis Jackson of Boston at the time he joined the abolitionist movement in 1835:

> Mobs and gag laws . . . betray the essential rottenness of the cause, they are meant to strengthen. . . . Happily, one point seems already to be gaining universal assent, that slavery cannot long survive free discussion.

Hence the efforts of the friends and apologists of slavery
to break down this right. And hence the immense stake,
which the enemies of slavery hold, in behalf of freedom
and mankind, in its preservation. The contest is therefore
substantially between liberty and slavery.[18]

Closely linked with the abolitionist defense of free speech,
and presenting the same ethical problem, was another tactic
used somewhat less often but frequently enough to compel our
attention. The sometimes sensational articles in antislavery
papers about slaves who were white[19] may be interpreted as
evidence that the abolitionists, despite their protests against
race prejudice, felt the enslavement of a white person somehow more deplorable than the enslavement of a Negro. Perhaps the accusation has merit in some cases. It should be noted,
however, that these news items were sometimes the subject of
separate editorial comment to the effect that the white reader
must realize that slavery was no distant danger, that he himself
could be seized and sold South on the claim of a slave catcher,
that slavery knew no bounds of color.[20] It is clear that the
purpose of at least some of these articles was to force the
reader to put himself imaginatively in the place of the slave.
This would be the first step toward his learning that the black
man felt the degradation of slavery as he himself would.

When abolitionists attempted to induce empathy with the
Negro in Northern whites who opposed slavery only pas-
sively, they were consciously trying to meet the greatest challenge to their cause, the widespread fear that unconditional
emancipation would bring social equality in its wake. According to one student of Northern public opinion, "The key to
the explanation of anti-abolition is race prejudice." Most
Northerners, he explains, were opposed at the same time to
slavery and to race equality and therefore supported the
American Colonization Society.[21] Abolitionists, realizing this,
always saw their struggle to discredit colonizationism as part
of their fight against racism. In fact, their slogan of immediate
and unconditional emancipation ought itself to be understood
as, among other things, an assertion of the equality of the
races. White-supremacist Northerners at the time understood

this better than modern historians who have assumed that the
slogan represented a naive call for a revolutionary transformation they thought could come in the near future.[22] Barnes, for
example, criticizes the abolitionists for adopting the immediatist slogan, because it repelled those who might otherwise
have been converted to antislavery. But the abolitionists' aim
was not chiefly to convert masses to *antislavery*; if all the
Northerners who already believed slavery to be evil had entered the movement in the 1830s, that movement would have
rivaled the Whig party in size—and been no more effective in
ending slavery. Abolitionists knew this. Nathaniel P. Rogers,
for one, blamed "color-phobia," of which colonizationism was
one type, for anti-abolition. Color-phobia, he wrote,

> abhors slavery in the abstract—wishes it might be done
> away, but denies the right of any body or any thing to
> devise its overthrow, but slavery itself and slaveholders.
> It prays for the poor slave, that he might be elevated,
> while it stands both feet on his breast to keep him
> down.[23]

The differences between that "antislavery" multitude and the
abolitionists were first, that the abolitionists saw slavery as a
sin, and second (the relevant point here), that they asserted
the equality of the races. Hence much of their propaganda
effort, often in the form of the empathy theme, was directed
at inducing Northern whites to see the Negro as their brother.[24]

They also proclaimed that Northern racism hurt the interests of white labor; by identifying manual labor with a despised caste, it made labor itself disreputable.[25] Hence abolition of chattel slavery, which produced the caste system, was
in the interest of the Northern working class. But the abolitionists, as is well known, made little headway in enlisting the
labor movement in their crusade, and part of the explanation
for their failure lies in their emphasis on the empathy theme.
That theme was no doubt an aid to commitment, but it did not
help the abolitionists' understanding of the nature of the evil
they were committed to destroy. It influenced them to regard
the slaves as suffering individuals (see their ritual repetition of
phrases such as "bleeding humanity"), but it threw no light on

the cause of the suffering. In fact, the empathy theme may have impeded that understanding, because it encouraged abolitionists to see the oppressors too as individuals, whose behavior could be explained solely in terms of individual sin and guilt. Despite their repeated use of the term *slave power* and their recognition that the slaveholders were a self-conscious oligarchy that acted as one in defense of its interests, there is little evidence in the abolitionists' writings of insight into the social sources of ideology or the class nature of the slave system. Spokesmen for labor such as George Henry Evans were committed to a social philosophy and program for change that denied the very premises of the abolitionists' crusade. The labor reformers stressed interest where the abolitionists stressed principle, talked of classes where the abolitionists talked of individuals, urged reform of institutions where abolitionists preached repudiation of sin. It is no wonder that the abolitionists failed, so far as the workingmen's movement was concerned, in their effort to combine interest with principle by means of the empathy theme.

It is this conflict in philosophy, rather than the abolitionists' failure to sympathize with Northern labor, that explains why the two movements were not allied. Some abolitionists did in fact sympathize with underpaid American workers, starving Irish peasants, and disfranchised English factory operatives.[26] Garrison, for one, was shocked to learn that British abolitionists did not as a matter of course support the Chartists' demand for electoral reforms, and when he learned the cause of the hostility between the Chartists and the British abolitionists, he sided with the former.

The issue was presented to him for the first time in July 1840 as he entered a hall in Glasgow to attend an antislavery public meeting. Someone handed him a leaflet entitled *Have We No White Slaves?* In his speech at that meeting Garrison answered the question, No! British workers are not slaves, you own your own wages, are permitted to learn to read and write, and can better your condition. The leaflet asked, Are we not grievously oppressed, starving in the midst of abundance? Garrison replied, Yes! And, according to his account of the incident, he "called upon British abolitionists to prove themselves the true friends of suffering humanity abroad, by showing that they were the best friends of suffering humanity at home." He then asked the audience whether British abolitionists were not friends of their own suffering countrymen and was surprised to hear "No! no! no!" from all parts of the hall, whereupon he said, "Then I am very sorry to hear it—I hope that it is not true of all of them—I am sure it is not true of the abolitionists of the United States; for they sympathize with the oppressed, as well as the enslaved, throughout the world."

He went on to advise British workers to help their cause by self-reform; it is at this point that the philosophic chasm separating abolitionists from workers' spokesmen becomes evident. Shortly after that meeting in July, Charles M'Ewan, a Chartist, published a handbill in the form of a letter to Garrison, to whom he sent a copy. Garrison commented on it in *The Liberator,* first paying tribute to its "bold and manly style." M'Ewan objected to Garrison's call for self-reform, and Garrison, in his editorial reply, asked whether self-reform would not help the British worker.

> That "a great amount" of the suffering of the laboring population in England (including Scotland and Ireland, of course,) arises from intemperance, it is idle for Mr. M'Ewan to deny; that they are too frequently induced to seek the intoxicating bowl, in consequence of their ignorance, destitution and severe toil, is also doubtless true; that the temperance cause has reclaimed thousands of them from drunkenness, banished from their domestic hearths no small portion of their misery, and qualified them to carry on the cause of political reform, is a delightful fact; and that they are far more ready to adopt the "tee-total pledge" than the more opulent classes, I most cheerfully bear witness.[27]

This incident has been commented on by historians; what has been overlooked is that passage in Garrison's reply in which he blamed the intemperance on the workers' circumstances and not their circumstances on their intemperance, while of course asserting that the intemperance worsened the conditions that caused it. And he suggested that self-reform might improve the laborer's ability to work for political reform, not make political reform unnecessary. M'Ewan's chief complaint seems to have been that Garrison mentioned self-reform at all, for he thereby gave a weapon to the enemy. But American abolitionists chronically thought in terms of appeals to individuals—oppressor and oppressed alike—and in terms of individual reformation rather than of a struggle for power, and it is clear that Garrison simply did not see M'Ewan's point.

The Glasgow rally was addressed by other abolitionists, British and American. One of the latter, Nathaniel P. Rogers of New Hampshire, said during his speech that he had learned that some British newspapers opposed the cause of universal freedom and he hoped that none of the gentlemen on the platform with him supported such papers. M'Ewan's letter attempted to enlighten Rogers and other Americans who shared his ignorance of the British abolitionist movement: "It may be astonishing, but the fact stands uncontrovertible, that none of them read any thing else but papers either directly or indirectly opposed to universal freedom."

Garrison's accompanying editorial mentioned that he had recently read that Chartists and socialists had broken up several British antislavery meetings. He could understand their conduct, he wrote, but he condemned their use of force.

> In their struggle to obtain those rights and privileges which belong to them as men, and of which they are now ruthlessly deprived, I sympathize with all my heart, and wish them a speedy and complete victory! But I cannot approve of any rude behaviour, or any resort to violence, to advance their cause: that cause is just, and can best be promoted by moral and peaceable instrumentalities—by appeals to reason, justice, and the law of God—by an unwavering reliance upon that truth which is mighty to the pulling down of strong holds.[28]

His attitude toward the wage worker was identical, then, to his attitude toward the slave, so far as their mode of redress was concerned.

It is clear that he did not see the free workers as a down-trodden class, but neither did he see the chattel slaves as a downtrodden class. He did see both as aggregations of suffering individuals, and in that light the chattel slaves were certainly more in need of a movement to champion their interests. Given the personal terms in which the abolitionists saw the problem of oppression, the slave deserved priority over the free worker because enslavement was personally more degrading than mere oppression. In their propaganda the abolitionists always stressed the degradation rather than the poverty of the slaves. Their individualistic and religious frame of reference happened to direct their primary attention to precisely that aspect of the slave's status which the free worker did not share, and it caused them to portray as secondary those evils which the slave suffered in common with the free worker. That is, both were poor (the abolitionist was willing to admit that some slaves were better off in a material way than some workers), but the slave's poverty resulted from his status; although the abolitionists differed as to how much the worker was responsible for his own poverty, they agreed that that poverty was at least not a necessary evil which he had no legal right to ameliorate. The slave was a chattel; the worker was a man with some freedom to better his lot. The slave could not plead his own cause. Deprived of legal rights, he could not, except by escape, do much to change his condition; others must agitate in his behalf. The free worker had all the legal prerogatives that the abolitionist had and could use the ballot in his own interest.[29] Hence the criticism of the abolitionist for his selective compassion misses the point; given his frame of reference, his choice is unassailable. Those who, like John A. Collins, did come to see the white workers as an oppressed class left the abolitionist movement.[30] There was no necessary conflict between a movement to abolish wage slavery and another to abolish the more extreme form of class oppression, chattel slavery. But the individualistic terms in which the abolitionists saw their task, their enemy, and the beneficiaries of their efforts made common cause impossible in practice.

When the abolitionists declared that the free worker, unlike the slave, had the legal right to improve his condition, especially in the United States where he possessed the ballot, and hence was partly to blame for his poverty, the latter's spokesmen replied that the worker was as much a slave as the Negro; hunger was as compelling an inducement to forced labor as was the whip and made him the slave of the capitalist class rather than of an individual master. The opposing views became the subject of a heated debate in the columns of *The Liberator* in 1846 and 1847.[31] It began while Garrison was in Britain and Edmund Quincy was editing the paper. In the issue of September 4, 1846, Quincy reprinted a letter Wendell Phillips had addressed to George Henry Evans, editor of *Young America*, explaining that he had for some time subscribed to Evans's paper and agreed with some of its doctrines, especially its advocacy of distribution of public lands. But he now had to protest Evans's tenet that a man robbed of his land was worse off than a man robbed of himself. Evans replied in an editorial, reprinted by Quincy:

> If it be true, as I most firmly believe it is, that wages slavery, in its legitimate results of crowded cities, debasing servitude, rent exactions, disease, crime, and prostitution, as they now appear in England and in our Northern and Eastern States, are even more destructive of life, health, and happiness than chattel slavery, as it exists in our Southern States, then the efforts of those who are endeavoring to substitute wages for chattel slavery are greatly misdirected. . . .

Evans went on to say that "the usurpation of the soil . . . makes the working classes the slaves of wages" and that "men robbed of their land *are* robbed of themselves most effectually. The National Reform measures would not merely substitute one form of slavery for another, but would replace every form of slavery by entire freedom."

Evans was seconded by another National Reformer, William West of Boston, in one of many of his letters to *The Liberator*. In the issue of September 25, West explained that the National Reformers did not condemn wage slavery solely because it caused poverty.

They oppose it because it holds the laboring classes in a state of abject dependence upon capitalists, not only for the bread it is their right to eat and the work it is their duty to do, but for the continuation of their lives, and the preservation of their morals, begetting starvation, pauperism, prostitution, infanticide, parricide, suicide, murder and piracy, and rendering necessary governments of violence and religions of fraud, with the pauper receptacles for the living and the dead, and then, Home Missionary and Tract Societies, their vindictive penal codes and their revengeful "eye for eye, tooth for tooth" creeds, their turnkeys and hangmen, their soldiers and marines, and this condition of the laboring classes they conceive to be far worse than that of horses and oxen, which is the worst possible condition chattel slaves ever can be reduced to. . . . Their rallying cry is, *"Down with all slavery, both chattel and wages,"* and their single object is, the "FREEDOM OF THE LAND."

West added that the progress of slavery could never be arrested and reversed until monopoly of the soil was abolished. Abolitionists must therefore unite with the National Reformers to limit the amount of land an individual might own, exempt it from execution for mortgage and debt, and make it inalienable except to the landless. Slaveowners would have to free their slaves because enormous plantations would disappear. Many plantations would become vacant, and the freedmen would settle on them and become yeomen farmers.

The following March, Garrison, back from Europe, joined the debate. "The evil in society," he wrote, "is not that labor receives wages, but that the wages given are not generally in proportion to the value of the labor performed." When capital draws the lion's share, it makes human interests "antagonistical, instead of co-operative; and those who can obtain power are disposed to oppress the weak." Various schemes, he said, had been proposed to cure society's ills—distribution of public lands, voting every man a farm, Fourierism, preaching the gospel, free trade, abolition of money—and he agreed a social reorganization was necessary. But "we cannot yet see that it is wrong to give or receive wages; or that money, which is in itself harmless, is the source of almost every human woe (though we think that ignorance and selfishness are). . . ."[32]

A few months later it was Wendell Phillips's turn. "Except in a few crowded cities and a few manufacturing towns," he wrote in *The Liberator* of July 9, "I believe the terms 'wages slavery' and 'white slavery' would be utterly unintelligible to an audience of laboring people, as applied to themselves." Workers as a class were neither wronged nor oppressed, and in any case they possessed ample power to defend themselves.

> Does legislation bear hard upon them?—their votes can alter it. Does capital wrong them?—economy will make them capitalists. Does the crowded competition of cities reduce their wages?—they have only to stay at home, devoted to other pursuits, and soon diminished supply will bring the remedy. . . . A wiser use of public lands, a better system of taxation, disuse of war and of costly military preparation, and more than all, the recognition of the rights of woman, about which we hear next to nothing from these self-styled friends of labor, will help all classes much. But to economy, self-denial, temperance, education, and moral and religious character, the laboring class, and every other class in this country, must owe its elevation and improvement.

And he added an admonition that the condition of the American worker must not be equated with that of the disfranchised European worker.[33]

Three months later Edmund Quincy contributed the last major polemic in the debate (it continued for a while in the form of occasional letters to the editor). Replying to a recent editorial in *Young America*, he denied that the need to work made the laborer as dependent as the slave. Yes, he was dependent on his employer, but no more than the employer was dependent on him. This was true in a slave society too; but there capital owned labor, whereas in free society labor owned itself and was free to make the best possible bargain with capital. Proof of this was the continual fluctuation in wages according to the state of the labor market. Further, the large annual immigration into the United States, wrote Quincy, proved that even the poorest workers could move about freely.

> The very paper, which has furnished the text for this Discourse, is established for the purpose of arousing these very *wages-slaves* to redress their wrongs, and establish a better state of things by POLITICAL ACTION! *Slaves* "voting themselves farms," and altering the laws of the land by their ballots! . . . If the white laboring men in America are *slaves*, whose fault is it? They are Slaves that hold the sceptre of Sovereignty in their own hands. . . . Is it so with the chattel Slaves?

And, as if to dispel any remaining doubt that he had failed completely to grasp the labor spokesmen's essential thesis, he asked the question that repeatedly appears in abolitionist arguments on this subject: If wage slaves are worse oppressed than chattel slaves, why do we not see them clamoring for owners?[34]

That Garrison, Phillips, and Quincy spoke for large numbers of Garrisonian abolitionists was demonstrated when antislavery meetings passed resolutions endorsing their views and defeated others representing the doctrines of the National Reformers.[35] A resolution accurately expressing the Garrisonian attitude toward the Northern working class was approved at a meeting in 1849:

> Whereas, the rights of the laborer at the North are identified with those of the Southern slave, and cannot be obtained as long as chattel slavery rears its hydra head in our land; and whereas, the same arguments which apply to the situation of the crushed slave, are also in force in reference to the condition of the Northern laborer—although in a less degree; therefore
>
> Resolved, That it is equally incumbent upon the working-man of the North to espouse the cause of the emancipation of the slave and upon Abolitionists to advocate the claims of the free laborer.[36]

When Garrisonian abolitionists favored advocacy of the claims of the free laborer they meant, of course, improvements in his condition, not change in his status.[37] The radical change they looked forward to, discussed in Chapter 4 above, was of a totally different sort from that demanded by the secular, class-conscious labor spokesmen, but it was radical for all that. It was an early nineteenth-century analogue of modern Christian anarchism; they both envisioned a fundamental change in the social structure and social values but endeavored to construct the good society not by seizure of power from one class by another, but by acts of individual compassion and individual conversion, acts that were to have an ever widening impact until brotherhood and cooperation had quietly transformed the social system. It is in the light of this vision, and not opposition to labor's objectives, that Garrison's "hostility" to labor must be understood.[38] And labor's "hostility" to abolitionism was likewise due, not to opposition to the abolitionists' objectives, but to its preoccupation with its own grievances and program. The gains the labor movement was fighting for were all ameliorative in nature, would not have affected the power of the slaveholders, and were therefore irrelevant to the needs of the slaves; and hence labor's tactics had little relevance to those the abolitionists had adopted. According to Joseph Rayback, outright hostility to abolition was not typical of labor leaders.

> Really typical was a disinterested attitude which had a deeper motivation. Its roots could be found in an awakened class consciousness, one that suggested the possibility of the emancipation of labor through strong trade unions, ten-hour days, mechanics' lien laws, anti-garnishee legislation, prohibition of child labor, land limitation, free grants of the public domain to actual settlers, abolition of chartered monopolies, and universal education. These matters held far more vital importance to workingmen than the liberation of three or four million black men.[39]

The "awakened class consciousness" to which Rayback refers ought perhaps to be called *partial* class consciousness, for all the demands he lists were reformatory, not radical; they could have been (and have been) realized with a less drastic change in American society than was required by the abolition of slavery. When the more far-seeing labor leaders asserted that black labor could never be completely freed by a movement that did not work for the interests of white labor, they were right.[40] And when abolitionists declared that white labor could not emancipate itself unless it worked also for the emancipation of the chattel slaves, they were right. But neither movement took to heart this admonition by some of its own theorists, and one suspects that the theorists themselves did not grasp the full meaning of the principle they stated; it was a propaganda device of each movement to secure the help of the other.

The philosophic difference between the radical abolitionists and the radical labor spokesmen suggests an inconsistency in the abolitionists' analysis of the nature of slavery. Utopian socialists argued that the worker's legal freedom was a mockery when circumstances conspired to crush his spirit and destroy his incentive to rise; the profit system fostered competitiveness and selfishness, and that system must be changed if love and cooperation were to characterize human relations. No, thundered Garrison; a theory that makes a man the creature of circumstances denies that he is responsible to God for his actions. Such a theory could absolve the slaveholder of guilt for his free choice to continue holding his slaves.[41] It could absolve Northerners of their guilt of complicity with the slave power.

Yet the abolitionists incessantly denounced the slave system for, among other things, fostering brutality, indolence, and arrogance in the masters[42] and demoralization in the slaves.[43] The system, moreover, by requiring the slaves to be illiterate and ignorant, diminished their chances of hearing the word of God and achieving salvation.[44] Fugitives like Frederick Douglass were considered especially worthy of admiration for their success in overcoming the stultifying effects of slavery; how many potential Douglasses, as well as Shakespeares and Luthers, had wasted away their lives in the cotton fields?

The abolitionists' difficulty on this point can be illustrated by articles written by two Garrisonians in *The Liberator*. In a letter to Garrison, printed in the issue of August 27, 1847, Henry C. Wright told of a conversation he had recently had with Robert Owen and concluded by denouncing as "a self-evident *untruth*" Owen's "fundamental principle that *man is the creature of circumstances,* and the necessary inference from it . . . that he is therefore *irresponsible.*" Five issues later, Edmund Quincy wrote that associationism and Land Reform both erred "in vastly exaggerating the evils that environ the life of the white laborer, while they strangely undervalue those that crush the minds as well as the bodies of the chattel slaves."[45] It might be argued that the abolitionists blamed the sinful slaveowners and not the slave system for these crimes. But a slave doomed to hell (although perhaps not the lowest level of it) because his owner had prevented him from hearing the saving gospel was as damned, through no fault of his own, as he would have been had the system prohibited the propagation of Christianity. In either case he was a victim of "circumstances." But Garrison spoke for many abolitionists when he scornfully referred to "Robert Owen's absurd and dangerous dogma, that men are 'the creatures of circumstances'—not sinful, but unfortunate—not inwardly corrupt, but outwardly trammelled."[46]

When an abolitionist discussed specific examples of prejudice he usually explained that prejudice was the result of slavery. But when he discussed the religious duty to abolish slavery, he often characterized prejudice and slavery as twin products of the unregenerate soul, manifested in love of domination and in a perverse rejection of the Christian message of brotherhood. In the former case, it would follow that slavery must be abolished in order that prejudice might be eliminated and brotherly feeling made possible. In the latter case, conversion, generating love of all men as brothers, must create the will to abolish slavery. When the abolitionist debated the labor spokesman, he emphasized the advantage of the free worker over the slave by denying that the former was the victim of circumstances. But when he described the effects of slavery he was forced to recognize the effects of circumstances on the mind and soul of the slave; that is, one of the things he most hated slavery for contradicted his own reason for rejecting the "doctrine of circumstances." We need not wonder at the abolitionists' failure to solve the problem of free will versus determinism that has baffled philosophers. It is doubtful, however, that they were even aware of its existence in their rationale.[47] They were agitators, not systematic thinkers, and although most of their theories did form a coherent whole, especially in Garrison's case, they drew from an arsenal of arguments as the specific incident or the weekly editorial required.[48]

WHEN WE TURN from an examination of how the abolitionists saw the problem of converting Northerners, to an examination of how they saw the problem of converting slaveholders, we make a surprising discovery: the two approaches were the same, with minor variations. On second thought, this should occasion no surprise; the reasons have already been made clear. First, they considered Northerners deeply involved in the sin of slavery and saw no essential difference between Northern and Southern attitudes toward the Negro.[49] Second, a number of abolitionists—several of the Lane Rebels, James G. Birney, the Grimké sisters, and others—were reformed slaveholders, and abolitionists understandably believed that many more could be induced to follow their path.[50] Third, the individualistic and evangelical terms in which they defined both their task as agitators and the nature of conversion to abolitionism assured them that the conscience of even the most unregenerate slaveholder could be awakened by the redeeming truth if only the channels of communication were kept open and flooded by unremitting propaganda that permitted the guilty soul no hiding place. Those abolitionists who finally gave up hope of converting the South did so, it appears, not because they had lost faith in the power of their message to work conversions but because Southern leaders prevented the message from reaching its intended audience.[51] Southern postmasters and local leaders who could burn *Liberators* and intimidate subscribers could not stop private correspondence, and individual abolitionists with slaveholding

acquaintances continued by letter the efforts they were prevented from exerting in an organized way.[52]

The abolitionists' approach to the South has been the occasion for some rather blatant errors of the "presentist" type
among historians. Antiabolitionist scholars, noting the hopelessness of converting the South and the uselessness of converting the North, contemn the whole abolitionist enterprise.
Proabolitionist scholars, noting the hopelessness of converting
the South, diligently search for and find justifications for
agitation confined to the North. Those justifications are, I
think, better founded than the motive that led to their discovery.[53] Howard Zinn, for example, argues that "only the
hypothesis of common interest for the entire population can
justify an appeal to the opponent on the basis of reason, asking
him to perceive his interest more accurately"; therefore Garrison was justified in using harsh language, for a radical cannot
hope "to please that element of the population which cannot
possibly be pleased by anything short of total surrender of
principle, whose self-interest in fact dictates rejection of any
reform."[54] The fact is that during the period covered in the
present study it was not at all clear *to the abolitionists* that
large numbers of slaveholders were past saving, and it was
clear *to the abolitionists* that slaveholders, slaves, and Northerners did have common interests—in salvation and social
justice.[55] "The *one* question for us to ask," wrote Mrs. Child,

> is, What is our duty? What course will best promote the
> true interests of the slave and the slaveholder? Whoever
> looks upon the subject in the light of principle and
> reason, will see that the interests of those two classes,
> fearfully as they now clash, would, in a right order of
> things, be most harmonious.[56]

Further, the harsh language used by Garrison and most
other abolitionist propagandists, in denouncing the sin of
slavery, was not defended on the ground that the chief sinners
would reject all appeals in any case and hence need not be
considered so far as tactics were concerned. On the contrary,
abolitionists repeatedly explained that the slaveholders' con-

sciences could be reached in no other way than the plain—and therefore harsh—declaration that their relation to their chattels was sinful and must be abandoned if the wrath of God were to be averted.

> You may go to the profligate man [explained Amos A. Phelps], and tell him it is for his interest to reform, and he will be a profligate still. So with the slave-holder. You must reach his conscience, and in order to [do] this, you must tell him the plain truth in regard to the moral character of his conduct.[57]

Added the Rhode-Island Anti-Slavery Society: "We expect not to dissuade men from their sins by concealing from them the fact that their conduct is sinful. . . ."[58] The evangelical cast of most abolitionists' thinking provided the initial urge to employ the strong language of the preacher warning his flock of the consequences of their persistence in sin. The preacher saw no incompatibility between the sinner's present intransigence and the possibility of his eventual conversion; in fact, it was the existence of both facts that made the harsh language necessary. Similarly, the abolitionist accepted both the present intransigence of the slaveholder and the phenomenon of conversion; his own harsh language was to be the bridge between the two.

There was more than one path to the slaveholders' consciences, however; interest was one. It is important to understand that when the abolitionists explained to Southerners that slaves were less productive than free workers, that the poverty of the South was due to the slave system,[59] that the civilized world condemned them, and that bloodshed might result from their failure to emancipate their bondsmen, they were not replacing their principled appeals by others that had a better chance of being heeded.[60] On the contrary, if the South, wrote Elizur Wright, Jr., was compelled, solely by considerations of interest, to abolish slavery, the sin would be unrepented and the reformation only nominal.[61] But appeals to interest could open the door by jarring the slaveholder from his complacency; the abolitionist might then open the door a bit wider by showing the troubled sinner the link between his worldly and his eternal interests.

But how could he reach the slaveholder's ear after the South had imposed its intellectual embargo on antislavery propaganda? By imposing a "moral embargo" on the South. Elizur Wright, Jr., formulated thus the theory concurred in by many of his coworkers:

> It were idle to expect to convert the mass of slaveholders by a diffusion of pamphlets; that can only be done by placing them under a moral embargo—by letting them see the image of their crime thrown back upon them from the moral sentiment of every non-slaveholder they meet. The work lies chiefly at the North.[62]

The work lay partly in Britain as well, according to Frederick Douglass in a speech that he delivered over and over, with variations in wording:

> I am met by the objection, that to do so [organize abolition societies in England] is to excite, irritate, and disturb the slaveholder. Sir, this is just what I want. I wish the slaveholder to be irritated. I want him jealous: I desire to see him alarmed and disturbed. Sir, by thus alarming him, you have the means of blistering his conscience, and it can have no life in it unless it is blistered.[63]

In short, if the slaveholders refused to allow direct appeals to their consciences, the abolitionists must find an indirect route. They must ostracize Southerners at Northern resorts like Newport, refuse fellowship with them in churches, proclaim their iniquity throughout the world via platform and printing press, demonstrate that slavery was in the long run destructive to the soil of the South as well as the soul of the Southerner, and perhaps make that system unprofitable in the short run by boycotting slave-grown produce. It was hoped that slaveowners, deprived of the friendship, fellowship, and patronage that lulled their consciences, would be forced to see themselves as the civilized world saw them, and examine the morality of their way of life. At that point they would become receptive to appeals to their sense of justice and their fear of God.[64] Interest would yield to principle. It will be

noted that this tactic was identical to the one used to convert
the North; there too appeals to interest were to plow the
ground in which the seed of principle would be planted.

After the South imposed its blockade on abolitionist propaganda, it became clear that the seed of principle must first take
root and the crop be harvested in the North to make the same
process possible in the South. Hence, the abolitionists' concentration of effort to abolitionize the North did not represent an
abandonment of the Southern field; rather, it was seen as a
precondition for converting the South.[65] On this tactic all
abolitionists concurred. They differed on how an abolitionized
North could have an impact on the South, but most of them
remained convinced, throughout the period covered by this
study, that abolitionist propaganda not only could but did have
that impact. Repeatedly they quoted statements by eminent
Southerners expressing fears that such propaganda was trou-
bling slaveholders' consciences and damaging their morale. The
Annual Report of the AASS in 1836, for example, noted the
burning of antislavery literature in Charleston and President
Jackson's message to Congress in which he recommended passage of a law prohibiting circulation in the South of literature
intended to instigate slave revolts. The report commented that
Southern leaders knew that abolitionists did not direct their
propaganda to the slaves or favor insurrections, but that the
literature was intended to appeal to the consciences of the
whites. It quoted Duff Green, editor of the *United States
Telegraph,* "one of the most authoritative organs of *Southern*
opinions," to the effect that the South had nothing to fear
from slave revolt and that the abolitionists neither intended to,
nor could if they would, incite rebellion. "We believe," it
quoted Green as saying, "that we have most to fear from the
organized action upon the CONSCIENCES and fears of the slaveholders themselves. . . . It is only by alarming the *consciences* of the weak and feeble, and diffusing among our own
people a morbid sensibility on the question of slavery, that the
abolitionists can accomplish their object." The report then
quoted John C. Calhoun to the same effect. Angelina E.
Grimké quoted the same words by Green and Calhoun, in a

pamphlet published in 1837, and added similar statements by other Southerners. Two years later a pamphlet by William Jay quoted the editorial which Green may by then have regretted ever having written.[66]

Ralph E. Morrow has drawn attention to a fact that makes abolitionist efforts to convert slaveholders appear reasonable: that white Southerners were not united and thoroughly convinced of the rightness of slavery. True, the abolitionists attributed Southern qualms of conscience to what remained of real Christianity in the South and to their own agitation, whereas Morrow shows that they were largely due to the persistence of Jeffersonian thought.[67] But the qualms were there, and abolitionists were quite correct in inferring that not all slaveholders' minds were absolutely shut to their message. Morrow also quotes a statement by the eminent proslavery theorist George Fitzhugh that suggests another defense of abolitionist tactics against criticism by modern historians. Fitzhugh wrote that since many Southerners suspected slavery to be morally wrong, "we must vindicate [the] institution in the abstract."[68] If Fitzhugh was right, so were the abolitionists in attacking slavery in the abstract, that is, as a moral wrong, for such a tactic struck at the slaveholders' most vulnerable spot.

It is interesting to speculate what the result would have been if a large part of the abolitionist movement had not weakened the moral focus of its propaganda and accepted the compromises dictated by political expediency. I am not arguing that the slaveholders could have been converted en masse by attacks on slavery as a sin; I think Garrison was right when he said that no oppressor class ever had given up its power and the American slaveholders would be no exception. But one cannot help wondering whether the abolitionist movement did not yield too much when the major part of it, during the 1840s, played down the purely agitational sort of tactics in favor of a type of political action that gave increasing emphasis to pragmatic alliances with politicians who would not denounce slavery in the abstract. One wonders whether a perseverance in the tactic of agitation and conversion would not have helped to weaken the slaveholders' will to fight.

NOTES

[1] *Fifth Annual Report of the Board of Managers of the Massachusetts Anti-Slavery Society*, p. vii.

[2] The therapeutic function of conventions is mentioned in Elizur Wright, Jr., to Theodore D. Weld, April 2, 1836, in Barnes and Dumond, eds., *Weld-Grimké Letters*, I, 291; circular letter from New-Jersey Anti-Slavery Society, July 16, 1841, Weld Papers, Box 7, UM; L. B. C. Wyman and A. Wyman, *Elizabeth Buffum Chace, 1806–1899: Her Life and Its Environment* (Boston, 1914), I, 137. Elizur Wright, Jr., in a letter to his father, September 20, 1834, Wright Papers, LC, advocated a plan whereby individuals would contribute 12½¢ a month to the cause: "Not the least advantage of this plan is involved in the law of human nature, 'that our sympathy for the suffering is in proportion to what we do for their relief.' Those who *give systematically* will *feel*. And *their* feelings will not grow cold." During the petition campaign, abolitionists sometimes pointed out that a person who could be induced to sign his name would feel committed thereby and become more receptive to further propaganda.

[3] Walter M. Merrill, *Against Wind and Tide*, p. 192. John L. Thomas, *The Liberator: William Lloyd Garrison*, pp. 339–40, mentions the incident but offers no comment other than that Garrison was glad he was a Bostonian.

[4] *The Liberator*, February 14, 1840.

[5] Garrison to George W. Benson, September 4, 1835, Garrison Papers, BPL.

[6] I do not contend that this verse appears more often than any other. In fact, abolitionist writings prior to 1850 reveal thorough familiarity with the Bible; many essays (by Garrison, especially) contain dozens of scriptural phrases incorporated integrally in the writers' own sentences, to such an extent that it is clear that the Bible provided the frame of reference for much abolitionist thinking in the 1830s and 1840s. But Hebrews 13:3 appears often enough to have special significance. A few examples are: Wyman and Wyman, *Elizabeth Buffum Chace*, I, 94 (quoting journal entry by Mrs. Chace in 1842); Garrison, "Repeal of the Union," *The Liberator*, May 6, 1842; letter to the editor from Noah Jackman, telling of a circular, adopted at an antislavery meeting in Massachusetts and sent to ministers to be read to their congregations, *ibid.*, February 16, 1844; Garrison, "Gerrit Smith's Constitutional Argument. No. III," *ibid.*, October 4, 1844; "Annual Report of the Weymouth Female Anti-Slavery Society," *ibid.*, October 17, 1845; Garrison, in introduction to "Letter from Another Martyr in the Cause of Freedom," *ibid.*, June 8, 1848; Beriah Green, *Things for Northern Men to Do* (1836), excerpted in Pease and Pease, eds., *The Antislavery Argument*, p. 186; Nathaniel P. Rogers, "Color-Phobia" (1838), *ibid.*, p. 319; Elizur Wright, Jr., to Beriah Green, March 29, 1836, Wright Papers, LC; Samuel J. May in *Fourth Annual Report of the Board of Managers of the Massachusetts Anti-Slavery Society* (Boston, 1836), pp. 4–5; [An-

gelina E. Grimké], *An Appeal to the Women of the Nominally Free States* (New York, 1837), p. 18; James Forten, *An Address Delivered before the Ladies Anti-Slavery Society of Philadelphia*, on the Evening of the 14th of April 1836 (Philadelphia, 1836), p. 13, as quoted in Keith E. Melder, "The Beginnings of the Women's Rights Movement in the United States, 1800–1840," Ph.D. dissertation, Yale University, 1964, p. 158; two letters from women's antislavery societies to the Anti-Slavery Convention of American Women (see *Proceedings of the Anti-Slavery Convention of American Women* [Philadelphia, 1838], pp. 17, 18).

7 Wyman and Wyman, *Elizabeth Buffum Chace*, II, 283.

8 *Things for Northern Men to Do*, in Pease and Pease, eds., *The Antislavery Argument*, p. 186. New York abolitionists, in a fund-raising appeal to children, asked them to act as if "their own fathers and mothers were in chains and bleeding beneath the whip" (*Emancipator Extra*, June 6, 1835, quoted in Bertram Wyatt-Brown, "The Abolitionists' Postal Campaign of 1835," *Journal of Negro History*, L [October 1965], 228).

9 "I could wish that bro. Foster would exercise more judgment and discretion in the presentation of his views; but it is useless to reason with him . . ." (Garrison to his wife, November 27, 1842, Garrison Papers, BPL). Edmund Quincy also disapproved of Foster's tactic of disturbing church services; see his "Divisions of Abolitionists," *The Liberator*, December 30, 1842.

10 Foster presented a resolution at a meeting in 1845: "Resolved, That as the Constitution of the United States guarantees the support and protection of the slave power, all who acknowledge allegiance to the federal government are, emphatically, slaveholders, and as such, are justly chargeable with all the guilt inherent in the slave system." The motion was tabled (*Twelfth Annual Report Presented to the Massachusetts Anti-Slavery Society, by Its Board of Managers* [Boston, 1844], p. 89). The restraint doubtless shown by Foster because this was a meeting of an antislavery society was absent when James Boyle presented the following resolution passed at meeting of "New Covenant Believers from various parts of the country" at Hartford in 1843: "Resolved, That no member of the church of Christ has ever held a slave or apologized for slavery, has ever practised or advocated war, physical resistance to evil—has ever practised or advocated intemperance, or manufactured drunkards, has ever practically or theoretically taught the inferiority of woman or the rightfulness of her subordination to man, or has claimed exclusive possession of any thing in heaven or earth or sea." (*The Liberator*, March 31, 1843) See also a Foster resolution, as reported *ibid.*, September 17, 1841. Abby Kelley, whom Foster married a few years later, was the butt of some good-natured chaffing based on a tongue-in-cheek application of domino logic. Miss Kelley of course approved of recent antislavery resolutions condemning most American churches as "brotherhoods of thieves" and "bulwarks of slavery." According to a letter from one Garrisonian to another, Miss Kelley at breakfast one day "was telling us of her going to Mtg. in Deacon somebody's carriage—whereupon J. G. Gibbons pencilled the following 'Whereas Abby Kelly [*sic*] did by her own confession, ride in a

Deacon's carriage, said Deacon being a member of the Bulwarks.—
Therefore,—Resolved that she has *not* come out & separated herself
from the American Church & is "striking hands"—with living body
snatchers—and cat o' nine tail devils.'" (Sarah Pugh to Richard and
Hannah Webb, June 17, 1842, Anti-Slavery Letters, BPL)

11 For example, see editorial "Progress of the Anti-Slavery Movement," *The Liberator*, January 28, 1842, in which Garrison refers to "the
still more guilty North."

12 *Seventeenth Annual Report, Presented to the Massachusetts Anti-
Slavery Society, by Its Board of Managers* (Boston, 1849), p. 11.

13 *Ibid.*, p. 10. Almost every issue of every antislavery newspaper
contained these and similar arguments. See Julian P. Bretz, "The Economic Background of the Liberty Party," *American Historical Review*,
XXXIV (January 1929), 252–57, for analysis of antislavery propaganda
aimed at proving that the depression that began in 1837 was the fault of
the slave power. Russel B. Nye, *Fettered Freedom, passim*, describes in
great detail the abolitionists' efforts to show the North that its own
freedom of speech was doomed if slavery were not abolished. For the
portrayal of the North as willing victim of the South, see, for example,
Elizur Wright, Jr., to Beriah Green, March 29, 1836, Wright Papers, LC.
Wright wrote that abolitionists would "be both *wicked* and *weak*" if
they neglected to show the North the danger of a certain legislative
action on the part of defenders of slavery (emphasis in original). See
also two editorials by Garrison, "Shall Texas Be Annexed to the Union?
—No. 1," and "The Texas Question," *The Liberator*, June 30, 1837, in
which he wrote that Northerners were not ignorant of their part in
upholding slavery but were ignorant of how that complicity threatened
their own freedom; racism had blinded them. Hence it was their interest
as well as their duty to fight against slavery. In the decade before the
Civil War the verse from the Epistle to the Hebrews appears less often
than before, partly because the religious motive was less important, but
also, one suspects, because events were convincing the North that it *was*
a victim of the slave power.

14 Birney to Myron Holley, Joshua Leavitt, and Elizur Wright, Jr.,
May 11, 1840, *Birney Letters*, I, 567–71.

15 Abolitionists did, of course, help *Northern* Negroes assert those
rights, as, for example, when two of them protested when Frederick
Douglass was ejected from a railroad car; they were thrown out along
with him and then tried in vain to ride in the Jim Crow car with him.
That incident and others are described in a letter to the editor from
John A. Collins, *The Liberator*, October 15, 1841. Another article in the
same issue prints protest resolutions passed at public meetings. Other
items of this nature can be found from time to time in *The Liberator*.
Abolitionists were also active in efforts to repeal the anti-intermarriage
law and the law permitting Jim Crow accommodations on public carriers
in Massachusetts and in efforts to integrate Boston public schools.

16 A good example of this argument is in *Proceedings of the Rhode-
Island Anti-Slavery Convention* (Providence, 1836), pp. 55–56.

17 Abolitionists recognized the ethical problem involved. Ellis Gray
Loring, for instance, wrote an essay intended to show the legitimacy of

appealing to other interests of Northern whites as well—the esteem in which labor was held, the prosperity of the Northern economy, the morals of the young, and the peace of the community. "I would never, even in argument," he wrote, "subordinate conscience to interest. . . . Nevertheless, I would take pains to let men see that it is no less a part of God's truth, and, according to the order of his Providence, that a community will not be the poorer for righteousness, than it is that it is the duty of a community to be righteous." (*The Liberator*, November 5, 1841)

¹⁸ Jackson to Samuel J. May, November 25, 1835, in Ruchames, ed., *The Abolitionists*, p. 120.

¹⁹ *The Liberator* occasionally printed such items in its section reserved for miscellaneous reprints of news items from other papers.

²⁰ See especially Garrison's editorial "The Declaration of American Independence," *The Liberator*, September 5, 1835, in which he mentioned instances of whites having been enslaved and stated that he had been shocked to encounter such cases, "not because I deemed it a more heinous crime in the sight of God to enslave a white than a black man, or to lacerate a white than a black woman, but because it revealed the utter insecurity in which the liberty of all my countrymen was placed, especially those whose skins are less transparent than others." Any of us, he added, including the swarthy Daniel Webster, might be kidnapped and sold; for at what shade could one draw the line? There were thousands of slaves whiter than their masters. See also Gerrit Smith's speech reported in *Third Annual Report of the American Anti-Slavery Society* (New York, 1836), pp. 17–18. Abolitionists were fond of quoting the 1835 message of Governor George McDuffie to the South Carolina legislature in which he defended slavery as the best status for all laborers, "bleached or unbleached." Garrison printed the speech in *The Liberator*, December 12, 1835. Two of many instances of its use in abolitionist propaganda are: *Proceedings of the Rhode-Island Anti-Slavery Convention*, p. 37; and William Goodell, *Slavery and Anti-Slavery*, p. 413. A similar point, in somewhat different context, is made by Jules Zanger, in "The 'Tragic Octoroon' in Pre-Civil War Fiction," *American Quarterly*, XVIII (Spring 1966), 63–70, especially pp. 64–67.

²¹ Lorman Ratner, "Northern Opposition to the Anti-Slavery Movement, 1831–1840," Ph.D. dissertation, Cornell University, 1961, pp. 212, 31.

²² Younger historians are reading the sources with deeper understanding. See Martin Duberman, "The Northern Response to Slavery," in Duberman, ed., *The Antislavery Vanguard*, pp. 402–6; and the brilliant article by Anne C. Loveland, "Evangelicalism and 'Immediate Emancipation' in American Antislavery Thought," *Journal of Southern History*, XXXII (May 1966), 172–88. According to Miss Loveland, "historians have usually misconstrued the immediatist slogan, interpreting it as a temporal rather than a moral and religious requirement. They have read into it a deadline for emancipation that misses the point and purpose of the abolitionist demand." "When abolitionists demanded immediate emancipation, they were . . . arguing that abolition was fully

within man's power and completely dependent upon his initiative," and "since action was the test of belief, true repentance virtually entailed the abolition of slavery" (pp. 173, 184, 185). An excellent formulation of this function of the immediatist slogan, by an abolitionist, is in Samuel J. May to Amos A. Phelps, March 18, 1834, Phelps Papers, BPL. See also James G. Birney to Gerrit Smith, November 14, 1834, in *Birney Letters*, I, 148.

[23] Nathaniel P. Rogers, "Color-Phobia" (1838), in Pease and Pease, eds., *The Antislavery Argument*, p. 319. See also Merton L. Dillon, "The Failure of the American Abolitionists," *Journal of Southern History*, XXV (May 1959), 165–67. Here is one of the few points at which a parallel can be drawn between the abolitionist and black-power movements.

[24] One of many documents that support the abolitionists' approach as well as Ratner's thesis (see note 21 above) is an article in the *Wilmington Loco-Foco* which Garrison appropriately reprinted in his "Refuge of Oppression" column, *The Liberator*, July 23, 1841. The *Loco-Foco* proclaimed its devotion to the principle of universal liberty as formulated in the Declaration of Independence, the U.S. Constitution, the constitution of every state, and the platform of the Democratic party. But, "Phrenology has established the disparity of the different castes of the human race on too firm a foundation for abolitionism to overthrow, a union between which is naturally abhorrent and repugnant to the human heart; . . . and while this natural repugnance exists, the superior caste will bear the palm." Since the *Loco-Foco* felt it would be unjust to continue enslaving Negroes or to expatriate them forcibly, it concluded that the problem "must be left to the inscrutable wisdom of Him, who, in his all-wise providence," would ordain the solution.

[25] For example, [Edmund Quincy], "Chattel Slavery and Wages Slavery," *The Liberator*, October 1, 1847; and Garrison, "Lyman Beecher," *ibid.*, August 6, 1836.

[26] Anti-Slavery Letters, BPL, include letters by James Mott, Edward M. Davis, and Wendell Phillips written during the potato famine, strongly sympathizing with the Irish and deploring the circumstances that forced so many to emigrate. On the other hand, some abolitionists seem to have been amazingly ignorant of New England workers' conditions. See, for example, John Greenleaf Whittier's pamphlet *Justice and Expediency* (1833), as excerpted in Ruchames, ed., *The Abolitionists*, pp. 46–57; on p. 54 he contrasts the slave system to "the beautiful system of free labor as exhibited in New England, where every young laborer, with health and ordinary prudence, may acquire by his labor on the farms of others, in a few years, a farm of his own." Whittier's automatic identification of free labor with rural employment may perhaps be excused in view of the early date of his pamphlet.

[27] *The Liberator*, December 18, 1840.

[28] *Ibid.* See also Garrison's editorial "The London Convention," *ibid.*, October 23, 1840, in which he expressed his low opinion of British abolitionism (excepting individuals such as George Thompson, Harriet Martineau, and Charles Stuart) as motivated by "nothing more than the

natural humanity of the people." In England, he wrote, "it costs no effort to denounce that which does not exist on her soil at home, to wit, slavery. Her abolitionism 'walks in silver slippers,' is *patronized* by her majesty the Queen, receives the condescending support of Prince Albert. . . . Hence, individuals may be very zealous and devoted there in the anti-slavery cause . . . and yet be as hostile to the spirit of freedom, and as unwilling to encounter odium and persecution by espousing an unpopular and radical reform at home, as is the pro-slavery party in the United States." Chartists who broke up antislavery meetings "have not been actuated by any hostility to the anti-slavery enterprise; but, perceiving that some of those who are most vociferous in denouncing oppression abroad, care nothing for suffering humanity at home, they have been stirred up to acts of violence, in their disgust at such hollow-hearted philanthropy. Their conduct is not to be justified, but it certainly admits of some palliation. The Chartists, in their struggle for emancipation, are the abolitionists of the United States; and they are as much hated and feared by all that is conservative, inhuman or despotic." Edward M. Davis, in a letter to Elizabeth Pease, February 15, 1842, Anti-Slavery Letters, BPL, asked, "Why are not the abolitionists of G. Britian [sic], chartists repealers & ultra democrats? If hatred of oppression has taken root in the *soul* not in the *fancy*, will not those who cherish it, favour political as well as personal and I may ask religious liberty? There is no beauty in that love of liberty which sympathises with the American slave and forgets the oppressed at home."

29 The fact that American workers had the vote and British workers did not helps explain American abolitionists' greater sympathy for the latter and their willingness to agree that British workers were oppressed. See, for instance, speeches by Charles Lenox Remond and John A. Collins, reported in *The Liberator*, July 30 and August 6, 1841.

30 Collins's letters to Garrison, in Anti-Slavery Letters, BPL, during his British tour in 1840 and 1841, show his gradual change in views and growing interest in communitarian socialism. Wendell Phillips ridiculed those views in a letter to Elizabeth Pease, August 24, 1843, same collection. Collins's departure from the abolitionist movement is mentioned in "Chattel Slavery and Wages Slavery," editorial by [Edmund Quincy] in *The Liberator*, October 1, 1847. His disillusionment with communitarianism is explained in his article "Ourselves," reprinted from his paper, *The Daytonian* (Dayton, Ohio), in *The Liberator*, August 28, 1846.

31 The March 27, 1846, and July 10, 1846, issues contain minor items on the subject before the real debate began.

32 "Free and Slave Labor," *The Liberator*, March 26, 1847. See also Garrison to his wife, May 20, 1840, Garrison Papers, BPL, in which he describes extremes of wealth and poverty he has observed on his trip to New York City and attributes the suffering to selfishness.

33 The article is reprinted in John R. Commons and others, eds., *A Documentary History of American Industrial Society*, VII (*Labor Movement: 1840–1860*) (New York, 1958), 219–21. Phillips stressed the difference between working conditions in Britain and the United States more than most of his associates, perhaps because he had traveled more

extensively and sojourned longer in Britain and on the Continent and
unconsciously emphasized the greater oppression of European labor by
exaggerating the opportunities open to American labor. For example, see
his letter to Richard Webb, January 13, 1848, Anti-Slavery Letters, BPL,
in which he enumerated certain categories of British labor paid so little
that such workers could be considered "*unpaid*, uncompensated, in any
just sense."

[34] "Chattel Slavery and Wages Slavery," *The Liberator*, October 1,
1847.

[35] See accounts of the New England Anti-Slavery Convention of
1847, *ibid.*, June 4, 1847; and of the annual meeting of the AASS the
following year, *ibid.*, May 19, 1848. Cf. George Bradburn's scorn for
"such men as Edmund Quincy and Wendell Phillips, the latter of whom
has expressed the opinion, that all the people of this country, excepting
the slaves, may easily become 'capitalists' by a little 'piety' and 'economy'; and the former gentleman tells us, in the last Liberator I received,
that it is purely the fault of the masses themselves, if every thing is not
right with them, in this glorious country of ours!" Bradburn to Gerrit
Smith, October 8, 1847, Gerrit Smith Miller Collection, SU.

[36] "Seventeenth Annual Meeting of the Massachusetts A. Slavery
Society," *The Liberator*, February 2, 1849. Before the resolution was
voted on, a member said most of the workers' problems were due to
drinking and that this was especially true of the Irish. The mover,
Charles Stearns, defended his resolution with remarks on the sufferings
of Northern workers. The incident is reported also in *Seventeenth
Annual Report, Presented to the Massachusetts Anti-Slavery Society, by
Its Board of Managers*, pp. 85–86. See also Garrison's resolution, reported
in *Fifteenth Annual Report, Presented to the Massachusetts Anti-Slavery
Society, by Its Board of Managers* (Boston, 1847), p. 91: "*Resolved*, That
of all classes in this country, to whom the three millions of our enslaved
and chattelized countrymen have a right confidently to look for
sympathy, aid, and complete deliverance from their horrible servitude,
THE WORKING-MEN of the North constitute that class; and so long as they
stand aloof from the Anti-Slavery enterprise, they will not only be
guilty of manufacturing yokes for the necks, and fetters for the limbs, of
the Southern Slave population, but will fail in all their efforts to remove
those burdens and monopolies, under which they themselves are
groaning."

[37] For example, Samuel J. May and Garrison believed the laborer had
to work too hard and too long, and they wished he had more than one
day off each week. Garrison to May, January 10, 1848, Garrison Papers,
BPL; and May to Garrison, January 15, 1848, Anti-Slavery Letters,
BPL.

[38] Cf. David Donald's interpretation in "Toward a Reconsideration of
Abolitionists," in *Lincoln Reconsidered* (New York, 1956), p. 31, which
is different from but compatible with mine.

[39] Joseph Rayback, "The American Workingman and the Anti-
slavery Crusade," *Journal of Economic History*, III (November 1943),
152–63; the quotation is on p. 155. The fullest discussion of the relation

abolition to the workingmen's movement is Bernard Mandel, *Labor, Free and Slave: Workingmen and the Anti-Slavery Movement in the United States* (New York, 1955).

40 See Rayback, p. 159, for a statement to that effect by a utopian socialist paper in 1843.

41 See, for example, "The Constitution—Political Action. Number III," *The Liberator*, May 1, 1846, in which Garrison wrote, "There is no necessity imposed on any man to be a villain, or to sanction villany [*sic*]."

42 Slaveholders' "understandings have become brutish, their consciences seared as with a hot iron, and their hearts harder than adamant" (Garrison to Joseph Pease, August 3, 1840, Garrison Papers, BPL). The tendency of slavery is "adverse to the improvement of master as well as slave. Slavery takes away the spur of intellectual, not less than of physical enterprise. . . ." (*Second Annual Report of the American Anti-Slavery Society* [New York, 1835], p. 58)

43 "[S]uppose it true what has been asserted, that the vast majority [of slaves] are contented and happy—*this* contentment and happiness should be considered not as the best, but as the very worst and most deplorable effect of slavery." ("Address to the People of the United States," by a committee of the New-England Anti-Slavery Convention, *The Liberator*, September 6, 1834)

44 This is one of the most frequently encountered indictments of slavery. One instance of its use is in Theodore S. Wright, "Prejudice against the Colored Man" (1837), in Ruchames, ed., *The Abolitionists*, p. 137.

45 "Chattel Slavery and Wages Slavery," *The Liberator*, October 1, 1847.

46 Garrison to Henry C. Wright, April 1, 1843, Garrison Papers, BPL. He was specifically criticizing Owen's doctrine that, as Garrison put it, "it is by association alone, in a distinctive community formed on the basis of equal rights and equal property, that the regeneration of the world is to be effected." Garrison was sympathetic to the Northampton community of which his brother-in-law, George W. Benson, was a member; however, members of that community did not own its property in common (see William Bassett to Elizabeth Pease, July 22, 1844, Anti-Slavery Letters, BPL), and Garrison in any case saw such communities as results rather than causes of individual regeneration. Ten years later Garrison expressed the same conviction: at a Woman's Rights Convention in Cleveland in 1853, he replied thus to Ernestine Rose's statement that "society" was to blame for oppression of women: "Society! I know nothing of society. I know the guilt of individuals. Society is an abstract term: it is made up of individuals, and the responsibility rests with individuals." (Elizabeth Cady Stanton and others, eds., *The History of Woman Suffrage* [New York, 1881], I, 139)

47 The only evidence of such awareness that I have seen is Garrison's letter to Henry C. Wright, December 16, 1843, in Garrisons, *Garrison*, III, 94n–95n. After criticizing Collins's recent conversion to communitarianism, Garrison wrote: "He holds, with Robert Owen, that man is the creature of circumstances, and therefore not deserving of praise or blame for what he does—a most absurd and demoralizing doctrine, in my

opinion, which will make shipwreck of any man or any scheme under its guidance, in due season. Still, it cannot be denied that circumstances are often very unfavorable to the development of man's faculties and moral nature; and if, by a reorganization of society, these can be rendered more favorable,—as doubtless they can, let it take place. But it is an internal rather than an outward reorganization that is needed to put away the evil that is in the world."

48 The abolitionists' dilemma concerning their rejection of the "doctrine of circumstances" while recognizing the effects of slavery on the slaves finds an interesting parallel with the dilemma of modern liberal historians who recognize the effects of environment on personality, as a general proposition, yet assume (sometimes unconsciously) an inherent love of freedom or an irreducible human dignity impervious to environmental conditioning. See the perceptive critique of Kenneth Stampp's *Peculiar Institution* in Stanley Elkins, *Slavery*, p. 23, for a similar point.

49 Nathaniel P. Rogers used this common abolitionist proposition to argue against Garrison's disunionist policy: "Why should they [the North and the South] separate? Are they not *agreed?* Are they not alike? Are they disagreed as to *slavery*,—or any other iniquity? . . . They shouldn't separate on the slavery question, for they don't differ on it. The North is a little more servile and pro-slavery than the South, to be sure, but not enough to *warrant any quarrel*." Reprint from *The Herald of Freedom*, of "New-England Convention," *The Liberator*, June 21, 1844.

50 See Theodore D. Weld to James Hall, May 20, 1834, in Barnes and Dumond, eds., *Weld-Grimké Letters*, I, 138–39. Of the eighteen speakers at the Lane Seminary debates, Weld wrote, eight had been born and lived all their lives in slave states; the other ten had lived in slave states, six from one to six years. The states in which these students had gained their firsthand knowledge of slavery were Virginia, the Carolinas, Alabama, Tennessee, Missouri, Kentucky, Louisiana, Arkansas (territory), Maryland, and Mississippi. The *First Annual Report of the American Anti-Slavery Society*, pp. 49–50, cited the Lane episode as proof that slaveholders could be converted, reported evidence from various parts of the South that abolitionist literature was having an effect, and pointed to recent efforts in Kentucky and Tennessee to abolish slavery gradually (the report argued the fallacy of gradualism but praised the good intentions manifested). *Proceedings of the Rhode-Island Anti-Slavery Convention* (1836), p. 52, cited Birney's conversion as proof that slaveholders' consciences could be reached.

51 There were exceptions, however. Garrison seems to have vacillated between confidence in the power of the truth—a confidence required by his religious tenets—and pessimism resulting from his realistic appraisal of evidence. One expression of this pessimism is in his letter to Joseph Pease, August 3, 1840, Garrison Papers, BPL, in which he wrote "that there is no instance recorded . . . in which the oppressors and enslavers of mankind, except in individual cases, have been induced, by mere moral suasion, to surrender their despotic power, and let the oppressed go free." West Indian emancipation was no exception, for "it was effected by the colossal power of the mother country, and in opposition

to the feelings and wishes of the West India planters." There was, he added, no more chance of converting the mass of American slaveholders by appeals to conscience and reason than of transforming "wolves and hyenas into lambs and doves, by the same process." See also Garrison to Elizabeth Pease, November 6, 1837, in Garrisons, *Garrison*, II, 183–84. Lydia Maria Child early became convinced that slavery would end only by violence. See her letter to Abby Kelley, October 1, 1838, in Stephen S. and Abby Kelley Foster Papers, AAS; and to Angelina G. Weld, October 2, 1838, in *Weld-Grimké Letters*, II, 704. James G. Birney had periods of pessimism and depression in which he lost hope of converting slaveholders. For one such period, see his letters to Gerrit Smith, July 14 and September 13, 1835, in *Birney Letters*, I, 202, 243. Angelina G. Weld wrote to Elizabeth Pease, August 14, 1839 (*Weld-Grimké Letters*, II, 784–85), that she was beginning to fear the slaveholders would not repent and that abolition must come by violence. It should be noted that these doubts were expressed only in private letters. Except for Mrs. Child, the doubters were not fixed in their pessimism, in the period covered by this study.

52 See, for example, copy of Gerrit Smith to General John H. Cocke, December 11, 1840, Gerrit Smith Miller Collection, SU; and *Correspondence between the Hon. F. H. Elmore, One of the South Carolina Delegation in Congress, and James G. Birney, One of the Secretaries of the American Anti-Slavery Society* (New York, 1838). Betty Fladeland, in *James Gillespie Birney*, pp. 162–63, explains the circumstances surrounding Birney's correspondence with Elmore.

53 Louis Filler, eager to demonstrate the reasonableness of the abolitionists, states that their problem in the 1830s "was not to persuade the South to emancipate its slaves. Only a few persons were infatuated enough to imagine that Southerners might do so. The problem was to persuade the North to permit the abolitionists to voice their testimony against slavery" ("Nonviolence and Abolition," *University Review*, XXX [March 1964], 172). The reference to conversion of slaveholders is clearly inserted as polemic against antiabolitionist historians, for the two tasks are not mutually exclusive. But Filler may in his eagerness have hurt his cause by stating that those who believed efforts to convert slaveholders might succeed were "infatuated"; there are innumerable statements proving that that is precisely what they believed (see note 58 below). Inability in the 1830s to survey the problem from a twentieth-century perspective is no proof of infatuation.

54 "Abolitionists, Freedom-Riders, and the Tactics of Agitation," in Duberman, ed., *The Antislavery Vanguard*, pp. 434–35. Elsewhere in the essay Zinn does, in my opinion, convincingly defend Garrison's harsh language; the quoted passage does not, however, strengthen the defense, since it is based on an erroneous assumption.

55 David Brion Davis, in "The Emergence of Immediatism in British and American Antislavery Thought," *Mississippi Valley Historical Review*, XLIX (September 1962), 229, explicitly links the evangelical approach to conversion to abolitionism with the abolitionists' rejection of the "doctrine of circumstances" discussed above: "Whereas the gradualist saw man as at least partially conditioned by historical and

social forces, the immediatist saw him as essentially indeterminate and unconditioned. The gradualist, having faith in the certainty of economic and social laws, and fearing the dangers of a sudden collapse of social controls, was content to wait until a legal and rational system of external discipline replaced the arbitrary power of the slaveowner. The immediatist, on the other hand, put his faith in the innate moral capacities of the individual." Although Davis is not here discussing conversion of slaveholders, it is clear that this attitude on the part of abolitionists would cause them to assume that innate moral capacities of slaveholders would permit conversion regardless of economic interest in holding their slaves. On p. 228, Davis explains: "Acceptance of immediatism was the sign of an immediate transformation within the reformer himself; as such, it was seen as an expression of inner freedom, of moral sincerity and earnestness, and of victory over selfish and calculating expediency." Surely, the same process could take place within the slaveholder.

⁵⁶ [Lydia Maria Child?], "Dissolution of the Union," reprinted from *The National Anti-Slavery Standard* in *The Liberator*, May 20, 1842.

⁵⁷ *First Annual Report of the American Anti-Slavery Society*, p. 4.

⁵⁸ *Proceedings of the Rhode-Island Anti-Slavery Convention*, p. 43. This determination to show the slaveholders the sinfulness of their conduct implies an assumption that such efforts were not foredoomed to failure. According to Filler, "few persons" shared that assumption. A quick survey of the 1833–1850 sources shows that these "few" included: Lewis Tappan, 1839 and 1843; Garrison, 1834; the Massachusetts Anti-Slavery Society's board of managers, 1835 and 1838; Newburyport Anti-Slavery Society, 1836; Sarah M. and Angelina E. Grimké, 1837; James S. Gibbons, 1842; Essex County Women's Anti-Slavery Society, 1842; a large group of Unitarian ministers, 1845; Theodore D. Weld, 1834, 1836, and 1838; James G. Birney, 1834 and 1835; John G. Whittier, 1833; Elizur Wright, Jr., 1833; Dr. Charles Follen, 1836; Sereno Streeter, 1836; the American Anti-Slavery Society in its annual reports for 1835 through 1838; and Henry B. Stanton, 1839. See Lewis Tappan, "A Third Political Party" (letter to the editor), *The Emancipator*, November 14, 1839; Lewis Tappan to John Scoble, March 1, 1843, in Annie H. Abel and Frank J. Klingberg, eds., *A Side-Light on Anglo-American Relations, 1839–1858* (n.p., 1927), pp. 114–15; *The Liberator*, November 22, 1834, August 22, 1835, October 29, 1836, July 21 and August 25, 1837, August 10, 1838, May 13 and 27, 1842; "Protest" against slavery by Unitarian ministers, 1845, in May Papers, BPL; Weld to Birney, June 19, 1834, and September 10, 1834, in *Birney Letters*, I, 120–21, 133–35; Introduction to *Emancipation in the West Indies* (1838), in Ruchames, ed., *The Abolitionists*, p. 152 (though originally written by others, the book was completely revised and shortened by Weld, who presumably wrote the introduction); Whittier, *ibid.*, pp. 49, 53; Elizur Wright, Jr., *ibid.*, p. 60; Follen, *ibid.*, p. 134; Streeter to Weld, August 9, 1836, in *Weld-Grimké Letters*, I, 326; *Annual Reports of the American Anti-Slavery Society*: 1835, p. 64; 1836, pp. 46–47; 1837, p. 55; 1838, pp. 108–9; Stanton in *Sixth Annual Report of the American Anti-Slavery Society* (New York, 1839), p. 12. See also sources cited elsewhere in this chapter.

⁵⁹ Examples of such arguments are too numerous to need citation.

One remarkable passage warrants quotation, however, for its modern-sounding analysis of the propensity to consume characteristic of pre-capitalist landed aristocracies: "The slave labor system is notoriously unfavorable to the accumulation of capital. In the management of resources, every thing is sacrificed to present profit. The habit of despotic control generates one of free expenditure." Slaveowners who deviate from this pattern, added the writer, are usually Northern-born. "But to keep up the value of slaves, it is necessary that employment should be found for them, increasing in the same geometrical ratio as the slaves themselves; and to give this employment, far more capital is required than to employ free labor. Whence is this capital to come? From the free states. But will it go from the free states, after slavery comes to be placed on a moral footing with *piracy?*" (*Fifth Annual Report of the Executive Committee of the American Anti-Slavery Society* [New York, 1838], p. 110)

60 Wendell Phillips was an exception. See his letter to George Thompson, July (?), [1839], Anti-Slavery Letters, BPL, in which he wrote that those who were deaf to appeals to principle could be forced by economic distress; they might close their ears to the pulpit, but they would listen to the voice of the market place (he was advocating encouragement of cotton-growing in India).

61 "On Abstinence from the Products of Slave Labor," *Quarterly Anti-Slavery Magazine*, I (July 1836), 399. James G. Birney expressed the same thought in a letter to Gerrit Smith, November 14, 1834, in *Birney Letters*, I, 148: if emancipation were demanded "as a matter of policy, worldly policy, the cause of holiness gains nothing—even if you were to succeed, which I hold to be impossible in the South-West—for you have not put to death, and rendered odious, the *sin* of Slavery by leading those who have committed it to repentance before God." Hence, he added, the failure of all gradualist schemes, for gradualism cannot "lay hold of mens consciences." And hence, he wrote later in that letter (p. 151), the need for denunciation and violent language: "Do you not think it probable, that very gentle and calm measures would not have been sufficient to rouse up from its torpor the public sentiment of this nation, and make it, in spite of itself, look steadfastly at the sin and injustice of Slavery?"

62 "Advance of the Abolition Cause," *Quarterly Anti-Slavery Magazine*, I (October 1835), 103.

63 Farewell Speech to the British People, 1847, in Foner, ed., *Life and Writings of Frederick Douglass*, I, 227. See also Douglass's letter to Horace Greeley, April 15, 1846, *ibid.*, pp. 144-49; a speech in Moorfields, England, 1846, *ibid.*, pp. 162-65; another in New York before the AASS, 1847, *ibid.*, p. 237. In his public letter to his former master, 1849, Douglass wrote that "the heart of the slaveholder is still within the reach of the truth" (*ibid.*, p. 404). The letter from Phillips cited in note 60 above suggests another reason why British abolitionism could affect American slavery: Britons could not be accused of selfish motives, as American abolitionists were, although falsely. Slavery, he wrote, was most often defended from the Bible. "If we construe a text in favor of Liberty—it is set down to partiality and prejudice." But "Your appeals sink deep—they

can neither be avoided nor blunted by any such pretence & their final
result must be conviction. Distance lends them something of the awful
weight of the verdict of posterity."

[64] One example of this line of reasoning is in an article by Sarah and
Angelina Grimké, 1837, in *Weld-Grimké Letters*, I, 366–72.

[65] One of many expressions of this view is in "Letters to Catherine E.
Beecher. No. VIII," by Angelina E. Grimké, *The Liberator*, August 25,
1837: ". . . we know that when public opinion is rectified at the North,
it will necessarily throw an anti-slavery light from its millions of reflecting surfaces upon the heart and soul of the South, through a hundred
thousand different mediums of influence and communication. Public
opinion at the North will be the vehicle by which moral truth will be
rolled in upon the South, a blazing shield turning every way and exhibit-
ing to the eye of every slaveholder in our country the unchangeable and
imperishable principles of justice and truth." The South, added Miss
Grimké, knew full well what the abolitionists were aiming at and feared
the moral power of the North and the world. See also *Fifth Annual
Report of the Executive Committee of the American Anti-Slavery
Society*, pp. 108–9.

[66] *Third Annual Report of the American Anti-Slavery Society*, pp.
46–47; [Angelina E. Grimké], *An Appeal to the Women of the Nominally Free States*, pp. 4–5; William Jay, *A View of the Action of the
Federal Government, in Behalf of Slavery*, 2nd ed. (New York, 1839),
pp. 220–21.

[67] Ralph E. Morrow, "The Proslavery Argument Revisited," *Mississippi Valley Historical Review*, XLVIII (June 1961), 83–84. See also
Charles G. Sellers, Jr., "The Travail of Slavery," in Charles G. Sellers,
Jr., ed., *The Southerner as American* (1960; New York, 1966), pp. 40–71;
on p. 53 he quotes Duff Green's statement quoted on page 259 above.

[68] Fitzhugh, *Cannibals All! or, Slaves without Masters* (Richmond,
Va., 1857), pp. 294–95, as quoted in Morrow, "The Proslavery Argument
Revisited," p. 86.

Afterword

"THE DEMOCRATIC PROCESS"

DISCUSSING GARRISON'S denunciation of both candidates in the 1836 presidential election, John L. Thomas remarks:

> Faced with a decision that involved choosing the lesser of two evils—a cardinal rule in democratic politics—Garrison refused to take the step which he believed an abandonment of principle. In thus committing his followers to a boycott of elections he was in effect challenging the democratic process.[1]

I believe a more pertinent comment on Garrison's policy is to be found in George Santayana's *Character and Opinion in the United States*, in a passage that does not refer specifically to the abolitionists. "The practice of English liberty" (which in this context means the same thing as Thomas's "democratic process") "presupposes," writes Santayana,

> two things: that all concerned are fundamentally unanimous, and that each has a plastic nature which he is willing to modify. If fundamental unanimity is lacking and all are not making in the same general direction, there

can be no honest co-operation, no satisfying compromise. . . . To put things to a vote, and to accept unreservedly the decision of the majority, are points essential to the English system; but they would be absurd if fundamental agreement were not presupposed. Every decision that the majority could conceivably arrive at must leave it still possible for the minority to live and prosper, even if not exactly in the way they wished. . . . In a hearty and sound democracy all questions at issue must be minor matters; fundamentals must have been silently agreed upon and taken for granted when the democracy arose. To leave a decision to the majority is like leaving it to chance—a fatal procedure unless one is willing to have it either way.[2]

When Garrison proclaimed the choice between two proslavery candidates and parties in 1836 a choice between evils, he was challenging not the democratic process but the fundamental consensus within which that particular democratic process took place. His many statements, quoted elsewhere in this book, on the differences between the Whig and Democratic parties on issues other than slavery, demonstrate that he would have been willing to function within a democratic process that had silently agreed upon antislavery and nonresistance fundamentals.

When the fundamentals are agreed upon, a choice made within the democratic process is not between the lesser and the greater evils (both bad), but between the lesser and the greater goods (both acceptable), with the successive choices, in the eyes of the reformer, leading the society step by step closer to an ideal approximation of the fundamental principles silently agreed upon at the start. But what of the radical, as opposed to the reformer—the radical to whom the fundamentals silently agreed upon are qualitatively evil and to whom a quantitative advance toward realization of those principles is at best irrelevant and at worst a betrayal of his cause? The fundamentals, Santayana points out, are never put to a vote, because the opposing sides are not "willing to have it either way." In the antebellum United States slavery was one of those fundamentals, and in fact slavery was not abolished by the democratic process, for by the middle of the century it could never have been put to a vote. When antislavery was, in Elkins's word, "democratized" in a major part of the country, revolution became inevitable—"revolution," that is, in the literal sense of a change in the fundamentals, and not necessarily in the sense of a violent overthrow—for the fundamentals were no longer silently agreed upon, and a new consensus had to come into existence.

Thomas contends that Garrison "more than any other American of his time . . . was responsible for the atmosphere of moral absolutism which caused the Civil War and freed the slave."[3] If Garrison helped to destroy the antebellum consensus (which remains to be proved by a study of the abolitionist movement's impact on public opinion), it was not because he helped to make Northern public opinion reject compromise and gradual abolition but because he helped to make Northern public opinion actively antislavery. There is no reason to believe that in the 1850s Northern public opinion, including that of the majority of abolitionists and Garrison himself, would have rejected gradual emancipation procedures on the basis of an antislavery consensus; there is ample evidence that most slaveowners would have, for it was not immediate abolition they opposed, but abolition on any terms. The point, then, is not that Garrison created an atmosphere of moral absolutism, but that the choice which the nation faced was objectively between absolutely antagonistic moral systems. And Garrison's real choice was not between democratic and undemocratic, or fanatical and reasonable, agitation; it was between antislavery agitation and silence.

NOTES

[1] *The Liberator: William Lloyd Garrison*, pp. 220–21. Cf. Barrington Moore, Jr., *Social Origins of Dictatorship and Democracy:* "In the circumstances of midnineteenth-century American society, any peaceful solution, any victory of moderation, good sense, and democratic process, would have had to be a reactionary solution" (pp. 131–32), and "An

attitude, a frame of mind, without a realistic analysis and program is not enough to make democracy work even if a majority share this outlook. Consensus by itself means little; it depends what the consensus is about" (p. 139).

² New York, 1920, pp. 205–6.

³ Thomas, *The Liberator: William Lloyd Garrison*, p. 4.

Bibliographic Note

Although the abolitionist movement is one of the favorite fields of specialization for American historians, there are surprising gaps in the literature. There is no satisfactory modern survey of the movement's history, and many of the important abolitionists have not yet found their biographers. Furthermore, much of the scholarly work written in the past generation has been flawed by distorting biases and angry partisanships greater than those to be found in almost any other field in American history. For these reasons the nonspecialist, faced with such abundance of books and articles, should not be misled into assuming that a reading of a few of the most recent works will provide him with an adequate grasp of the history of abolitionism. The best bibliography easily available is that in Louis Filler, *The Crusade against Slavery, 1830–1860* (New York, 1960). Many valuable works have been published since that book came out, the direction of which is well represented in the articles in Martin Duberman, ed., *The Antislavery Vanguard: New Essays on the Abolitionists* (Princeton, 1965).

In this study I have paid little attention to personalities and none at all to the way in which individual abolitionists' thinking evolved. I omitted these topics because I wished to examine the tactical ideas and problems on their merits; that is, to deal with abolitionism as a case history of an American agitational movement, focusing on the problems it shared with other movements and playing down those characteristics that were peculiar to it. But a more comprehensive understanding of the abolitionist movement cannot be achieved without consideration of personalities and their development. The reader who wishes to trace the evolution of Garrison's thinking should consult the two recent biographies: John L. Thomas, *The Liberator: William Lloyd Garrison* (Boston, 1963), and Walter M. Merrill, *Against Wind and Tide: A Biography of William Lloyd Garrison* (Cambridge, Mass., 1963). Both attempt to correct the fashion, begun with the publication in 1933 of Gilbert H. Barnes's *The Anti-Slavery Impulse, 1830–1844*, of minimizing Garrison's importance. Both are valuable works, but Merrill's, in my opinion, explains far too many of Garrison's mature views as reactions to his unhappy childhood.

Thomas's brilliant work, on the other hand, repeatedly points out connections between Garrison's beliefs and his intellectual milieu, between contradictions in his thought and ambivalences within the abolitionist movement. I feel, though, that Thomas tends to see contradictions where they do not exist. For example, on p. 136 he states that Garrison's

> disavowal of violence was something less than unequivocal. A month after the [Nat Turner] revolt, he wrote, "I do not justify the slaves in their rebellion: yet I do not condemn *them*, and applaud similar conduct in *white men*. I deny the right of any people to fight for liberty, and so far am a Quaker in principles. Of all men living, however, our slaves have the best reason to assert their rights by violent measures, inasmuch as they are more oppressed than others."

Earlier (pp. 135–36), he offers another example of what he calls Garrison's "ambiguous allegiance to the peace cause." Garrison condemned David Walker's *Appeal*, a tract published in 1829 which called upon the slaves to revolt. Garrison, writes Thomas,

> criticized it as "a most injudicious publication" while admitting that its incitement to violence was "warranted by the creed of an independent people." Although he

"deprecated its circulation," he was forced to admire its "impassioned and determined spirit" and "the bravery and intelligence" of its author.

The first example shows, I believe, Garrison's use of a common propaganda technique: publicizing contradictions in the enemy's ideology. Garrison never lost an opportunity to show white Americans the hypocrisy implicit in their applause for the violent patriots of '76 and their horror at the thought that the slaves, infinitely more aggrieved than the Revolutionists, might emulate them. In pointing out that contradiction, he did not equivocate in his condemnation of all violence. In his comments on Walker's *Appeal*, Garrison made precisely the same point and incidentally gave evidence of a trait that his scholarly critics have denied he possessed: the ability to admire and to see the point of view of someone he disagreed with. I do not interpret this as ambiguity in his allegiance to his own point of view.

In short, I believe that Thomas's work, by far the best extant biography of an abolitionist and one of the most stimulating books on the movement ever written, is limited by its author's inability to empathize with his subject and especially with Garrison's radical cast of mind.

A few other works which can provide the reader with insights into the personalities and the development of the thinking of abolitionists who were important before 1850 are: Russel B. Nye, *William Lloyd Garrison and the Humanitarian Reformers* (Boston, 1955); Betty Fladeland, *James Gillespie Birney: Slaveholder to Abolitionist* (Ithaca, N.Y., 1955); Ralph V. Harlow, *Gerrit Smith, Philanthropist and Reformer* (New York, 1939); Benjamin Thomas, *Theodore Weld, Crusader for Freedom* (New Brunswick, N.J., 1950); Irving H. Bartlett, *Wendell Phillips: Brahmin Radical* (Boston, 1961); Benjamin Quarles, *Frederick Douglass* (Washington, 1948); and Bertram Wyatt-Brown's forthcoming biography of Lewis Tappan, to be published by The Press of Case Western Reserve University.

Recent works that I highly recommend as correctives to the by now standard misconceptions in this field are: Martin B.

Duberman, "Abolitionists and Psychology," *Journal of Negro History*, XLVII (July 1962), 183–91; Anne C. Loveland, "Evangelicalism and 'Immediate Emancipation' in American Antislavery Thought," *Journal of Southern History*, XXXII (May 1966), 172–88; "Of Slavery and Morality," the Epilogue in Donald G. Mathews, *Slavery and Methodism: A Chapter in American Morality, 1780–1845* (Princeton, 1965): C. Vann Woodward, "The Antislavery Myth," *American Scholar*, XXXI (Spring 1962), 312–28; Bertram Wyatt-Brown, "William Lloyd Garrison and Antislavery Unity," *Civil War History*, XIII (March 1967), 5–24.

INDEX

AILEEN S. KRADITOR was born and brought up in Brooklyn, and attended Syracuse University, Brooklyn College, and Columbia University, where she received her M.A. in philosophy. Between the years 1951 and 1958, she worked in various jobs in factories and offices, and returned to Columbia in 1957 to study American history; she received her Ph.D. in history in December 1962. From 1963-1967 she was assistant professor of history at Rhode Island College, and spent a year as visiting professor in history at Sir George Williams University, Montreal, in 1968. Professor Kraditor is the author of *The Ideas of the Woman Suffrage Movement, 1890-1920* (which received the Ansley Award from Columbia University), and *Up from the Pedestal: Selected Writings in the History of American Feminism*.

VINTAGE HISTORY—AMERICAN

VINTAGE POLITICAL SCIENCE
AND SOCIAL CRITICISM

A free catalogue of VINTAGE BOOKS *will be sent at your request. Write to* Vintage Books, 457 Madison Avenue, New York, New York 10022.

VINTAGE BIOGRAPHY AND AUTOBIOGRAPHY

A free catalogue of VINTAGE BOOKS *will be sent at your request. Write to* Vintage Books, 457 Madison Avenue, New York, New York 10022.